DECOLONIZATION IN PRACTICE

DECOLONIZATION IN PRACTICE

Reflective Learning from Cross-Cultural Perspectives

Edited by Ranjan Datta

Toronto | Vancouver

Decolonization in Practice: Reflective Learning from Cross-Cultural Perspectives
Edited by Ranjan Datta

First published in 2023 by
Canadian Scholars, an imprint of CSP Books Inc.
180 Bloor Street West, Suite 1401
Toronto, Ontario
M5S 2V6

www.canadianscholars.ca

Copyright © 2023 Ranjan Datta, the contributing authors, and Canadian Scholars.

All rights reserved. No part of this publication may be reproduced, stored in a retrieval system, or transmitted, in any form or by any means, without the prior written permission of Canadian Scholars, under licence or terms from the appropriate reproduction rights organization, or as expressly permitted by law.

Every reasonable effort has been made to identify copyright holders. Canadian Scholars would be pleased to have any errors or omissions brought to its attention.

Library and Archives Canada Cataloguing in Publication

Title: Decolonization in practice : reflective learning from cross-cultural perspectives / edited by Ranjan Datta.
Names: Datta, Ranjan, 1977- editor.
Description: Includes bibliographical references.
Identifiers: Canadiana (print) 20230509177 | Canadiana (ebook) 20230509266 | ISBN 9781773383804 (softcover) | ISBN 9781773383828 (EPUB) | ISBN 9781773383811 (PDF)
Subjects: LCSH: Canada—Race relations. | LCSH: Canada—Ethnic relations. | LCSH: Decolonization—Social aspects—Canada. | LCSH: Colonization—Social aspects—Canada. | LCSH: Social justice—Canada. | LCSH: Reconciliation. | LCSH: Immigrants—Canada. | LCSH: Indigenous peoples—Canada. | LCSH: Colonists—Canada.
Classification: LCC FC104 .D43 2023 | DDC 305.800971—dc23

Cover art by Dolly Peltier. *Ojibwe Floral*. 2010. Acrylic on Wood. Wikwemikong, Ontario.
Cover design by Rafael Chimicatti
Page layout by S4Carlisle Publishing Services

23   24   25   26   27   5   4   3   2   1

Printed and bound in Ontario, Canada

Canadä

Dedication

This book is dedicated to all decolonial and anti-racist educators, scholars, and activists fighting to create justice for all. We are all responsible to Indigenous people and land in our decolonial journey.

Contents

Author Biographies   xi

Introduction   1

Part I   **Indigenous Community Reflections on Decolonization in Practice**   9

Chapter 1   Dance of a Transformative Shiibaashka'igan Pedagogy within the Academy   11
Karen Pheasant-Neganigwane
Miskwa Aanakwad Kwe/Pêkâc Kâpimohtêt Yôtin Iskwêw

Chapter 2   Decolonizing University Pedagogical Approaches through Indigenous Storying   29
Christine Fiddler

Chapter 3   First Nations Control of First Nations Education: Using Land as a Foundation for Scholastic Achievement while Reinforcing Cree Culture, Language, and Ways of Knowing   48
Herman Michell, Lisa Antoine, and Delano Mike

Chapter 4   The Pedagogy of Decolonization through a Paradigm Shift in Birth Work from an Indigenous Woman's Perspective   63
Kristie Billard

Chapter 5   An Indigenous Journey: From a Colonized Mindset to Decolonized Dreams   77
Ryan Whitford

Chapter 6   Spiralling In to Spiral Out: Teaching in a Land-Based Mohawk Immersion School   91
Gabrielle Yakotennikonhrare Doreen

Part II	**Racialized Immigrant Women and Children Community Reflections on Decolonization in Practice** 113
Chapter 7	Learning the Importance of Indigenous Meanings of Land Acknowledgement: A Racialized Colour Settler Woman's Decolonial Reflection 115 *Jebunnessa Chapola*
Chapter 8	Responsibility to Build a Decolonial Community: From a Colour Settler Woman's Perspective 131 *Priyanka Mahey*
Chapter 9	Decolonizing Digital Citizen Science: Driving Self-Governance via Data Sovereignty of Historically Colonized Populations 150 *Jasmin Bhawra*
Chapter 10	Land-Based Learning as Cross-Cultural Youth Community Building: A Cross-Cultural Children's Learning Journey 177 *Prarthona Datta and Prokriti Datta*
Part III	**Colour Settler Refugee and Disabled Women Community Reflections on Decolonization in Practice** 189
Chapter 11	Learning the Importance of Building a Decolonial Community: From and within a Colour Settler Former Refugee Woman's Reflections 191 *Najla Mohammadi*
Chapter 12	Decolonial Lived Experiences in Bangladesh and Canada: Navigating Race and Disabilities 205 *Tasnim Jaisee*
Part IV	**Black and Asian Immigrant Community Reflections on Decolonization in Practice** 223
Chapter 13	Decolonizing Meanings of Climate Risks: A Learning Experience from and within Sub-Saharan African Immigrant Communities' Perspectives in Western Canada 225 *John B. Acharibasam and Ranjan Datta*

Chapter 14 Aligning Anti-Racism Efforts with Decolonization: Reflections from Organizing in Vancouver's Chinatown   241
Yi Chien Jade Ho

Part V   **Anti-Racist Organization Reflections on Decolonization in Practice   257**

Chapter 15 Responsibility to Build Decolonial Community(ies): A Learning Journey through Anti-Racism Education and Action with the Multicultural Community in Saskatchewan   259
Rhonda Rosenberg

What Is Next? (Moving Forward)   275

Index   277

Author Biographies

Ranjan Datta, PhD, is a Canada Research Chair in Community Disaster Research and an assistant professor of Indigenous Studies in the Department of Humanities at Mount Royal University, Alberta, Canada. Ranjan's research interests include advocating for decolonial community disaster research, responsibilities for decolonial research, Indigenous environmental sustainability, critical anti-racist climate change resilience, land-based education, and cross-cultural community research.

John Bosco Acharibasam, BA, MA, PhD, is a post-doctoral fellow at the Johnson Shoyama Graduate School of Public Policy, University of Regina. His work focuses on community-based research that advances the health and well-being of BIPOC populations in Canada. As a Black immigrant scholar, he acknowledges the need to build cross-cultural bridges among BIPOC communities in Saskatchewan, Canada. His research also addresses decolonizing methodologies, education, climate change, environmental justice, and anti-racial issues.

Lisa Antoine is a Plains Cree from the Beardy's & Okemasis' Cree Nation within Treaty 6 Territory. At the time of the writing of this article, Lisa is employed as the mental health and wellness coordinator at Willow Cree Health Services. She is a registered social worker, with a bachelor's degree in Indigenous Social Work from the First Nations University of Canada. Lisa is currently working on completing a bachelor's degree in Sociology. She has a strong passion in working with First Nations people. She believes all answers to health and wellness are rooted within the land and Cree cultural traditions. She states, "Land-based teaching encompasses who we are as Indigenous people; it is the most priceless resource we can learn and share with our nations."

Jasmin Bhawra, PhD, is an assistant professor at the School of Occupational and Public Health at Toronto Metropolitan University, Ontario, Canada. As director of the CHANGE Research Lab, she leads cutting-edge, interdisciplinary digital health research. Using mixed methods and a citizen science approach, her research prioritizes disadvantaged and vulnerable populations, including BIPOC communities, children, and youth. Her research takes a health equity lens to active living, nutrition, chronic disease prevention, and health policy. Dr. Bhawra works closely with community partners to co-conceptualize program and policy solutions to complex health problems. Dr. Bhawra received a Banting Postdoctoral Fellowship (2020–2021) at the University of Saskatchewan.

Kristie Billard is an Indigenous woman of colour living and working in Treaty 7. Kristie has spent the last 22 years working in laboratory medicine and is currently volunteering as a doula at Juniper Midwives, a Mètis-owned and -run midwifery clinic, working to help others bring back midwifery to Indigenous Nations in Treaty 7. Kristie's passion for midwifery access and the rights of Indigenous women and healthcare comes from her experiences having her three children. A common theme in her writing is the injustices and inequalities faced by First Nations regarding health and well-being, access, and sovereignty to their medicines, customs, and bodies and how it echoes the colonial destruction of Indigenous land.

Jebunnessa Chapola, PhD, is SSHRC postdoctoral fellow at the Johnson Shoyama Graduate School of Public Policy, University of Regina, Saskatchewan, Canada. She is a community builder, a decolonial social justice feminist activist, transnational cultural activist and performer, community radio host, and interdisciplinary community-engaged scholar, rooted in Saskatoon and in Calgary, in Canada.

Prarthona Datta is a 16-year-old and Grade 11 youth activist. She advocates for youth responsibilities for climate change solutions and learning about Indigenous land-based sustainability. She is a second-generation racialized immigrant child and has been involved in a cross-cultural community garden with her family for the last eight years. She is a climate change advocate, encouraging others to become more responsible for climate change and the land.

Prokriti Datta is in Grade 10 and has many experiences with social and environmental learning from a community garden, including direct learning from soil, various insects and plants, gardener friends, and parents. She is interested in the history of Canada as she is a second-generation child and has a responsibility for the land she is living on. The land has helped her to learn who she is today and who she wants to be.

Gabrielle Yakotennikonhrare Doreen is turtle clan, Kanienke'há:ka from Tyendinaga Mohawk Territory in Ontario. She is a mother of five and a Tota (grandmother). Gabrielle's passion for learning and teaching as well as language and culture revitalization has influenced her academic and professional path. She holds diplomas in Early Childhood Education and Kanien'ké:ha Language. Gabrielle's undergraduate degrees include Art (Indigenous studies) and Education. She also holds a master's degree in Indigenous Land-Based Education and is currently a PhD student at the University of Saskatchewan. Gabrielle is the recipient of Trent University's Bagnani Medal (2011) and Vanier Canada Graduate scholarship (2021).

Christine Fiddler is from the Treaty 6 Territory of Waterhen Lake First Nation. She teaches English at the First Nations University of Canada while she pursues her PhD in History at the University of Saskatchewan. Her PhD dissertation explores Indigenous understandings of health and healing as practised by Cree peoples living in northwest central Saskatchewan in the early 20th century. Through her consulting business, Free the Spirit Consulting, she facilitates workshops on personal development and Indigenous insights and most recently offers her knowledge in programs, policy development, and projects involving Indigenous people. One of these projects in 2023 includes Heritage Saskatchewan's *Relationship Building and Reconciliation through Living Heritage* project in partnership with the Office of the Treaty Commissioner and Aboriginal Friendship Centres of Saskatchewan.

Yi Chien Jade Ho 何宜謙 is a PhD candidate in the Faculty of Education at Simon Fraser University (SFU), British Columbia, Canada. She is also a labour and housing justice organizer, working both with precarious teaching and research staff at SFU and tenant-led organizations such as the Vancouver Tenants Union. Jade's doctoral work centres on developing a radical pedagogy of place through decolonial lenses focusing on settlers of colour and their connection to place, land, and identity.

Tasnim Jaisee identifies as an immigrant woman of colour with disabilities. Her research focus is on intersectional feminist understandings of race, gender, and disabilities. She is a lifelong learner and an activist. Her background is in Political Studies and Women's and Gender Studies through the University of Saskatchewan. She has formerly served at the University of Saskatchewan Students' Union, both as the Women's Centre Coordinator and president of the organization in consecutive terms. Currently, she is serving as an equity, diversity, inclusion project specialist for the Office of the Provost and Vice-President Academic at University of Saskatchewan. She has been working on menstrual equity, building accessible physical spaces, and overall creating an inclusive campus.

Priyanka Mahey was born in Calgary, Alberta, to second-generation immigrants from Punjab. Going through diverse experiences at a young age allowed Priyanka to witness the disparity and inequality that exists for Indigenous and minority groups. She has always been passionate about social justice and helping give back to the community through hands-on approaches. Priyanka believes decolonial narratives and pedagogies are essential in learning and unlearning settler colonial narratives. Land-based learning and connecting to the land is not only a precedent to reconciliation, but essential to building connections.

Herman J. Michell, PhD, is an independent scholar. He was formerly an associate professor with tenure at First Nations University of Canada and also the president CEO of the NORTEP program in Laronge, Saskatchewan. He is a member of the Barren Lands Cree Nation, former executive director of the Northern Teacher Education Program—Northern Professional Access College, and originally from the small fishing/trapping community of Kinoosao on the eastern shores of Reindeer Lake in northern Saskatchewan. Dr. Michell is a university educator, published author, researcher, consultant, lecturer, and conference speaker. Dr. Michell shares the view that "land-based education is not a trend." It is a life-giving force critical to the survival of the Cree peoples. Cree culture, worldview, language, ways of knowing, stories, ceremonies, values, beliefs, and practices are rooted in the land. The land is considered a teacher and healer. Dr. Michell is a writer with numerous published books and articles. He grew up on Reindeer Lake, Treaty 10 Territory. He is a member of the Barren Lands First Nation.

Delano Mike is a member of the Beardy's & Okemasis' Cree Nation, Treaty Six Territory. At the time of writing this chapter, Delano is a band councillor/headman for his Nation. His education is in the Indigenous Social Work field, where he has worked for the past 10 years. As a residential school survivor, his passion is to create platforms that educate band members on breaking the cycles of intergenerational trauma. Cultural identity development is critical in the aftermath of residential schools and colonization. Delano is a big advocate for First Nation youth, and his work includes planting the seeds of health and wellness in youth.

Najla Mohammadi is a colour settler feminist woman residing in Treaty 7 Territory, Alberta, Canada. She is from the Shia Hazara Imami Ismaili community in Kabul, Afghanistan. She is passionate about learning and working with Indigenous communities as well as refugees and immigrants with the UNHCR in the future.

Karen Pheasant-Neganigwane (Anishinaabe/Three Fires Confederacy) is honoured as a Nokomis of eight grandchildren, from her three children. She dedicates her life's work, of mino-bimaadiziwin, in keeping with the 8th Fire prophecy, as a 7th Fire prophecy community member. Karen's path to social action and scholarly work started as a youth during the height of the civil rights era of the '70s (Toronto). Her activism, she attributes to both her parents—both survived the Indian residential school experience. Her early social justice engagement, established in idealism, artistic spirit, and free speech, provided a crucial beginning for her inquisitive spirit. Karen left Toronto and lived a life as a dancer, artist, and educator. She spent the past 40 years mentored by iconic Indigenous scholars from the Great Lakes of her people to Treaty 3, Treaty 6, and currently in Treaty 7. She currently is an assistant professor at Mount Royal University, cross-appointment with Humanities and Liberal Arts/Education, Calgary, Alberta.

Rhonda Rosenberg is the executive director of the Multicultural Council of Saskatchewan (MCoS). She has been working with the multicultural community in Saskatchewan since 1995 in a variety of roles. She has experience in anti-racism education, youth leadership, experiential education, cross-cultural education, non-profit management, and policy governance. Rhonda has worked intensively using transformative drama with youth and adults to explore racism and discrimination and find opportunities for positive change. Rhonda is a recipient of the Saskatchewan Council for International Cooperation's Global Citizen Award, the 2020 Saskatchewan Human Rights Commission Champion award, and the 2022 Queen's Platinum Jubilee Medal.

Ryan Whitford is a Cree/Métis/French student who resides in Calgary, Alberta, Canada, with his wife, Stephanie, and son, Sullivan. Ryan is currently attending Mount Royal University and working towards a Bachelor of Social Work. After getting sober, Ryan reconnected with his Indigenous roots and now fully represents what it means to see through an Indigenous lens.

Introduction

I invite readers to consider *decolonization in practice* as lifelong learning, unlearning, and relearning responsibilities from all of our cross-cultural communities (i.e., Indigenous, settlers, Black, transnational immigrants, new immigrants, and refugee communities). Many academic researchers introduced decolonization in their work; however, they have not explained what it means to think of decolonization as a source of reflective learning from and within our everyday practice. While reading our stories in this book, I request readers to rethink, relearn, and reflect on the following questions in their practice: *Why should we take responsibility for decolonizing our ways of knowing and doing? How can our decolonial practice build a strong sense of community? What does it mean to understand "decolonization"—a system of reciprocal social relations and ethical practices—as a framework for reconciliation? Why do we need to be decolonial to achieve social justice? How does our learning, unlearning, and relearning benefit us?* In this edited volume, our collective decolonial reflective stories from our everyday practice discuss the above questions.

The authors, as part of decolonial cross-cultural communities, shared our stories to not only challenge our static mindsets about our learning and actions from our everyday practice but also take the responsibility to rethink, reshape, and relearn who we are and who we need to be through building respectful relationships with cross-cultural communities; respecting Indigenous Treaty rights; taking actions to decolonize our ways of knowing and acting; learning the role of colonized education processes; protecting our land and environment; creating an intercultural space for social interactions, taking responsibilities to be part of anti-racist and Indigenous land-back movements, and advocating justice for all.

Contributors from cross-cultural communities, including Indigenous, settler, immigrant, and refugee communities, use many engagement methods from their everyday learning reflections. For example, we do narrative research: when working with a community, we tell a story together and equally own that story. The scholarship that came out of this research also looks very different—and its audience isn't restricted to scholars. The outputs have a social impact on the community and are defined in collaboration between researchers and community members. One of the goals of this edited collection is to promote learning that leads to social action from anti-racist solidarity as part of the decolonization process.

In these decolonial reflective stories, we (Indigenous, settlers, Black, and minority immigrant community practitioners and scholars) share our personal journeys and stories of inspiration, resistance, unlearning, relearning, and transformation—with influences on personal, theoretical, philosophical, and global narratives, which have shaped our thinking and being—as empowered Indigenous people, immigrants, and refugees making a difference in the anti-racist solidarity processes that create all of the belongingness with care, respect, and responsibilities towards building decolonial communities.

A JOURNEY OF RESPONSIBILITIES

As an editor of this collective collection, I hope that my reflective learning about the importance of "decolonization in practice from and within community reflections" may help our readers to understand how I came to realize our decolonial learning and practice from and within our everyday practice can transform *who we are and who we need to be* for achieving social and environmental justice. The journey of responsibility to honour Indigenous cultures, languages, identities, and spirituality while learning Western knowledge and skills to create our belongingness with Indigenous lands and peoples.

Responsibility to Learn Meanings of Decolonization

From my 12 years of learning experience as a decolonial and anti-racist educator, scholar, and community activist, I learned that our reflective meanings of decolonization in practice could provide many opportunities to rethink, relearn, and reshape who we are and who we need to be. Our responsibility to learn the meanings of decolonization from and within our everyday practice can also help answer the following essential questions: *Who owns the land we walk/live on? What does decolonization mean to us? What are the Indigenous histories of Canada? What did colonizers do to the Indigenous people of Canada? How does reconciliation look for me? How can reconciliation occur between Indigenous and non-Indigenous people? Why do we need land-based education to achieve social justice?* I hope our readers find our decolonization in practice stories helpful in many ways: decolonizing our ways of knowing, decolonizing ways of connecting, decolonizing ways of learning, decolonizing ways of doing, and decolonizing ways of reflecting. Our learning responsibility may make us strong, collaborative, and responsible.

Responsibility to Decolonize Everyday Practice

Decolonization in practice centres from and within community everyday practice. Rethinking, relearning, and reclaiming opportunities in everyday practice may help us rebuild meaningful relationships with Indigenous land and people. For instance, to explain the meanings of decolonization in everyday practice, Indigenous scholars Eve Tuck and K. Wayne Yang (2013) have argued that decolonization is set apart from other social justice issues due to its additional imperative of "land back." Our everyday reflective stories showcase how our decolonial responsibility can help us be part of land-back movements and create our belongingness with land and Indigenous people. This book helped us realize that we need to be change-makers within and from our learning and practice before we can ask others to make a change.

Responsibility to Be a Lifelong Learner

Decolonization in practice teaches us that decolonization is not a trend or a box to be ticked; it's not a single gesture, action, or statement; it's not about blame or guilt; and it's not someone else's responsibility. Decolonization in practice helps us to relearn how to live together, how to respect each other, how to protect each other's rights, how to create belongingness with the land and people, how to take responsibility, how to protect Indigenous land rights, how to speak up against injustice, and how to protect land and water.

Responsibility to Be a Land-Based Learner

Decolonization in practice helps us to learn the importance of Indigenous land-based learning. Indigenous land-based learning is deeply interconnected with Indigenous knowledge, culture, and Indigenous treaty rights. Indigenous land-based learning also means living in harmony with the environment, respecting animals, and taking only what we need (Datta, 2019). Decolonization in practice in land-based learning also helps us to learn that we all have a responsibility to give back land to Indigenous people.

Responsibility to Be Anti-Racist

Decolonization in practice can help us learn why we all need to be part of anti-racist movements. For instance, critical anti-racist scholar St. Denis (2007) discusses why anti-racist education is essential for deconstructing our static mindset. For example, she explains, "Racism is socially constructed through power relation, embedded in colonial legacies, and connected with ongoing colonization" (p. 1071). She also says, "(Racialization) is a process that has been used 'to justify inequality and oppression of Aboriginal peoples'" (p. 1071). Another anti-racist scholar, Creese (2019), explains that the processes of racialization are linked to power relations that are "deeply rooted in histories of colonial domination" (p. 1481). According to St. Denis (2007), by taking responsibility in everyday practice, we could eliminate racism by challenging systems, organizational structures, policies and practices, and attitudes and behaviours so that power and opportunity are redistributed and shared equitably. St. Denis (2007) suggests that our anti-racist learning can help us understand why and how race matters, understand colonial processes, and develop cross-cultural awareness training. Our edited collection also explains how to build anti-racist solidarity by presenting the following learning objectives: *I identify how I may unknowingly benefit from racism; I promote and advocate for policies and leaders that are anti-racist; I speak out when I see racism in action; I educate my peers about how racism harms our profession; I do not let mistakes deter me from being better; I yield portions of power to those otherwise marginalized; I surround myself with others who think and look differently than me.*

Responsibility to Be a Reflective Learner

Decolonization in practice can help us to be reflective learners. For instance, we may ask ourselves: *What does Indigenous knowledge mean to me? Why are these meanings important to me? What are the challenges in our everyday practices? What does decolonization mean to me for understanding the implications of Indigenous knowledge? What is/are our worldview(s) (i.e., theoretical frameworks)?* These reflective learnings can help our self-determination and strengthen our decolonial community.

Responsibility to Be Indigenist

Learning decolonization from practice can help us realize why we all need to be Indigenist researchers and educators. Being an Indigenist researcher, I have reaped many benefits, such as learning how to build relationships with non-humans (i.e., plants, animals, insects, rocks, and so on); understanding the importance of relationships from Indigenous perspectives; learning to respect and honour Indigenous worldviews, knowledge, and practice; understanding relationships as responsibilities; learning to take a political stand for Indigenous land-water rights; building solidarity with Indigenous rights movements; learning from Indigenous Elders and Knowledge Keepers; and protecting Indigenous treaty rights.

Responsibility to Respond to the TRC's Calls to Action

Decolonization in practice explains why all Canadians should take responsibility to:

1. Learn about the Truth and Reconciliation Commission (TRC) of Canada's 94 calls to action and how to practice them in our everyday lives.
2. Know and honour Indigenous treaty rights and build solidarity with Indigenous movements for enforcing governments to implement extended-due treaty rights.
3. Acknowledge and respect Indigenous rights and titles.
4. Know and let go of negative perceptions and stereotypes.
5. Acknowledge the past, learn about Indigenous histories, and ensure that history never repeats itself.
6. Recognize the intergenerational impacts of colonization, attempts at assimilation, and cultural genocide.
7. Know the critical roles Indigenous Peoples have held in the creation of Canada and their contributions to world wars to protect Canada.
8. Respect Indigenous Elders' and Knowledge Keepers' knowledge and practice.
9. Support the reclamation of identity, language, culture, and nationhood.
10. Build trustful relationships with Indigenous people.

In this book, collective decolonial responsibility in our everyday practice is a response to the call of the TRC that meaningful engagement among Indigenous Peoples and non-Indigenous people will be vital in advancing reconciliation through anti-racist solidarity. Various cross-cultural, community-oriented activities will showcase how to understand and take responsibility for building anti-racist solidarity; we can begin to identify areas of opportunity and current obstacles to progress.

This book will encourage readers to understand the importance of decolonization and make us responsible for transforming our learning into action as a lifelong process. I also hope our decolonization responsibilities may help rethink and relearn that practice should be a complex, critical, and continuous process. At the same time, it should also be relational and political with the land and Indigenous people we live with. We hope this book showcases why we should not take our decolonial learning as an event but as a lifelong process, and why it is everyone's responsibility.

WHO CAN BENEFIT FROM THIS BOOK

This book's collective decolonial stories may benefit many readers: Indigenous and non-Indigenous educators, students, faculty, researchers, activists, environmental professionals, and anyone who works with anti-racist policies. It also provides particular value to diverse communities, who, up to this point in time, have had to spend inordinate amounts of time "teaching" Western-trained educators, professionals, and immigrant and refugee citizens about their basic understandings of the world before the knowledge they bring to the table could be understood and valued.

In this book, collective decolonial stories may be helpful for critical readers in education, environmental sociology, anthropology, interdisciplinary studies, postcolonial studies, ethnic studies, environmental sustainability, and Indigenous and women's studies. Since this book will not be produced without building upon and working within several fields—including postcolonial theories, Indigenous methodologies and methods, sustainability theory and practices, decolonization, community-based practice, youth practice, and Indigenous knowledge and practice—it will also appeal to different disciplinary, interdisciplinary, and transdisciplinary academics and practitioners.

Collective decolonial stories contribute to the debate on appropriate ways to teach and practice building anti-racist communities as resiliency. Scholars are currently divided on whether decolonization should be a subject area of its own or integrated into all other subject areas. Others believe decolonization is separate from work as it is emotionally laden and reflection driven. In this book, contributors suggest that building a decolonial community from and within our everyday practice can transform our learning into action for achieving our social and environmental justice goals. As each story builds anti-racist communities as a form of resiliency in appropriate ways and shares what the author has learned with others, more groups can imagine different ways of living with and caring for their lands.

INNOVATIVE EDUCATIONAL LEARNING

In this book, collective decolonial stories are innovative in many ways:

First, they focus on decolonization from and within cross-cultural community reflections; this joins recent comparisons on Indigenous and transnational community-based perspectives.

Second, focusing on Indigenous land-based learning and practice, our decolonial stories offer a bridge between Indigenous and Western (including social and engineering) perspectives, which nicely fit in Canadian Scholars' rich tradition of publications.

Third, decolonial collective stories are inspired by an exchange with Mi'kmaw Indigenous scholar Marie Battiste (2013), decolonizing our ways of knowing, thinking, and acting; this book is a fundamental shift in thinking of reconciliation and environmental sustainability as a continuous process that belongs to everyone. It has enormous implications and possibilities for reimagining environmental sustainability as our relationships with humans and non-humans.

This book shares community perspectives and our personal journeys and stories of inspiration, resistance, unlearning, relearning transformation, and the personal, theoretical, and philosophical influences that have shaped our thinking and being.

REFERENCES

Battiste, M. (2013). *Decolonizing Education: Nourishing the learning spirit*. Purich Publishing.

Creese, G. (2019). "Where are you from?" Racialization, belonging and identity among second-generation African-Canadians. *Ethnic and Racial Studies, 42*(9), 1476–1494. https://doi.org/10.1080/01419870.2018.1484503

Datta, R. (2019). Clarifying the process of land-based research, and the role of researcher(s) and participants. *Ethics in Science and Environmental Politics, 19*, 1–11. https://doi.org/10.3354/esep00187

St. Denis, V. (2007). Aboriginal education and anti-racist education: Building alliances across cultural and racial identity. *Canadian Journal of Education/Revue canadienne de l'éducation, 30*(4), 1068–1092. https://doi.org/10.2307/20466679

Tuck, E., & Yang, K. W. (Eds.). (2013). *Youth resistance research and theories of change*. Routledge.

PART I

INDIGENOUS COMMUNITY REFLECTIONS ON DECOLONIZATION IN PRACTICE

Indigenous community perspectives on decolonization are vital for this book. Thousands of years of Indigenous communities have proven how vital their knowledge and sustainable practices are for all Canadians (i.e., Indigenous, settlers, immigrants, racialized immigrants, and refugee communities). The chapters in this part share critical community reflections and guidelines regarding how to practice decolonization in our everyday practice. Indigenous communities' reflections on decolonization may be helpful for students, teachers, professionals, and community members to understand that we all have a responsibility to both Indigenous people and the Indigenous land that we are living on. These chapters suggest why and how to ask ourselves how we know what we know and why and how to learn and do things differently in our everyday practice.

1. **Karen Pheasant-Neganigwane** showcases how Indigenous dance can be decolonial transformative Shiibaashka'igan pedagogy within the academy.
2. **Christine Fiddler** examines how decolonizing university pedagogical approaches through Indigenous storying cultivates resilience in the Indigenous students who read them in university.
3. **Herman Michell**, **Lisa Antoine**, and **Delano Mike** (as First Nations Elders, educators, scholars, and land protectors) provide an introduction to some of the key elements of land-based education rooted in the traditional territories of First Nations peoples.
4. **Kristie Billard**, using her lived experience, explains the need for anti-racist community building.
5. Using decolonial Indigenous lived experience, **Ryan Whitford** discusses how to transform from a colonized mindset to decolonized dreams.

6. Explaining Indigenous teaching from a land-based framework, **Gabrielle Yakotennikonhrare Doreen** provides core elements of Rotinonhsonníh land-based education, advocates for the importance of Indigenous languages, and highlights the benefits of project-based learning as reclaiming Indigenous praxis.

CHAPTER 1

Dance of a Transformative Shiibaashka'igan Pedagogy within the Academy

Karen Pheasant-Neganigwane

Miskwa Aanakwad Kwe/Pêkâc Kâpimohtêt Yôtin Iskwêw[1]

Dedication: To both my parents, Rosemary Mishibinijima and Moses Wassegijig (Lavallee), who thrived after their residential school experience, who lived fully with audacity, belief, and certainty.

BOOZHOO, BOOZHOO, BOOZHOO, BOOZHOO

> Centering stories uncovers a longstanding and active history of narrative continuance embodying Anishinaabeg practices and ways of being—sometimes even in the most challenging of circumstances. In traditional frameworks, this is often described as practices embodying *Mino-bimaadiziwin*, or "the good life." (Doerfler et al., 2013, p. 171)

Both my parents were severely and traumatically impacted by Canada's education policies, particularly as attendees of the residential schools. These colonial policies created mayhem for most, if not all, First Nations people. Regardless of these tragedies, my parents sought their own way to find a life of mino-bimaadiziwin, then instilled that belief in me in turn as a youth activist, community worker, and now as an academic, with my dance life threaded throughout my journey. Since childhood, dance has held meaning for me far beyond an aesthetic expression.

Both social and ceremonial, dance nurtures and restores my body, mind, and soul. Beyond the pleasing aesthetics, the healing elements of being a dancer, a Shiibaashka'igan dancer, impart a transformative solace into my being.

I teach within the intersections of upholding Anishinaabe Inendamowin and as an educator in a Canadian, Western postsecondary institution. It is at this place of positionality (Sensoy & DiAngelo, 2017, p. 29) that I pose my research question: "What is the potential for inspiring a transformative pedagogical practice as an Anishinaabe educator, from a Shiibaashka'igan paradigm? Since the release of the Truth and Reconciliation Commission (TRC) of Canada's 2015 report and its 94 Calls to Action, universities have been on a "journey to reconciliation" (Steinhauer, 2019, p. 119). Indigenous scholars, with their distinct *Inendamowin*, are required to have conscious engagement with the reconciliation process. It is the intention of this research to seek and define a transformative Anishinaabe pedagogy to contribute to this journey within the academy.

IDENTITY AND TERMINOLOGY

I use the adjectives "Indians," "First Nations," "Native American," "Indigenous," "Native," and "Aboriginal" interchangeably in my writing. While all these terms are colonial descriptors for the Indigenous peoples of Canada and the United States, "First Nations" and "Aboriginal" are more commonly used in Canada while "Native American" and "Native peoples" are more commonly used in the United States. I also use the term "Anishinaabe" or "Anishinaabek" (plural), which I explain later in this chapter. Either term can be a nation identifier or can reference the collective whole of original peoples of Turtle Island, depending on context. For my generation, "Indian" was the commonly accepted label assigned to Anishinaabek. Indian refers to those who are legislated within the federal *Indian Act* (1876), who have registered treaty status, or who are federally recognized with a "Certificate of Indian Status." I was socialized, from a familial, communal, and societal perspective, as an "Indian" and so I sometimes use this term when it is contextually appropriate to do so.

SITUATING MYSELF

My research is informed by several elements of my being, some visibly present and others unseen. First, I write as an Anishinaabe kwe of the Three Fires Confederacy (Ojibway, Odawa, and Pottawattimi), the daughter of intergenerational Indian residential school survivors. I am also a Shiibaashka'igan knowledge keeper, which is the jingle dress dance, which is symbolic of a reverent and healing dance—a Shiibaashka'igan. Finally, I am a teacher in several capacities: in communities on and off-reserve, as a Nokomis, and as a postsecondary educator since 2002.

The more I study, the more I realize the extent to which cultural genocide and my parents' Indian residential school experience has shaped our shared realities. During my earlier attempts with my research, I continually retraumatized myself with the research literature and attempts to situate my place to define the problem. The intensity or realization of the concept of *soul wound* was foreign to me. Psychologists Duran et al. (1998) define soul wounds as

> The core of Native American Awareness was the place where the soul wound occurred. This core essence is the fabric of soul and it is from this essence that mythology, dreams, culture emerge. Once the core from which soul emerges is wounded, then all of the emerging mythology and dreams of a people reflect that wound. (p. 45)

Jo-Ann Episkenew (2009) further explains, "problems that Native Americans suffer today are a direct result of the soul wound" (p. 8). I came to realize that my lived experience is an extension of a soul wound, a result of the harmful legacy of Duncan Campbell Scott, the deputy superintendent of the Department of Indian Affairs from 1913 to 1932, otherwise known as the "architect of Canada's most destructive Aboriginal policies" (Abley, 2013). Between discussions with my mother, teaching about the historical and contemporary reality of Aboriginal issues and challenges, and deciding on my research question, these experiences triggered many emotions in me, as I had spent a lifetime attempting to "mask" myself at the intersection of my Indigeneity while navigating formal academic contexts. Since 2013, I have painstakingly reflected on Scott's policy decisions and the reality of my positionality in relation to a renewed insight on Indigenous education issues.

The essence of my scholarly research journey is thus profoundly inspired by both my parents and the territories where I have resided, beginning with my home on Manitoulin Island, the original home of my ancestors. I am the eldest daughter of Moses Wassegejig (Lavallee) 'bah and Rosemary Lavallee (Mishibinijima). He is Ojibway, she is Odawa. This is the land of my mother's Nokomis,[2] Agatha Pangowish, wife of Ziimo Pangowish, who is the nephew of Mack-E-Te-Be-Nessy (Andrew J. Blackbird). Additionally, my maternal grandparents, Alfred Mishibinijima and Mary Jane Pangowish, and my paternal grandparents, Sophie Ewewii and Dominic Wassegejig, are all from Manitoulin Island.

This is my family and, like them, I am Anishinaabe. My late dad's friend, Cecil King, explains what it means to be Anishinaabe:

> We call ourselves Anishinaabek ... which literally means, "I am a person of good intent," or "I am a person of worth." Our people believe that we and other human beings are all fundamentally "good." While we take pride in being Anishinaabek, we see ourselves as part of the larger human community. We recognize all humankind as creations of Kizhe Manito (King, 2013, p. 1). Anishinaabe scholar Brenda Child (Leech Lake, Minnesota) (2012) describes Anishinaabek as "a highly evocative term that originates in sacred stories and holds stronger spiritual association. To be Anishinaabe is to be human" (p. xvii). For me, this is a passion for my Anishinaabe identity. Thus, nationhood identity forms the fundamental foundation of my Anishinaabe axiological, cosmological, epistemological, and ontological self.

Additionally, I have explicit cultural lived experiences within three other Indigenous territories: Treaties 3, 6, and 7. Thus, these lived learned experiences with seen and unseen beings bring a pivotal cultural grounding construct to my approach regarding both my pedagogical considerations and scholarly research. Thus I include other Indigenous doctrines as part of my own epistemology, as they remain constant, dynamic contributors. This engagement has nurtured a mental shift from a framework of colonial deficiencies and the pathologizing of Anishinaabek to validation and reclamation of passion, optimism, and triumph as an *Ogichidaa kwe*[3] within the academy.

PROBLEM STATEMENT: CRISIS OF DISBELIEF

The Canadian education system, from curriculum to school resources to pedagogical considerations, requires institutional and systemic change, which was reported in the historical report, *Indian Control of Indian Education* (ICIE; NIB, 1972). The Canadian school system's role in perpetuating and indoctrinating students into white supremacy requires critical assessment and repair, not only for Indigenous students. Justice Murray Sinclair, chair of the TRC, explains that

> All of the aspects of how colonialism has negatively impacted all Canadians, not just people of colour, not just Indigenous people, but all Canadians have been impacted by this history of colonialism, and one of the historical truths that I

speak about, and I challenge people to debate it with me, if they wish, is that our public school system, since the 19th century, has been teaching white supremacy. And we don't know it. We don't realize it. They only talk about the historical impact and historical benefits of having white people in this country. They never talk about the history of Indigenous People. (Paikin, 2020)

When I share the above statement with my students, they are dismayed. They often share their disbelief in class discussions and reflection papers that "this happened in Canada." The term "colonization" generally acquires a new meaning for my students; with a realization of the infliction of colonial policies on Indigenous peoples, they have what Makokis et al. (2010) calls a "crisis of disbelief" (p. 34).

The crisis of disbelief that Leona Makokis names is a reality for many of us, who as Indigenous educators also have been challenged to believe in ourselves, our own Inendamowin. According to Makokis (2010), "Colonization has created a crisis of disbelief—we don't believe in ourselves, our knowledge, our language, our institutions, our people" (p. 34). While attending a law conference on my home campus at the University of Alberta, I heard social activist, scholar, and Sixties Scoop survivor Raven Sinclair speak to the impact of Indigenous stereotypes, which Heidi Kiiwetinepinesiik Stark (2020) argues are grounded in "historical conceptions of Indigenous peoples as savage and criminal" (p. 77). Within these stereotypes are deficit labelling, and as Sinclair states, "if you get told [labelled] enough times, you begin to believe it" (Stark, 2020). Unfortunately, I am no exception to falling victim to negative stereotypes. However, I believe that now, during this era of decolonization and Indigenization, is the time to bring into the academy the confidence in our own epistemologies, to bring our knowledges into the forefront not only to create change, but to heal ourselves.

As Anishinaabek, we have always been unjustly considered within society (Blackbird, 1887). Daniel Heath Justice defines the impact of this regard as *colonial fragmentation* (Justice, 2018, p. 2), an undeniable effect of attempted cultural genocide (TRC, 2015), which produces extreme poverty, oppression, and trauma for Indigenous peoples—myself included. Socioeconomic conditions forced me to leave Wikwemikong, my community. Being within a huge educational institution such as the University of Alberta was in some respects a dream come true, as I believe in the Anishinaabe prophecy of the 8th Fire, "an eternal fire of peace, love, brotherhood and sisterhood" (Benton-Banai, 1988, p. 93). Within our educational institutions I had been socialized to believe that universities were places of intellect, integrity, and objectivity—not a place where ignorance could fester. When I arrived, I came into a different "crisis of disbelief" in which I was challenged to believe in the academy.

Sometimes, when ignorance arises, I remain optimistic and believe it is an oversight. Wendy Rodgers, the University of Alberta Deputy Provost, described the process of disbelieving. When speaking about the academy and ignorance, she spoke about her own awakening, which began as she confronted her ignorance around the damage done by our colonial heritage.

> I see the world differently … recognizing that our university, like our country, has absorbed some of the colonial assumptions about the superiority of white, Western ways and the inferiority of Indigenous peoples and their cultural practices. We have to work to unlearn these assumptions. (Rodgers, as cited in Gillespie, 2018)

Although Rodgers admits to an "awakening" to colonial superiority within the academy, I remain unsure that this newfound awareness will lead to immediate transformative change. The statements of academic administrators such as Rodgers have me recall Anishinaabe scholar Sheila Cote-Meek (2020), who attests that, "most, if not all post-secondary institutions are in the process of dialogue and engagement on how best to respond to the Truth and Reconciliation Commission of Canada's (TRC) 94 Calls to Action" (p. xi). This research is propelled by my optimism and contribution towards evolving an 8th Fire nuance in the academy. As well, bringing in an Indigenous pedagogy to contribute to the decolonizing and Indigenizing of the academy (DIA) process, which is secured in the recognition that "education and culture are inextricably bound together, each compliments the other and one is the other. The time to realize this simple fact is long overdue for Native people" (Waubageshig, 1970, p. vii). Or, as I recently told a colleague—after 500 years, it ain't fast enough!

Figure 1.1: The Soul and Spirit

RELEVANCE: APPROACHING GRAND ENTRY INTO THE ACADEMY

In this section, I share intentions, relevance, and hopefully the soul and spirit of why this research is necessary both at this point in colonial history and for my own lived experience within the academy. I use the term "soul" from a lens of recognition and affirmation that this embodied approach is a vital component of transformation.

In conversation with Indigenous scholar Pat Makokis, she reminded me that part of my conundrum is that I am operating within "the belly of the beast" (personal communication, December 21, 2020). The "belly" is an apt metaphor. Resmaa Menakem (2017) explains that

> When you feel anxious in the pit of your stomach; when you sense that something wonderful or terrible is about to happen; when something feels right or wrong in your gut; when your hearts sinks; when your spirit soars; or when your stomach turns in nausea—all of these involve your soul nerve. (p. 139)

When I dance, when I first approach the entranceway to the dance arena, at the Grand Entry point, I dance with full intention. There is a soulful engagement with the songs and the drum, a relationship of reciprocity with those who are witnessing the Grand Entry. The people in attendance are not audience members; they too capture the spirit brought about by the songs and dances. This discussion is about my entrance, where I bring my Anishinaabe axiological, cosmological, epistemological, and ontological self to the academy. These are the elements that contribute to an Indigenous pedagogy.

As an Anishinaabe educator researching and teaching within the academy, I sometimes find myself challenged being at this conflicting place. Standing on the threshold of the academy can be "ruthless" (King, 2013, p. 256) in relationship to my own Indigenous cultural pedagogical approaches. I find the TRC 94 calls to action promising at a time when increasing numbers of Indigenous scholars attest to "a resurgence in Indigenous education, and much more value is now placed on Indigenous pedagogy, andragogy and cultural knowledge" (Linklater, 2014, p. 93). I have a story that explores and uniquely provides the backstory and context of the ruthlessness of these conflicting issues, thus illustrating the soul–nerve conundrum at the intersectional location of being within a colonial educational institution. This is my soulful dance story, the beginning of my Grand Entry into the academy on my own terms. I intend to seek "soulful" elements within a kinesthetic practice such as dance that will contribute to an Indigenous pedagogical approach.

SHIIBAASHKA'IGAN: CULTURAL INTERSECTIONS, HEALING, AND THE WHITENESS OF THE WHITEBOARD

In December 2017, I was one of over a dozen instructors for the newly designed course—"Aboriginal Education: EDU 211," a required course within the university. We developed the mandatory course and, as such, it was progressive while fulfilling a "decolonizing" approach to create awareness for all pre-service teachers. Prior to this course, my teaching experience had primarily been within First Nation communities, with First Nation students; therefore, I was mildly intimidated to be within a non-Indigenous classroom. This new teaching experience caused me to doubt myself and question my teaching positionality with white students. Beginning the first year of the course in 2013, overt and covert racism tainted the classrooms. Although I approached this class with uncertainty, I was confident that my teaching experience would carry me through this induction into the mainstream academy.

It was my third year teaching this course. A requirement of the students in this course was to critically engage with a diverse range of topics through discussion forums and weekly reflection papers. The lecture hall of 440 students had completed 12 weeks of lectures and seminars as well as an experiential component led by Indigenous community-based teachers and educators. At the final course lecture, during a panel presentation by four instructors, including myself, I was the last speaker, addressing the topic of Aboriginal health and wellness.

The instructor who presented prior to me spoke about education, training, and employment, including statistics on postsecondary education completion, retention and attrition, and employability issues. The presentation included an anonymous polling exercise where all 440 students could respond to the instructor's whiteboard question: "From what you have learned in EDU 211, why might Indigenous peoples not go to university or be employed?"

Though certain responses were indicative of course content, I was disappointed at the number of students who stated that Indigenous peoples are "lazy, drunk, alcoholics"; I stopped counting the comments after a while. After a few "drunk" posts, I froze and rescinded into my mind, feeling a fleeting sense of shattering. Over 100 years ago, R. Baudin, principal of the residential school in my home community of Wiikwemikoong wrote, "Good and moral as they may be, they lack great mental capacity" (TRC, 2015, p. 61). I sat frozen, numb, in shock, in disbelief while in a higher learning classroom over 100 years later, witnessing the same colonial perpetuation of Indigenous stereotypes.

A stricken silence hit the lecture hall. One of the senior faculty course designers spoke up to express their dismay and took a moment to address the "discourse of denial" that was present in the room (Sockbeson, 2009). I sat on the sidelines amidst the other EDU211 instructors, grateful for their presence, which cushioned the assault to my psyche and soul.

Prior to this awkward moment, I had been sitting, waiting in anticipation to share my presentation. I was feeling proud, attired in my colourful ribbons skirt, and eagerly anticipating the opportunity to share my thoughts and feelings with the students. I often think of arriving at a lecture as akin to arriving for Grand Entry at a powwow. Grant Entry is a time to glimmer, share, and celebrate our resilience, sustainability, and culture. But as the final presenter, my topic—health and well-being—suddenly seemed ironic.

I slowly rose from my seat, leaving the protected space of my teaching colleagues, and cautiously approached the centre of the lecture hall stage. I paused, then lifted my eyes and scanned the breadth of the room. I stood front and centre, between the whiteboard and the 440 students, the vast majority of whom were white. I opened with these words: "How do I feel, when faced with the reality of

Figure 1.2: Anishinaabek—My Community, My Children, and My Grandchildren

our horrendous socioeconomic statistics and the stereotypical views that Canadian society has of who we are as Indians, as Indigenous people, as Anishinaabek—my community, my children, and my grandchildren?" My presentation title page replaced the previous awkward comments on the whiteboard screen. I raised and swept my arms across the lecture hall, as the whiteboard now had a beautiful photo of me holding my two-year-old grandson depicted behind me. In the photo, we are both wearing our best powwow dance wear. Then I gently said, "This is what I do … I dance …"

Within the constricted awkwardness of the lecture hall, a song came from within my being. I stepped forward and rhythmically secured a position on the lecture hall floor. I began to dance the Anishinaabe Shiibaashka'igan healing dance—the sidestep. I gathered solace, security, and calmness within me. My body claimed the tempo, and the spirit of a song entered my backbone, to my soul muscle, the psoas muscle. I am not sure how long I danced, maybe one or two push ups, which may have been a minute or longer of a song. The rhythm filling my body, my steps and mind, in the silence of the lecture hall. The feeling I captured was that of when I dance at a powwow, where I put all my energy into Grand Entry protocol to initiate the celebration. When I was finished, I looked up at the students and said, "I dance. I dance with my children, my grandchildren, to remind me how amazing, beautiful, brilliant, and intelligent we are as Anishinaabe, as Indigenous people." The lecture was hall was in a mode of a stifled, awkward silence, seemingly not sure how to respond to the impromptu lecture hall expression of Shiibaashka'igan, a dance of healing. I then began my presentation.

Without conscious thought, my body held an innate ability to know that "healing needs to occur on many levels" (Linklater, 2014, p. 43). My dance, and all the spirit that it entails, brings a sense of being best described by Mojica (2009): "It is significant that the healers as artists are the vanguard of this critical time. We are fertile minds from a living culture ancient as well as contemporary" (p. 149). As much as dance can be an artistic expression, the Shiibaashka'igan also represents a wisdom-based healing aspect.

The first time I shared this story was during a faculty hiring committee interview over a year after the original incident took place, where I again experienced the innate knowing of my body. Though I had not planned to do so, I shared the story as it happened and found myself dancing once again. Telling this story required my dance as a protective healing strategy. At the time, I was unaware of the potential psychological triggers that would happen for me when at a place of "intersectionality" (Sensoy & DiAngelo, 2017), being at the intersections between the academy and myself as an Indigenous scholar. Repeatedly, I recall a teaching: the answers we seek are always within us. I had kept this experience buried, a typical protective practice of mine. The dance and essence of Shiibaashka'igan that brings solace to my soul when I dance at cultural gatherings can be realized and transferred into the academy—albeit its form, structure, and application are yet to be determined.

The silence we as Indigenous peoples keep as oppressed peoples can be so stifling. The truth is, I rarely, if ever, tell anyone about the harsh experiences I have when teaching in the academy, as "systemic structural forces" tend to keep me silent (Willis, 2017). However, I shared the "whiteboard" story with my mom the day I first drafted it. After I finished telling my story, there was a lengthy silence. When she was ready, my mother, who responds to my writing in English, replied in Anishinaabemowin:

> It will take them a long time. They don't get it … They think it is just fun, they don't know, it's a way of life. The dance, those are not costumes. They don't know it's about kitchi manitou (Creator), that is what is going on with the dancer. It is gitchi inendamowin (deep thought/reflection) that is there with the dancer—they don't know that … miiyah (that is it). (personal communication with my mother, May 6, 2020)

This whiteboard experience, which I had kept silent about for some time, brought a sense of understanding that I came to realize as my mother's wisdom reflected in her response, as well as from an early mentor—Joe Couture, as he explains "sense-rooted thinking." Although not speaking about "dance" per se, I take this Shiibaashka'igan experience, as a part of "sense-rooted thinking that knows the world as a spiritual reality" (Couture et al., 2013, p. 107). I have since taken the Shiibaashka'igan concept as my own pedagogical approach. I know as I danced across the floor that I embodied an innate sense of passion, optimism, and triumph as I brought healing into the situation. Perhaps the students or faculty merely saw an artistic expression of dance, but however it was received or interpreted, it worked. Dance is an extension of biskaabiiyaang—a multisensory affirmation of being. Shiibaashka'igan touches my spirit, touches my soul. I hear it and know it when the songs touch my spirit and soul.

At one time, I lacked an appreciation for Western education, as I had an instinctive sense of the perpetuation of ignorance and white supremacy that exists in colonial institutions. Yet, these institutions of education are not only systems of oppression, as my story illustrates. As Yosso (2005) states, "schools most often oppress and marginalize while they maintain the potential to emancipate and empower" (p. 74). I am confident in my competency to teach within academia and am also unsettled by the compromises this requires. Noella Steinhauer (2019) captures this conflict best:

> We are forced to operate in a mainstream context if we wish to work or go to school, and we must learn to operate in both places—of epistemic privilege and gross system disadvantage. This means that we operate within two worlds—the First Nations world and the mainstream world—and we must continually transition between worldviews as a matter of survival. (p. 138)

Although my dance brought resolution and healing to me while teaching in the lecture hall and provided security when retelling the story in the faculty interview, I did not have my current confidence then. A default mode of survival and reaction to this inflicted experience was the norm within the intersections of the academy. It took several years of gestation for this story to teach me what I am now confidently starting to realize. The dance and essence of Shiibaashka'igan that brought solace to my soul when I danced at a cultural gathering can be realized and transferred to the academy—albeit its form, structure, and application is to be determined.

FINDING THE EXTRAORDINARY IN THE DANCE OF SHIIBAASHKA'IGAN: CONCEPTUAL FRAMEWORK

Throughout my research, I share stories that "are not separate from theory; they make up theory and are, therefore, real and legitimate sources of data and ways of being" (Brayboy, 2005, p. 426). I acknowledge the first theorists in my life were my parents and how their lives and stories contributed to my understanding of mino-bimaadiziwin (the good life) principles (Bell, 2016; Debassige, 2010; Gross, 2016; Hupfield, 2015; Rheault, 1999; Sinclair, 2013; Stark, 2021). The stories are akin to the jingle cones on my jingle dress—the Shiibaashka'igan. Collectively, they contribute to the conceptual framework of this research proposal.

> Most stories date the origin of the jingle dress to the post World War I era when the Spanish flu, brought home from Europe by returning soldiers, quickly spread across Canada, eventually killing over 50,000 people. The most vulnerable were those between 20–40 years of age. If ever there was a need for nanaadwi'in (healing) and for bagosenim (hope), it was then. (Shiibaashka'igan Exhibit, 2019)

From my Anishinaabe kwe lens of the Shiibaashka'igan, dance performance is more than a form of artistic expression. My investment of energy—whether creating via beading, sewing, or designing, or being within the spirit of Shiibaashka'igan—is of a transcendent healing nature. Kleiman (2010) explains it further, as "performance is not only an action and art form. In the discourses and practices ... it is also a field of study and a method of enquiry (or a way of knowing)" (p. 158). Kleiman further states,

> the importance of considering performance in relation to sustainability is that it is both a conceptual and practical terrain that has the potential to generate and provoke genuine shifts in attitude and behaviour by engaging the emotion and senses as well as the intellect, by disturbing attitudes and behaviours, and by making the ordinary extraordinary. (p. 159)

Likewise, I choose to create the extraordinary from the ordinary, from an Anishinaabe presence of the wisdom of the Shiibaashka'igan that lends itself to the conceptual framework of this research.

Typically, there are rarely, if ever, two jingle dresses that are the same. Each dancer creates their own Shiibaashka'igan dress to represent who they are as individuals. Just as each dance is an expression of one's spiritual connection to the drum, likewise with one's regalia; a jingle dress is intrinsically an extension of one's being. Perhaps for some, the glitz, colour, and sheer aesthetic beauty of a dancer's wear catches the eye. But for me, besides the bliss that comes from reciprocal relationship to a song, it is the healing essence of the tradition of the Shiibaashka'igan that is critical to my body, mind, and soul. Anishinaabe scholar Brenda Child (2020) describes this tradition:

> Ojibway people connect the jingle dress dance, tradition, to healing—and I should say that it's the dress, it's the dance, and it's also the songs. So, I call it a tradition because it's more than just the dress itself. Ojibwe people believe in the healing power of music. And the jingles—Ojibwe people believe that spiritual power moves through air. And, if [...] you've heard dozens of dozens of Ojibwe woman dancing together in jingle dresses, it makes an incredible sound. And so, the sound of the tinkling of jingle dresses is part of healing. But it is very much in line with how Ojibwe people view the world and how they view spiritual power. (3:11–4:07)

As a lifelong dancer, as well as being a Nokomis, I find the intrinsic qualities of my Anishinaabe cultural attributes bring an essence of insight and healing to constricted moments.

SUMMARY: COUNTING COUP

> To count or strike coup was to get in close physical proximity with an enemy. A coup was honored, not because of any result which accrued from the act itself, but because of the danger which had been successfully overcome, and the emphasis naturally fell upon the conditions under which the act was accomplished. (Smith, 1938, p. 427)

I consider my research as an expression of appreciation, a reverence, and a testament to the "knew" knowledge (Steinhauer, personal communication, 2021) as an Anishinaabe educator. Like my dance, when I come in Grand Entry, this is my coup. Anishinaabe scholar Dale Turner (2006) writes that "Word Warriors must protect these forms of knowledge from exploitation by Indigenous and non-Indigenous peoples and must do so mainly by engaging western European intellectual culture. Yet at the same time they must retain strong connections to their communities" (p. 10). My research is my coup. Anishinaabe communities have a term—*Ogitchidah kwe*—which means "warrior woman[4]" (Pheasant-Neganigwane, 2016). This role of the Ogitchidah kwe is further elaborated in a paper by McGuire Adams (2009):

> Ogitchidah was explained to me by Anishinaabe elder Willie Wilson. Willie is a fluent speaker of Anishinaabemowin. He explained, "If you translate Ogitchidah it means 'you are going over.' You are the one who makes things happen; You are the bridge to make things happen. This translation is essential to understanding a key aspect of our worldview as Anishinaabe. Our language is action oriented and therefore specific responsibilities may be attached to a word to reflect the word/actions intended." (p. 22)

Additionally, one of my Shiibaashka'igan sisters Winona LaDuke (2002) describes Ogichidaa kwe specifically, as "one who defends the people" (p. 196). The objective of this research is to defend Indigenous knowledge and its application within the academy, beyond the rising of some teepees and the hiring of "cigar store Indians" (Dewer, 1999). I humbly stand as an Anishinaabe kwe and introduce myself as an "Ogichidaa kwe" and take responsibility to share the intent of Shiibaashka'igan to bring healing into our academy. This is my counting coup.

Miigwech, Nahkaangenaw/All my relations

NOTES

1. Both my Indigenous names in Anishinaabe and Nehiyawak (Cree)
2. Grandmother
3. Ogichidaa kwe: Warrior woman in Anishinaabemowin, to be further discussed in this research proposal.
4. Ogitchidah kwe: Anishinaabe term for warrior woman, or lead woman. There are different interpretations and different spellings. I tend to go with my local Wiikwemikoong dialect (which still have several dialects, as my community is Odawa, Ojibway, and Potawatomi).

REFLECTION QUESTIONS

1. How do you understand decolonization? How is decolonization understood within your and your community's perspectives?
2. Why is decolonization critical in social movement struggles?
3. What are the outcomes we are seeking through decolonization?
4. What line of thinking influences your views on decolonization?
5. Who or what has influenced your understanding of decolonization?

SUGGESTED READINGS

- Carr, M. (2001). *Assessment in early childhood settings: Learning stories*. Paul Chapman.
- Formosinho, J., & Araújo, S. B. (2006). Listening to children as a way to reconstruct knowledge about children: Some methodological interpretations. *European Early Childhood Education Research Journal, 14*(1), 21–31. https://doi.org/10.1080/13502930685209781
- Horton-Deutsch, S., & Sherwood, G. D. (2017). *Reflective practice: Transforming education and improving outcomes* (Vol. 2). Sigma Theta Tau.
- Robinson, K., & Aronica, L. (2016). *Creative schools: The grassroots revolution that's transforming education*. Penguin.

REFERENCES

Abley, M. (2013). *Conversations with a dead man: The legacy of Duncan Campbell Scott*. Douglas & McIntyre.

Bell, N. (2016). Mino-bimaadiziwin: Education for the good life. In F. Deer & T. Falkenberg (Eds.), *Indigenous perspectives on education for well-being in Canada* (pp. 7–20). ESWB Press.

Benton-Banai, E. (1988). *The Mishomis book: The voice of the Ojibway*. Indian Country Press.

Blackbird, A. J. (1887). *History of the Ottawa and Chippewa Indians of Michigan: A grammar of their language, and personal and family history of the author*. Ypsilantian Job Printing House.

Brayboy, B. M. J. (2005). Toward a tribal critical race theory in education. *The Urban Review, 37*(5), 425–446. https://doi.org/10.1007/s11256-005-0018-y

Child, B. J. (2012). *Holding our world together: Ojibwe women and the survival of community*. Penguin.

Child, B. J. [College of Liberal Arts, University of Minnesota]. (2020, May 19). *The jingle dress, a modern tradition: An interview with Brenda Child* [Video]. YouTube. https://www.youtube.com/watch?v=b36QFGTlajk

Cote-Meek, S. (2020). Introduction: From colonized classrooms to transformative change in the academy: We can and must do better! In S. Cote-Meek & T. Moeke-Pickering (Eds.), *Decolonizing and Indigenizing education in Canada* (pp. xi–xxiii). Canadian Scholars.

Couture, J. E., Couture, R., & McGowan, V. (2013). *A metaphoric mind: Selected writings of Joseph Couture*. Athabasca University Press.

Debassige, B. (2010). Re-conceptualizing Anishinaabe mino-bimaadiziwin (the good life) as research methodology: A spirit centered way in Anishinaabe research. *Canadian Journal of Native Education, 33*(1), 11–28.

Dewer, J. (1999). The cigar store Indian. *Windsor Review, 32*(1), 34–40.

Doerfler, J., Stark, H. K., & Sinclair, N. J. (Eds.). (2013). Eko-niiwin Bagigigan: Stories as resiliency. In *Centering Anishinaabeg studies: Understanding the world through stories* (pp. 171–172). University of Manitoba Press.

Duran, E., Duran, B., Brave Heart, M. Y. H., & Yellow Horse-Davis, S. (1998). Healing the American Indian soul wound. In Y. Danieli (Ed.), *International handbook of multigenerational legacies of trauma* (pp. 341–354). Springer.

Episkenew, J. (2009). *Taking back our spirits: Indigenous literature, public policy, and healing*. University of Manitoba Press.

Gillespie, T. (2018). *Custodians of the internet: Platforms, content moderation, and the hidden decisions that shape social media*. Yale University Press.

Gross, L. W. (2016). *Anishinaabe ways of knowing and being*. Routledge.

Hupfield, J. (2015). *Indigenous education, mino-bimaadiziwin, and the fostering of relational space through Indigenous pedagogy* [Unpublished master's thesis]. York University.

Justice, D. H. (2018). *Why Indigenous literatures matter*. Wilfrid Laurier University Press.

King, K. A., & Hermes, M. (2013). Why is this so hard? Ideologies of endangerment, passive language learning approaches, and Ojibwe in the United States. *Journal of Language, Identity & Education, 13*(4), 268–282. https://doi.org/10.1080/15348458.2014.939029

Kleiman, P. (2010). Staging sustainability: Making sense of sustainability in HE dance, drama and music. In P. Jones, D. Selby, & S. Sterling (Eds.), *Sustainability education: Perspectives and practice across higher education* (p. 155–171). Earthscan.

LaDuke, W. (2002). *The Winona LaDuke reader*. Voyageur Press.

Linklater, R. (2014). *Decolonizing trauma work: Indigenous stories and strategies*. Fernwood Publishing.

Makokis, L. J., Shirt, M. V., Chisan, S. L., Mageau, A. Y., & Steinhauer, D. M. (2010). *mâmawi-nehiyaw iyinikahiwewin*. Blue Quills First Nations College.

McGuire Adams, T. (2009). *Ogichitaakwe regeneration* [Unpublished master's thesis]. University of Victoria.

Menakem, R. (2017). *My grandmother's hands: Racialized trauma and the pathway to mending our hearts and bodies*. Central Recovery Press.

Mojica, M. (2009). Theatre that heals wounded communities. In J. Episkenew (Ed.), *Taking back our spirits: Indigenous literature, public policy, and healing* (pp. 147–185). University of Manitoba Press.

National Indian Brotherhood / Assembly of First Nations. (1972). *Indian control of Indian education*. Ontario Native Education Counselling Association.

Paikin, S. (2020, December 7). *Murray Sinclair: Reflections on reconciliation* [Video]. TVO Today. https://www.tvo.org/video/murray-sinclair-reflecting-on-reconciliation

Pheasant-Neganigwane, K. J. (2016). Beyond the ebb and flow of the powwow dance arena: Rekindling the flame to cultural sustainability. *Canadian Journal of Native Education, 38*(2), 87–95.

Rheault, D. I. (1999). *Anishinaabe mino-bimaadiziwin—the way of a good life: An examination of Anishinaabe philosophy, ethics and traditional knowledge*. CreateSpace Independent Publishing.

Sensoy, O., & DiAngelo, R. (2017). *Is everyone really equal? An introduction to key concepts in social justice education*. Teachers College Press.

Sinclair, N. J. (2013). *Nindoodemag bagijiganan: A history of Anishinaabeg narrative* [Unpublished doctoral dissertation]. University of British Columbia.

Smith, M. W. (1938). The war complex of the Plains Indians. *Proceedings of the American Philosophical Society, 78*(3), 425–464.

Sockbeson, R. C. (2009). Waponahki intellectual tradition of weaving educational policy. *Alberta Journal of Educational Research, 55*(3), 351–364. https://doi.org/10.11575/ajer.v55i3.55332

Stark, K. J. (2020). Colonialism, gender violence, and the making of the Canadian state. In G. Starblanket, D. A. Long, & O. P. Dickason (Eds.), *Visions of the heart: Issues involving Indigenous Peoples in Canada* (5th ed., pp. 70–93). Oxford University Press.

Stark, K. J. (2021). Anishinaabe Inaakonigewin: Principles for the intergenerational preservation of mino-bimaadiziwin. *Montana Law Review, 82*(2), 2.

Steinhauer, N. (2019). Laying the foundations for success. In S. Carr-Stewart (Ed.), *Knowing the past, facing the future: Indigenous education in Canada* (pp. 119–142). Purich Books.

Truth and Reconciliation Commission of Canada. (2015). *Canada's residential schools: The final report of the Truth and Reconciliation Commission of Canada* (Vol. 1). McGill-Queen's University Press.

Turner, D. A. (2006). *This is not a peace pipe: Towards a critical Indigenous philosophy.* University of Toronto Press.

Waubageshig. (1970). *The only good Indian: Essays by Canadian Indians.* New Press.

Willis, P. (2017). *Learning to labour: How working class kids get working class jobs.* Routledge.

Yosso, T. J. (2005). Whose culture has capital? A critical race theory discussion of community cultural wealth. *Race Ethnicity and Education, 8*(1), 69–91. https://doi.org/10.1080/1361332052000341006

CHAPTER 2

Decolonizing University Pedagogical Approaches through Indigenous Storying

Christine Fiddler

This chapter[1] is based on both my university teaching experiences and on my research as a graduate student in the Department of Educational Foundations at the University of Saskatchewan. My research focused on the resilience of Indigenous people exemplified in the literary works of Indigenous authors written in a fictional or non-fictional autobiographical voice. I examined how these literary works, in turn, cultivated resilience within Indigenous students reading them in university. My first teaching experience during this master's degree was leading a seminar for the Indigenous Studies department. In my seminar, I had students push the tables to the side and arrange their chairs in a circle, with the aim to build trust with one another and allow for sharing of stories. I voiced my personal experiences as a First Nations person to reinforce what we were learning in the course readings. This sort of Indigenizing pedagogy embraces "a different style that allows for more student discussion and engagement and creates an atmosphere of ethical relationality wherein ... learners may come together with the instructor" (Pete et al., 2013, p. 111). The circle as one of the Indigenous ways of knowing used in classrooms creates space for Indigenous voice and contributes to learners' experiential, embodied understanding of decoloniality (Fellner, 2016, 2018, p. 291).

Within my seminar, several students remarked that they enjoyed the approach and it was evident this physical space facilitated a sense of belonging and relationality. Meanwhile, there were some students who expressed that they disliked the physical space component and strongly preferred fact-based learning over personal stories. Fellner (2018) indicates that "regardless of their ancestries, students in the Canadian context are used to learning through conventional Euro Western pedagogical processes ... [and] being challenged with both the content and processes of decolonial education is difficult for some" (p. 293). Several years later at the First Nations University of Canada, I taught classes composed of mainly Indigenous students. I did not model this class as before with discussions in a circle format; however, I invited Indigenous Elders as guest lecturers and used personal storying, Indigenous literature, and reflective journalling, which appeared to resonate with the worldviews and beliefs of the students as some of them freely shared their experiences verbally, and the majority through writing. These strategies correlate to what Archibald (2008) deems "storywork" in her efforts "to find a way to respectfully place First Nations stories within the academic and educational mileux" (p. 7). She states, "Stories have the power to make our hearts, minds, bodies, and spirits work together. When we lose a part of ourselves, we lose balance and harmony, and we may feel like Coyote with mismatched eyes. Only when our hearts, minds, bodies, and spirits work together do we truly have Indigenous education" (p. 12).

Professors (and teachers) have a significant role in fostering a strong grounding for students transitioning into "a social and economic environment dominated by an emphasis on information and knowledge work" (Riley & Ungerleider, 2012). The attributions and stereotypes that professors hold, particularly about Indigenous people, may be evident in their negative relations with Indigenous students and their views of Indigenous knowledge, worldviews, and methodologies as inferior or irrelevant in contemporary society. Systemic racism in this form leads to the creation of a hostile class environment and may contribute to Indigenous student dropout rates (Alfred, 2004; Brandon, 2002; Farkas, 2003; Garcia, 2001; Riley & Ungerleider, 2008, 2012; Willet, 2007). Additionally, "teaching decolonial curriculum using conventional Eurocentric approaches reinforces colonization through Eurocentric [pedagogies], implying Western Eurosettler superiority over Indigenous knowledge systems. Thus, decolonizing must occur through (re)claiming and (re)centering Indigenous traditions" (Fellner, 2018, p. 291; Wilson, 2004). Decolonizing curriculum means that professors actively challenge Eurocentric systems and encourage students to do the same, "working toward transformations that benefit Indigenous communities" (Fellner, 2018, p. 285).

Indigenous university students are more likely to experience steady struggles attributed to colonization, Eurocentrism, and institutional, systemic, and societal racism. Indigenous students' experiences are often marked by a history of colonization in the form of trauma and intergenerational impacts (Mordoch & Gaywish, 2011; Sitler, 2008; Stout & Kipling, 2003). Many Indigenous students hold Indigenous worldviews and perspectives that are completely contradictory to the Eurosettler colonial worldviews and perspectives accepted in universities (Dei et al., 2002; White et al., 2009). And they often deal with a variety of situations rooted in discrimination and societal and systemic racism (Cannon & Sunseri, 2011; Dei et al., 2002; Henry & Tator, 2006; Mordoch & Gaywish, 2011).

Systemic racism refers to both institutional and structural racism; the first of these refers to racial discrimination deriving "from individuals carrying out the dictates of others who are prejudiced or of a prejudiced society" (Henry & Tator, 2006, p. 352). Conversely, institutional racism refers to "the inequalities rooted in the system-wide operation of a society ... [and] to practices that exclude substantial numbers ... of particular groups from significant participation in major social institutions" (Cannon & Sunseri, 2011, p. xiv; Henry & Tator, 2006, p. 352). An example of systemic racism for Indigenous university students is the adverse treatment they are given by professors and how subjects about Indigenous people are handled in the classroom.

Including Indigenous literature in university courses is a decolonizing pedagogy. "Decolonizing curriculum may be conceptualized through the interconnected processes of deconstructing colonial ideologies and their manifestations, and reconstructing colonial discourse through Indigenous counternarratives" (Battiste, 2012; Donald, 2009; Fellner, 2018, p. 284; Madden, 2016). This approach reinforces to Indigenous students that their experiences are validated and may open discussions that help students to acknowledge and voice their struggles. Episkenew (2009) stated that all forms of Indigenous literature—whether autobiographical works, fiction, drama, film scripts, screenplays, or song lyrics—are aesthetically beautiful creations and compelling works that depict Indigenous reality. The literary works draw attention to the Indigenous experience and have the power to better the situations of Indigenous people, particularly through the processes of storying traumatic events and sharing an alternative collective myth in response to the settlers' authorized collective myth.

Stories also work for Indigenous people to describe their way of healing, health, and wholeness (Hart, 2002). Hart (2002) stated that through the lens of an Indigenous worldview, stories are utilized in three ways: sharing general stories, using humour, and role modelling. The sharing of general stories allows individuals to discover whatever meaning in the story relates to them personally. The use of humour supports the release of tension and energy, as well as knowledge development, since much can be learned from the laughter stemming from particular situations. Whereas role modelling, through telling stories, is "indirect, nonconfrontational and supportive" (Hart, 2002, p. 57). Thus, Indigenous literature has the power to help Indigenous students to begin to heal or to learn new ways of dealing with difficult circumstances, ways that may help them throughout their lifetime.

My research study has found that the storied experiences of Indigenous authors, in a fictional or non-fictional autobiographical voice, represent authors' life narratives and demonstrate to Indigenous students that others of Indigenous descent often persist through hardship without giving up hope. The study found that when professors include Indigenous literature in course content, Indigenous students benefit in three ways: the literature helps students to initiate healthy ways of coping with their struggles; it increases their engagement in university learning (with consideration of professors' approaches in validating Indigenous literature and experiences); and it leads to their personal growth and inner transformation. The study helped me to determine how a selected group of Indigenous students found a source of resilience in studying Indigenous literature at the University of Saskatchewan.

HISTORICAL AND CONTEMPORARY CONTEXT

There is a long-standing history of education for Indigenous people in this country. Education has come to take on a notable role for the advancement of our well-being; attaining education for Indigenous people has been marked by many challenges which continue to persist. Since treaties in Canada were signed, several Indigenous leaders have viewed education as a tool for preparing oneself for the future and "as a tool of self-determination" (Brant-Castellano et al., 2000, p. 213). For many Indigenous people, education is a form of empowerment and a way to help other Indigenous people recover from "the persistent results of long historical processes born of deliberate human actions and policies aimed at cultural suppression, oppression and marginalization" (McGuire, 2013, p. 63). There are deep roots to the underachievement among Indigenous students, largely attributed to the historical experiences and injustices experienced by Indigenous people in Canada that are connected to issues of land possession and dispossession. The US and Canadian governments have developed inhuman policies to subjugate and assimilate Indigenous people for the purpose of taking over the lands. Native Americans, First Nations, Métis, and Inuit experienced forced removal, confinement to reserves and reservations, the assimilative aims of residential schools, and the legal systems that enforced these colonial actions. Indigenous people adapted and resisted where they could but were for the most part powerless in escaping these policies and systems meant to destroy their former way of life before white settlers populated their home territories. (Hoxie, 2001; Milloy, 2017).

The residential school system "has been the most damaging of the many elements of Canada's colonization of this land's original peoples and, their consequences still affect the lives of Aboriginal people today" (Milloy, 2017, xxxviii). The Canadian government used education to assimilate Indigenous children into European ways when they were taken away from their families and sent to residential and boarding schools across Canada (Stout & Kipling, 2003). According to the National Centre for Truth and Reconciliation website, the 20 residential schools that were first opened in the 1860s and located in north, central, and south Saskatchewan began to be closed down by the government in the 1970s, but remained in operation until 1996. On a national scale, there were 139 residential schools across Canada at the peak of the system (Forsyth, 2013). In the vision of education developed by both church and state in the final decades of the 19th century, it was the residential school experience that would lead children most effectively out of their "savage" communities into "higher civilization" and "full citizenship" (Milloy, 2017, p. 22).

> In their lives after residential school, many adult survivors, the families and communities to which they returned, all manifest a tragic range of symptoms emblematic of, as the chief's statement said, "the silent tortures" that continued in their communities. Social maladjustment, abuse of self and others and family breakdown are some of the symptoms prevalent among First Nation Babyboomers. "Graduates" of the "Ste. Anne's Residential School" era are now trying and often failing to come to grips with life as adults after being raised as children in an atmosphere of fear, loneliness and loathing. (p. 297)

Indigenous youth in Saskatchewan (inclusive of university students) often show traumatic effects and behavioural patterns associated with their parents', grandparents', and—in some cases—their own experiences in residential schools. Stout and Kipling (2003) described such traumatic effects and behavioural patterns, including parental pathology, a high incidence of life stress, exposure to violence, low self-esteem, and "resorting to brittle or destructive coping strategies when faced with subsequent adversity" (p. 52). Many Indigenous students at the University of Saskatchewan are included in the number of descendants of Indigenous people who attended residential schools all over Saskatchewan.

The continual impact of the colonization process on the worldviews and belief systems of Indigenous people is compounded by an education premised on Eurocentric worldviews and values. Dei et al. (2002) reasoned that to "a disturbing extent, patriarchal Eurocentrism continues to masquerade as universalism" (p. 8).

This includes the way "institutions validate knowledge, recognize socialization within divergent cultures, regard first language influences, and accept different spiritual beliefs and world-views" (White et al., 2009, p. 212).

Mordoch and Gaywish (2011) posed a question in their study about the need for healing in the classroom and found that "a considerable number of mature students can potentially be experiencing complex post-traumatic syndrome that results in behaviours that interfere with achieving their academic goals" (p. 101). These conditions contribute to low academic achievement rates of Indigenous students and having them addressed in university education through Indigenous-centred pedagogies is beneficial.

Whether it is trauma in their own lives or that of their family, community, or peers, "students who are living with trauma may use a considerable amount of energy to conceal their situations and have less energy to engage in the classroom, needing all of their energy to get through the day" (Mordoch & Gaywish, 2011, pp. 101–102; Sitler, 2008). Trauma robs people of control, connection, and meaning, which help motivate people to set and attain goals; trauma may also sensitize Indigenous students to feelings of incompetence and devaluation of self and efforts (Herman, 1997; Mordoch & Gaywish, 2011). Furthermore, a barrier to addressing students' trauma is the common view of education and therapy as two distinct entities (Herman, 1997; Mordoch & Gaywish, 2011). Mordoch and Gaywish (2011) stated that education should respond to the potential of effects of both historical and ongoing trauma within classroom settings. The authors pointed to statistical evidence and accounts of the lived experience of Indigenous mature students to prove that "a percentage of Indigenous students will be experiencing the effects of both historical trauma and ongoing traumatic events" (p. 101). The education system can play a larger role by helping students to address these specific challenges in the classroom, particularly for adult learners in university.

These factors remain prevalent in Canadian society and institutions, working against Indigenous students' retention and graduation rates. Canadian institutions such as the University of Saskatchewan must address these factors by increasing their own awareness and understanding of Indigenous people and, in doing so, include Indigenous people in discussions as equals in order to develop strategies for greater Indigenous participation. Including Indigenous content in the form of Indigenous literature in university courses is relevant in this case because the storied experiences of Indigenous authors, in a fictional or non-fictional autobiographical voice, represent authors' life narratives and demonstrate to Indigenous students that others of Indigenous descent often persist through hardship without giving up hope.

USING AN INDIGENOUS METHODOLOGY IN A STUDY ON INDIGENOUS STUDENTS

Incorporating Indigenous methodologies in research studies such as this ensures that Indigenous worldviews, beliefs, and perspectives are valued in research outcomes and validated as holding truth, credibility, and esteem in the academic institution. As a *Nehiyaw* (Cree) person who is grounded in cultural teachings, I framed my study with a combination of Indigenous methodology and grounded theory methods to analyze and sort data. I used a conceptual research framework that was a metaphor for the *Nehiyaw* practice of *mosahkina wihkaskwa* (gathering sweetgrass) to outline the research preparation, methods, and procedure in order to demonstrate the theoretical and practical underpinnings of the research. *Mosahkina wihkaskwa* is a traditional *Nehiyaw* cultural practice that carries aspects of *Nehiyaw* knowledge and worldviews. *Wihkaskwa* is a type of grass that is picked in the summer for use in prayer and ceremony.

This research was also guided by the *Nehiyaw* concept of *Miyo-Pimatisiwin* (the good life; Hart, 2002) to examine the resilience of Indigenous students. While I looked at several theories to better understand the concept of resilience in terms of Indigenous students in higher education, I primarily focused on Hart's (2002) concept for the purposes of this study, as springing back from adversity and having a good life outcome is the essence of resilience for Indigenous people today. Hart (2002) refers to *Miyo-Pimatisiwin* as involving the four states of self: emotion, mind, body, and spirit, and the effort of maintaining a balance in the four areas to ensure wellness. For many Indigenous people, *Miyo-Pimatisiwin* translates into "the good life" and means "the overall goal of healing, learning, and life in general" (p. 44). Similarly, Fellner (2018) states that living a good life involves bringing Indigenous knowledges to life by helping ourselves, our communities, and the rest of society, increasingly moving "toward good relationships, healing, balance, wellness, and social and environmental justice" (p. 289).

Using an Indigenous methodology in this academic research also involved delineating the origin of my worldview and being specific when applying the *Nehiyaw* methodology according to my cultural values. I expected the research would be culturally safe and respectful to others (Martin & Mirraboopa, 2003, p. 4). To achieve this, I carried out the research while relying on the protocols and worldview I learned in my upbringing as a *Nehiyaw* person so that hopefully Indigenous participants felt their worldviews and beliefs were being respected. Furthermore, I ensured that I was responsible for protecting any kind of Indigenous knowledge that was shared by being reciprocal in my relationship with the participants. This included incorporating Indigenous practices such as organizing a meal for the time I spent debriefing with participants, giving them gifts in exchange for the stories they shared, as well as offering cloth, tobacco, and prayers to guarantee the research process went well.

Managing, organizing, and analyzing the data using grounded theory methods was consistent with a *Nehiyaw* methodology because it is comparable to the practice of sorting and braiding *wihkaskwa*. Grounded theory methods cut and analyze the data, which serve as an analytical tool to break down and fragment data and build it back up guided by Indigenous understanding. In this case, combining the grounded theory analysis with reflections on the Indigenous worldview was comparable to braiding the sorted piles of *wihkaskwa* into sections that fit well together. In addition, I continued to journal in parallel with data collection, note-taking, and coding (Dick, 2005). While initially five themes emerged from data analysis, I distilled these five themes down further to three themes with one subtheme. In the end, the three themes became comparable to the three sections of the *wihkask* (sweetgrass braid).

PARTICIPANT SELECTION

Selecting participants and hearing their stories was similar to gathering *wihkaskwa* (sweetgrass) from a field of grass. Just as the *wihkaskwa* is hidden in a field of various strands of regular grass and must be carefully selected, valuable pieces of the participants' individual stories were gathered and selected in much the same way. Purposive sampling allowed me to focus on six Indigenous undergraduate students at the University of Saskatchewan. This participatory group was currently enrolled at the University of Saskatchewan and completed a first-year course incorporating some aspects of Indigenous literature. As indicated in the following list, each participant chose a pseudonym with two participants deciding to use their spiritual names in their traditional language: *Nohkom Kanehkan Apit* (Cree for "Grandmother who sits at the front"), *Adjgaliaq* (Inuvialuktun for "Created by Hands"), *Chris*, *Jimmy*, *Cindy*, and *Raine*.

THE THREE WAYS INDIGENOUS LITERATURE INCREASES THE RESILIENCE OF INDIGENOUS STUDENTS

Three broad themes emerged during data analysis: coping with personal and academic challenges; engagement in learning, with a subtheme of professors' approaches in validating Indigenous literature and experiences; and personal growth and transformation. These themes directly answered the research question: How is the resilience of selected Indigenous students at the University of Saskatchewan influenced by the Indigenous literature currently taught in the post-secondary classroom?

COPING WITH PERSONAL AND ACADEMIC CHALLENGES

Personal and academic challenges inevitably arose for all the participants in their first year of university. Indigenous literature instilled a sense of hope in Nohkom Kanehkan Apit, Adjgaliaq, Chris, Jimmy, and Raine to effectively deal with challenges they encountered not only during their university studies but also prior to this. Reading Indigenous literature led them to believe they could persist through difficult life circumstances.

Chris reflected on first reading Indigenous literature and recalled a time in his childhood when he came across Campbell's (1973) book *Halfbreed*. Reading this particular literary work and other forms of literature gave him a sense of hope during difficult times in his life:

> Reading and books, and education were an escape for me because my home situation wasn't always great. I grew up in a rough situation and it wasn't always good. And for me, school was an escape. It was, I would rather be at school then at my current home situation. And yeah, books ... for me books became an escape and it wasn't just [Indigenous] books, it was other books. (p. 20)

In this case, the opportunities to read in school were a source of fulfillment for Chris and helped him to be resilient to get through difficult times.

All of the participants shared struggles they faced that at times were discouraging to them during their first years of university. Nohkom Kanehkan Apit, Adjgaliaq, Chris, Jimmy, and Raine said they were empowered to get through difficult situations when they read Indigenous literature, highlighting the extreme hardship that their Indigenous ancestors overcame and the resilience that was required to do so. When reading Indigenous literature, Nohkom Kanehkan Apit and Adjgaliaq stated how they were moved, as their struggles related to the characters' circumstances. Nohkom Kanehkan Apit said that although reading Indigenous literature such as *In Search of April Raintree* (Culleton, 1983) brought about strong emotions for her, she decided only to share certain things in university class discussions. She dealt with strong emotions privately as she read the literature and cried in response to the experiences resembling her own life.

White-Kaulaity (2006) stated that emotionally relating to Indigenous literature is common, as Indigenous authors are more likely to "write honestly about their experiences. Their voices evoke emotion while they express anger for being misunderstood, disrespected, oppressed, and colonized" (p. 12). Indigenous literature seemed to contribute to the personal growth of Nohkom Kanehkan Apit and Adjgaliaq when it caused them to recall emotions tied to their memories of life experiences.

Adjgaliaq said he reacted emotionally as he read Indigenous literature such as *The Lesser Blessed* (Van Camp, 1996) and he believed that there are healthy and unhealthy ways of dealing with strong emotions; "I recognized those emotions, where they came from and remembered the ways I coped with them before, if they were healthy ways I did the same, or if they were not, I found a healthy way to cope with them." Adjgaliaq said he recognized how reading Indigenous literature was bringing about strong emotions for him and, in this sense, healing "comes about through emotional expression, discharging turmoil and thorough cleansing and purifying oneself" (Hart, 2002, p. 102). Nohkom Kanehkan Apit and Adjgaliaq clearly stated how they experienced personal growth as they related emotionally to the texts and overcame personal circumstances that had a continual effect on them.

ENGAGEMENT IN UNIVERSITY LEARNING

Indigenous literature proved to be a major factor for increasing the participants' engagement with their university learning. They indicated that Indigenous literature increased their engagement when it allowed them to talk about their personal experiences and to share their perspectives in class discussions. They said that having Indigenous literature included in their courses captured their interest, especially when the literature reached them at an emotional level, whether it made them cry, laugh, or feel angry.

Cindy said Indigenous literature increased her engagement as she read about characters familiar to her, especially in her upbringing as an Indigenous person.

> I remember [reading] *Medicine River* (1990), I think, kind of made me feel … makes you think a bit more about Aboriginal relations and how you treat each other. Whereas the poetry [by Louise Halfe] was more like, it makes you feel more empowered and more stronger.

Indigenous literature engaged Cindy to a great extent in the class; she became more engaged when she was able to talk about her personal experiences and share her perspectives.

When Indigenous literature related to the lives of the students reading it and the lives of people in their communities, four participants said they became increasingly engaged in their learning because the content was relevant to their own experiences. Jimmy described his learning about the juxtaposition of traditional and religious beliefs in Indigenous literature:

> In all of these pieces of literature, it's all people trying to tell the discourse between the Native spirituality and the Christians is like the Christians trying to tell these people who they are. … So to me it's like, I don't want people to tell me who I am because yes I come from two different backgrounds. But I'm not going to let either side to try to force me into being something that, you know, that I'm not.

Jimmy became more engaged in the course as he clearly understood the conflict between people who follow Christianity and those who follow Indigenous spirituality that is oftentimes existent in Indigenous communities. The representation of this conflict in literature caused him to ask questions about his own beliefs and identity.

Nohkom Kanehkan Apit, Adjgaliaq, Chris, Jimmy, and Raine said that Indigenous literature engaged their interest when authors presented the graphic truth, the real-life experiences of Indigenous people presented by Indigenous authors. When Indigenous literature was also used as a teaching tool that valued Indigenous perspectives, all participants stated that they felt their worldviews and perspectives were affirmed and valued. The participants said they became more engaged in their university learning when they were invited to share their perspectives and when they felt they were contributing to the learning of others.

APPROACHES OF PROFESSORS VALIDATING INDIGENOUS LITERATURE AND EXPERIENCES

All the participants said that when they shared their responses to Indigenous literature in class discussions, the professor's approach greatly influenced how they learned about topics in Indigenous literature. The participants all agreed that they valued the learning more when professors demonstrated open-mindedness, approachability, and enthusiasm about what they taught.

The pedagogical approach used by the professor, the professor's open-mindedness, and the professor's interaction with the student determined the extent to which the majority of participants became invested in their university learning. The six participants were the most engaged when professors showed open-mindedness by accepting students' diverse perspectives, whether or not the professor agreed with what students said.

All the participants viewed professors as appropriately handling learning situations when they allowed students to voice their perspectives, which was a form of accepting those perspectives. In particular, professors' impartiality was demonstrated in accepting that Eurocentric worldviews, perspectives, and values were not the norm by acknowledging the relevance of Indigenous worldviews, perspectives, and values. The ability of the professor to be unbiased seemed to be the most critical factor in helping the participants become more engaged.

The extent of a professor's understanding of Indigenous worldviews and perspectives also impacted students' engagement in Indigenous literature. For instance, when Nohkom Kanehkan Apit shared her perspective on family relationships and what was acceptable or unacceptable, she felt her perspective was rejected by one of her non-Aboriginal professors when the professor stated her own view on family relations and conditional acceptance of illegitimate children. On the other hand, Nohkom Kanehkan Apit's other English professor allowed her to voice her perspectives freely and welcomed discussions in which students gave their perspectives to topics according to Indigenous worldviews and norms. Professors proved to effectively engage the Indigenous students participating in this study when they shared their own perspectives while respecting those of the students.

PERSONAL GROWTH AND TRANSFORMATION

All the participants indicated that reading Indigenous literature led to their personal growth or transformation in the form of a newfound awareness and understanding, an increased capacity for critical thinking, the recognition of a silenced voice that needed to be heard, and a greater understanding of the realities of other Indigenous people through real-life stories. Reading novels, plays, poetry, and short stories by Indigenous authors had the power to affirm their identities and free the majority of participants from feeling isolated and disconnected as they attended university.

Nohkom Kanehkan Apit, Adjgaliaq, and Chris said they began looking for other literature to further acknowledge their Indigenous worldviews and perspectives.

The inclusion of Indigenous literature in university courses indicated to all the participants that the recognition of Indigenous perspectives is valuable to society. This allowed them to see their contributions to society as valuable, and this new understanding was in itself a sense of personal transformation.

Reading Indigenous literature in first-year classes led to all the participants becoming more aware of the experiences of other Indigenous people. Reading about Indigenous authors' difficult life situations allowed all participants to reflect on their own beliefs and how this impacted their understanding of Indigenous identity. Although reading some of the literature proved difficult for three of the participants, they stated that these readings proved to build their awareness.

The Indigenous literature allowed all the participants to question the situations of Indigenous people presented in the literature and their relevance in past and present times. Raine stated that Indigenous literature offers a lot to Indigenous students who may have grown up in privileged homes or in non-Indigenous communities. The literature could help those students learn about the adversity that other Indigenous people experience and perhaps understand their own Indigenous identities better. He said that he learned from Indigenous literature in a similar way as an urbanized Cree-Métis youth:

> It heightens my learning, I believe it heightens also the peers that I'm taking classes with, because when you're taking these classes you're taking them with future social workers, future teachers, and future analysts. And that's what they need to … they need to be exposed to the Indigenous literature because it exposes the truth, it exposes the realities that some of us … face today.

Learning from Indigenous literature proved transformational for Raine, as was the case with all participants. Reading Indigenous literature increased his awareness of the historical realities of Indigenous people, particularly when the experiences were told from the point of view of Indigenous authors. Overall, Indigenous literature made it possible for all the participants to distinguish the differences between Indigenous and colonial worldviews more easily.

Indigenous literature helped all six participants to more clearly articulate the stereotypes and misunderstandings of Indigenous people formed by other groups in Canada. Common bias, racism, inaccurate perceptions, and stereotypes were evident to them through their personal experiences at the university. Reading Indigenous literature reaffirmed their personal experiences with racism and stereotypes and increased their engagement in university learning.

INDIGENOUS LITERATURE AS A SOURCE OF RESILIENCE FOR INDIGENOUS STUDENTS

Indigenous autobiographical literature often has an emotional impact on Indigenous readers and as a result has a profound resonance for those reading it. Reading Indigenous literature is empowering for Indigenous students because "reading literature by other Indigenous people who share the same experiences and who can articulate their feelings about those experiences can be a healing experience for both writers and readers" (Episkenew, 2009, p. 16). Reading Indigenous autobiographical literature helps Indigenous students manifest resilience in new ways as they undergo healing and learning during their university studies.

Maria Campbell, Louise Halfe, Tomson Highway, Thomas King, and Beatrice Culleton Mosionier are some of the foundational Indigenous authors of published literature who have set the stage for other authors. These Indigenous authors presented stories of characters dealing with trauma and emotional turmoil based on the colonial realities of Indigenous people in Canada. Indigenous autobiographical writing is an act of "reinventing" the colonizers' language, manipulating the English language and its literary traditions to narrate Indigenous experiences in an effort to heal from colonial trauma (Episkenew, 2009; Gold, 2001; Harjo & Bird, 1997; Pennebaker, 1997). Indigenous authors' acts of writing down the stories of Indigenous people often demonstrate the importance of believing in the possibility that things will get better even in the bleakest times. And even in stories that present Indigenous people defeated by trauma, these stories exemplify the realities in most Indigenous students' lives. Facing similar circumstances requires that they remain hopeful about the future and use positive coping strategies.

For the participants, resilience meant fighting for survival, working through obstacles, and finding ways to overcome challenges. As well it meant carrying on through everyday struggles, having a positive attitude, personal growth, independence, and self-motivation. And finally, the participants saw resilient students as those who managed their time effectively, took initiative, and saw their university experiences as rewarding. Collectively, the participants identified resilient individuals as those who can prosper and succeed despite struggles, learn life lessons through struggles, and find strength within themselves through helping others. These meanings of resilience related to the concept of *Miyo-Pimatisiwin* as "the overall goal of healing, learning, and life in general" (Hart, 2002, p. 44). For the participants, their resilience was attributed to ensuring their own health, happiness, and well-being, along with those around them.

CONCLUSION

Opening ourselves up to a larger reality requires teaching and learning while simultaneously respecting others and otherness (Ghosh, 2010). Therefore, it is problematic when education systems across Canada use curriculum that does not recognize and mis-recognizes the contribution of groups of people. Contemporary media, including films and literature, used in education "have the ability to influence the construction of personal identities, self-esteem, and ideas about the world around us" (Maslin, 2002, p. 6). Media continues to perpetuate stereotypes to a large extent by racializing behaviors along with phenotypic traits. In this way "the dominant group is able to justify the unequal treatment of racialized groups … based on what is viewed as the shortcomings of those members" (p. 13). Using Indigenous literature may help educators to better support Indigenous students. Episkenew (2009) described how "Indigenous life writing helps Indigenous readers heal from postcolonial trauma by helping them recraft their personal and collective myths" (p. 70). In particular, autobiographical literature and testimonial literature address present situations and look "for future solutions, to revolutionary solutions, and to a transformed society as envisioned by the witness telling [his or] her story" (Beard, 2000, p. 65).

Indigenous literature, as a form of Indigenous learning materials, corresponding to the Indigenous knowledge that Indigenous students are taught within their own families and communities (Chief, 2011; Clancy, 1995). Indigenous literature and content in classroom learning clearly influence Indigenous students' and teachers' identities and self-concepts and serve as a powerful tool to influence the identity and self-esteem of Indigenous students and teachers when included in the curriculum (Chief, 2011; Clancy, 1995; O'Reilly-Scanlon et al., 2004).

The pedagogical approaches of professors when teaching Indigenous literature are important for engaging Indigenous students in what they are learning. It is important for professors to value the knowledge that all students (Indigenous and non-Indigenous) bring with them into the classroom to create a feeling of belonging for optimal learning and to acknowledge their own power in shaping students' attitudes towards themselves as learners (Haug et al., 1992; O'Reilly-Scanlon et al., 2004). Indigenous students often draw inspiration from the stories of others; thus, reading Indigenous literature has the capacity to teach them how someone of their background was able to persevere over tragedy and hardship. They may be empowered to make use of their talents, abilities, and knowledge, which may help them to help others or to realize their purpose in life (Quigley, 2006).

I propose that Indigenous curriculum and university pedagogies be brought into classroom learning in the form of Indigenous literature, ensuring that this literature is taught in a way that is consistent with Indigenous worldviews, perspectives, and practices. Using Indigenous literature to teach Indigenous university students about resilience is essential for decoloniality and Indigenizing. Just as *mosahkina wihkaskwa* (gathering sweetgrass) serves to heal and strengthen individuals and communities, hopefully this research may serve the same purpose for better supporting Indigenous students in the university.

NOTE

1. An initial version of this article was published in *Education Matters*, *3*(1), 2015. Special Themed Issue: *Indigenizing Education*. https://journalhosting.ucalgary.ca/index.php/em/article/view/62959

REFLECTION QUESTIONS

1. How do the historical colonial situations shown in Indigenous literature continue to affect Indigenous people in Canada today?
2. How did the Indian residential school system achieve its intended purposes? In what ways have Indigenous people coped with the adversity and trauma of residential schools both as children and later as adults?
3. What are some of the Indigenous worldviews and cultural practices that have persisted despite the influences of colonialism and colonization? How do you see these worldviews and practices as beneficial to helping First Nations people recover from historic trauma and the intergenerational impacts of residential schools?
4. What is your understanding of racism and oppression (for example, what are three/four key ideas to understand and know)?

SUGGESTED READINGS

- Highway T. (1998). *Kiss of the Fur Queen*. Doubleday Canada.
- Highway T. (2021). *Permanent astonishment: Growing up Cree in the land of snow and sky*. Doubleday Canada.
- Miroux, F. (2019). Richard Wagamese's *Indian Horse:* Stolen memories and recovered histories. *Actio Nova: Revista de Teoría de la Literatura y Literatura Comparada*, *3*, 194–230. https://doi.org/10.15366/actionova2019.3.009

- Thistle, J. (2019). *From the ashes: My story of being Métis, homeless, and finding my way.* Simon and Schuster.

REFERENCES

Alfred, T. (2004). Warrior scholarship: Seeing the university as a ground of contention. In D. A. Mihesuah & A. C. Wilson (Eds.), *Indigenizing the academy: Transforming scholarship and empowering communities* (pp. 88–99). University of Nebraska Press.

Archibald, J. (2008). *Indigenous storywork: Educating the heart, mind, body, and spirit.* UBC Press.

Battiste, M. (2012, May). *Bringing Aboriginal education into conventional education: Nourishing the learning spirit* [Presentation]. Canadian Society for the Study of Education, Waterloo, ON, Canada.

Beard, L. J. (2000). Giving voice: Autobiographical/testimonial literature by First Nations women of British Columbia. *Studies in American Indian Literatures, 12*(3), 64–83.

Brandon, W. W. (2002). Interrupting racial profiling: Moving pre-service teachers from white identity to equity pedagogy. In J. S. Slater, S. M. Fain, & C. A. Rosatto (Eds.), *The Freirean legacy* (pp. 139–156). Peter Lang.

Brant Castellano, M., Davis, L., & Lahache, L. (2000). *Aboriginal education: Fulfilling the promise.* UBC Press.

Campbell, M. (1973). *Halfbreed.* McClelland & Stewart.

Cannon, M. J., & Sunseri, L. (2011). Not disappearing: An introduction to the text. In M. J. Cannon & L. Sunseri, (Eds.), *Racism, colonialism, and Indigeneity in Canada: A reader* (pp. xiii–xxvii). Oxford University Press.

Chief, T. (2011). *Inclusion of Aboriginal content into the curriculum: Student and teacher perspectives* [Unpublished master's thesis]. University of Saskatchewan.

Clancy, P. J. (1995). *A study of selected Canadian Aboriginal literature: Its implications for teaching Aboriginal students* [Unpublished master's thesis]. University of Saskatchewan.

Culleton, B. M. (1983). *In search of April Raintree.* Pemmican Publications.

Dei, G. J. S., Hall, B. L., & Rosenberg, D. G. (2000). *Indigenous knowledges in global contexts: Multiple readings of our worlds.* University of Toronto Press.

Dick, B. (2005). *Grounded theory: A thumbnail sketch.* Retrieved January 14, 2023, from http://www.aral.com.au/resources/grounded.html

Donald, D. T. (2009). Forts, curriculum, and Indigenous Métissage: Imagining decolonization of Aboriginal-Canadian relations in educational contexts. *First Nations Perspectives, 2*(1), 1–24.

Episkenew, J. (2009). *Taking back our spirits: Indigenous literature, public policy, and healing.* University of Manitoba Press.

Farkas, G. (2003). Racial disparities and discrimination in education: What do we know, how do we know it, and what do we need to know? *Teachers College Record, 105*(6), 1119–1146. https://doi.org/10.1111/1467-9620.00279

Fellner, K. D. (2016). *Returning to our medicines: Decolonizing and Indigenizing mental health services to better serve Indigenous communities in urban spaces* [Unpublished doctoral dissertation]. University of British Columbia. https://open.library.ubc.ca/collections/ubctheses/24/items/1.0228859

Fellner, K. D. (2018). Embodying decoloniality: Indigenizing curriculum and pedagogy. *American Journal of Community Psychology, 62*(3–4), 283–293. https://doi.org/10.1002/ajcp.12286

Forsyth, J. (2013). Bodies of meaning: Sports and games at Canadian residential schools. In J. Forsyth & A. R. Giles (Eds.), *Aboriginal peoples and sport in Canada: Historical foundations and contemporary issues* (pp. 15–34). UBC Press.

Garcia, R. L. (1984). Countering classroom discrimination. *Theory into Practice, 23*(2), 104–109.

Ghosh, R. (2010). Racism: A hidden curriculum. *Education Canada, 48*(4), 26–29.

Gold, J. (2001). *Read for your life: Literature as a life support system.* Fitzhenry & Whiteside.

Harjo, J., & Bird, G. (1997). Introduction. In J. Harjo & G. Bird (Eds.), *Reinventing the enemy's language: Contemporary Native women's writings of North America* (pp. 22–24). W. W. Norton.

Hart, M. A. (2002). *Seeking mino-pimatisiwin: An Aboriginal approach to helping.* Fernwood Publishing.

Haug, E. (2005). Critical reflections on the emerging discourse of international social work. *International Social Work, 48*(2), 126–135. https://doi.org/10.1177/0020872805050204

Henry, F., & Tator, C. (2006). *The colour of democracy: Racism in Canadian society* (3rd ed.). Thomson Nelson Canada.

Herman, J. (1997). *Trauma and recovery: The aftermath of violence from domestic abuse to political terror.* Basic Books.

Hoxie, F. (2001). *A final promise: The campaign to assimilate Indians 1880–1920.* University of Nebraska Press.

Madden, B. (2016). *(Un)Becoming teacher of school-based Aboriginal education: Early career teachers, teacher identity, and Aboriginal education across institutions* [Unpublished doctoral dissertation]. University of British Columbia.

Martin, K., & Mirraboopa, B. (2003). Ways of knowing, being and doing: A theoretical framework and methods for Indigenous and Indigenist re-search. *Journal of Australian Studies, 27*(76), 203–214. https://doi.org/10.1080/14443050309387838

Maslin, C. (2002). *The social construction of Aboriginal people in the Saskatchewan print media* [Unpublished master's thesis]. University of Saskatchewan.

McGuire, P. D. (2013). *Anishinaabe Gikeedaasiwin—Indigenous knowledge: An exploration of resilience* [Unpublished doctoral thesis]. University of Saskatchewan.

Milloy, J. S. (2017). *A national crime: The Canadian government and the residential school system, 1879 to 1986*. University of Manitoba Press.

Mordoch, E., & Gaywish, R. (2011). Is there a need for healing in the classroom? Exploring trauma-informed education for Aboriginal mature students. *[Indigenous Education] in education, 17*(3), 96–106. https://doi.org/10.37119/ojs2011.v17i3.75

O'Reilly-Scanlon, K., Crowe, C., & Weenie, A. (2004). Pathways to understanding: "Wahkohtowin" as a research methodology. *McGill Journal of Education, 39*(1), 29–44.

Pennebaker, J. W. (1997). *Opening up: The healing power of confiding in others* (2nd ed.). The Guilford Press.

Pete, S., Schneider, B., & O'Reilly, K. (2013). Decolonizing our practice: Indigenizing our teaching. *First Nations Perspectives, 5*(1), 99–115.

Quigley, L. (2006). Weaving common threads. *Rural Special Education Quarterly, 25*(1), 3–6. https://doi.org/10.1177/875687050602500102

Riley, T., & Ungerleider, C. (2008). Preservice teachers' discriminatory judgments. *Alberta Journal of Educational Research, 54*(4), 378–387.

Riley, T., & Ungerleider, C. (2012). Self-fulfilling prophecy: How teachers' attributions, expectations, and stereotypes influence the learning opportunities afforded Aboriginal students. *Canadian Journal of Education, 35*(2), 303–333.

Sitler, H. C. (2009). Teaching with awareness: The hidden effects of trauma on learning. *The Clearing House: A Journal of Educational Strategies, Issues and Ideas, 82*(3), 119–123.

Stout, M. D., & Kipling, G. (2003). *Aboriginal people, resilience and the residential school legacy*. Aboriginal Healing Foundation. Retrieved January 14, 2023, from https://www.ahf.ca/downloads/resilience.pdf

Van Camp, R. (1996). *The lesser blessed*. Douglas & McIntyre.

White, J. P., Peters, J., Beavon, D., & Spence, N. (2009). *Aboriginal education: Current crisis and future alternatives*. Thompson Educational Publishing.

White-Kaulaity, M. (2006). The voices of power and the power of voices: Teaching with Native American literature. *The ALAN Review, 34*(1), 8–16.

Willett, E. C. (2007). Ahkamēyimo (Persevere): The experience of Aboriginal undergraduates. [Doctoral dissertation]. University of Saskatchewan Indigenous Studies Portal. Retrieved January 14, 2023, from https://iportal.usask.ca/record/36184

Wilson, A. C. (2004). Reclaiming our humanity: Decolonization and the recovery of Indigenous knowledge. In D. A. Mihesuah & A. C. Wilson (Eds.), *Indigenizing the academy: Transforming scholarship and empowering communities* (pp. 69–87). University of Nebraska Press.

CHAPTER 3

First Nations Control of First Nations Education: Using Land as a Foundation for Scholastic Achievement while Reinforcing Cree Culture, Language, and Ways of Knowing

Herman Michell, Lisa Antoine, and Delano Mike

This chapter is focused on how "First Nations control of First Nation education" has been at the forefront of "nation-to-nation" treaties in Canada since the early 1970s. In this chapter, we (as First Nation Elders, educators, scholars, and land protectors) outline an introduction to some of the key elements of land-based education that is rooted in the traditional territories of First Nations peoples. The contents include a heavy emphasis on the decolonization and Indigenization of education as a way to challenge systemic racism and cultural genocide stemming from the impacts of residential schools and other assimilation policies.

Educators across Canada recognize the value of land-based education and healing as a way to reconnect with First Nations culture, language, and ways of knowing in a post–residential school era. However, land-based education is familiar for First Nations peoples. Teaching and "learning on the land," community-driven, and community-led approaches are the cornerstone of Indigenous education (Battiste & Henderson, 2000).

The literature on land-based education is growing (Michell, 2018; Tuck et al., 2014; Wildcat et al., 2014; Wilson & Wilson, 2010). It is the "community" that breathes life into land-based education. The mission is to create a "home away from home" school environment for teachers and students focusing on scholastic achievement. Many studies have been done on First Nations education. One of the most comprehensive was the Royal Commission on Aboriginal Peoples report (1996).

In this chapter, we are authors of Cree heritage. We outline the basic elements of land-based education. We are strong advocates for First Nations education and healing in the aftermath of residential schools. We strongly believe in community-based education approaches. We intend to add to the land-based education discourse with a focus on Cree Peoples' ways of knowing. First Nations are diverse across Canada. However, we have a shared history of colonization (Michell, 2015). We have a shared worldview of interconnectedness. We have a shared vision of self-determination.

First Nations peoples have always had their own education systems prior to contact. Our Elders and Knowledge Keepers say "we must go back" to the land in order to heal from the multilayered impacts of assimilation. Reconciliation is very much about reclaiming our own ways of teaching while healing from collective trauma (Michell, 2017). First Nations cultures, worldview, languages, knowledge systems, ways of knowing, ceremonies, values, history, and day-to-day practices are rooted in the land, lakes, and rivers we occupy.

First Nations people want their children to learn "who they are" while accessing the best education possible. We want our children to engage in "multiple-eyed seeing" in an increasingly global world. We want them to walk in "multiple worlds" with a sense of pride. Today, teachers follow provincial curriculum standards and outcomes as a guide. The province of Saskatchewan has a mandate to incorporate Indigenous content at the K–12 level. It is important to note First Nations peoples have an Inherent Right to develop school foundations that reflect their cultural ways of life while reinforcing academic excellence.

Curriculum theories have undergone significant changes "opening doorways" for Indigenous Knowledge(s) and ways of teaching and learning. More and more First Nations teachers are doing graduate-level training. Curriculum theories that inform teacher practice change as more research is done using Indigenous methodologies. Teachers, leaders, and parents must continue to engage in local dialogue about what it means to have "First Nations control of First Nations education" at a cultural, philosophical, theoretical, and practical level.

Land-based education begins with a "**teacher exploration and sharing**" on what it means to be "Cree" and why it is necessary to teach and learn about Cree ways of knowing.

- What does it mean to be located within a treaty territory?
- What does it mean to be situated on Cree lands and the history of the Cree peoples?

- What does it mean for what we teach?
- What does it mean for the way we teach?
- What does it mean to incorporate Cree language and ways of knowing in our families and school?

Community people and teachers of Cree heritage are encouraged to engage in Circle Conversations and a "remembering back" on how young people were educated during pre-contact times. These stories require documentation for curriculum development purposes. How can the land-based education approach be used to teach core subjects while strengthening Cree culture and language using the seasonal cycle? How can Cree education be strengthened using anti-racist and anti-oppressive approaches?

Duck Lake was home to one of the last operating residential schools in Canada, St. Michael's Indian Residential School (Duck Lake Indian Residential School), which closed in 1996. It was in existence for over 100 years. The disruption of First Nations cultures, worldviews, languages, family systems and ways of life caused by the residential school system created collective trauma. Children suffered horrific abuses. Today, it is about healing and reclaiming cultural identity and language while supporting learners and survivors.

As an original signatory to Treaty 6 (1876), the Beardy's & Okemasis' Cree Nation is situated near the national historic sites of Fort Carlton and Batoche—home of the Riel Resistance. It is one of the largest independent bands in Saskatchewan. Reserve lands extend from rich farmlands in central Saskatchewan to the resource-rich southeastern Saskatchewan. The community is located 80 kilometres north of Saskatoon adjacent to the town of Duck Lake. Population: 3,565. Registered band members as of 2019: 1,073 live on reserve. Their 18,368.5-hectare land base is located approximately 58 kilometres southwest of Prince Albert.

INDIGENOUS EDUCATION REQUIRES ACCESS TO LAND

Beardy's & Okemasis' Cree Nation is a perfect place for land-based approaches to teaching, learning, and healing. The traditional ecological knowledge (TEK) of First Nations people stems back to the beginning of time (Michell et al., 2021). There are mixed ecosystems: northern plains, boreal forest, and thousands of lakes, rivers, muskegs, and ponds. Cree people's lives revolve around buffalo, deer, elk, moose, geese, ducks, and other animals. There are diverse animal habitats and places to fish and gather medicines, berries, and natural foods. It is a region with a vibrant history from prehistoric times to the present day. The elderly have rich stories to share about living on the land.

Cree culture consists of hunting, fishing, trapping, gathering, and growing foods. Living off the land requires a sustainable and active physical lifestyle. Shared responsibilities, teamwork, and collaboration are important for survival. The weather can be cold and harsh in the winter. It is important to prepare students with survival skills before and during excursions. Safety of students is a priority. Students can be given swimming tests and taught the geography of the area, canoe safety, and first aid. They have opportunities to explore who they are through traditional activities, learn how to build a fire and shelter, and learn to harvest foods and medicines in a way that does not disturb the delicate balance of the natural world.

Indigenous education involves activities for mental, spiritual, emotional, and physical development. The focus is on whole-child development. Elders say multi-dimensional balance is important for health and wellness. Traditional land users and Cree Knowledge Keepers are the teachers of Cree ways of knowing. They have diverse knowledge and skill sets. They are role models. Teachers and students learn together on excursions while fulfilling provincial curriculum expectations. There is a balance of indoor and outdoor activities.

Until the early 1990s, most schools in Saskatchewan struggled with how to integrate First Nations cultural content. During the residential school era, local histories and local stories were absent from the curriculum. There needed to be more First Nations books, articles, and materials. "Pan-Indian" teaching approaches were common. Culture and language were considered an "add-on" to the curriculum. Today, integration comes in many forms. Raising the profile of Indigenous knowledge systems and the work of Knowledge Keepers is important at the community level.

Many advances have been made in First Nations education since the "1973 Indian Control of Indian Education Policy." This policy was adopted by the National Indian Brotherhood, now the Assembly of First Nations. First Nation communities are taking over their own education systems, developing school authorities, sitting on school boards, and creating Indigenous-based schools. Teacher capacity has been built. First Nations curriculum development is ongoing. The Truth and Reconciliation Commission (TRC) report on residential schools reinforces the need for the development of First Nations education systems (2012, 2015).

Strong administrative support is essential in First Nations education. Principals and teachers need to have a solid background on the social, historical, political, economic, cultural, and contemporary realities of First Nations across Canada. Educators are encouraged to actively connect and learn about their work community, culture, history, and traditional teaching practices through continuous professional development opportunities, orientations, and workshops.

Cree culture, Cree language, and Cree ways of knowing are rooted in the land, lakes, and rivers. Spiritual laws and natural laws are learned on the land. The concept of "community" extends to the natural world. In the Cree belief system, we consider animals and plants as our relatives. There are many teachings. Community involvement in curriculum development and implementation is essential. Parental involvement is linked to academic success. Federal government funding for land-based education is a moral and legal imperative in an era of reconciliation. Land-based education comes with costs that are beyond annual school budget allocations.

Land-based education is different in each school context. Teachers can take students out on short land excursions with minimal costs. Medicine Walks, in which students are shown how to identify traditional plants and edible foods, are common. Land-based education can include blocking off an hour, an afternoon, the whole day, or a four-day excursion. Land-based activities can also be done inside the classroom. Bring the land into the classroom. Balance is the key, as not all children are able to experience land-based activities.

Teachers need culturally appropriate resources and materials to be effective in the delivery of Indigenous education. A teacher resource and material repository website is needed so that sample lesson plans, activities, books, articles, videos, and documentaries are easily accessible. Other links can be showcased so that teachers have options based on their area of focus. One of the richest repositories is the National Centre for Collaboration in Indigenous Education (NCCIE.ca).

Land-based education is essential in reversing the impacts of colonization, residential schools, day schools, and Sixties Scoop experiences. The goal of residential schools was to "tear down the child" and make them into the likeness of European settlers. According to the TRC report, Canada committed cultural genocide. This assimilation approach to education resulted in a massive loss of cultures and languages. The psychosocial symptoms from abuse experienced in these schools are observable in communities. Elders say we must go back to the land to heal from the impacts, re-learn our cultural life ways, and strengthen our languages.

Spirituality is the foundation of Cree communities. Traditional spiritual practices are inseparable from school operations. Cree ceremonies, protocols, prayers, dances, songs, and stories are rooted in the land. Spiritual laws and Cree values are learned in ceremonies and community gatherings. Traditional values guide respectful ways of thinking and behaving. They reinforce a "sacred and relational" school environment based on respect for others regardless of race, culture, ethnicity, gender, and other social markers.

Community celebrations and community Pow Wows are important because they bring people together. Community gatherings "bring people home." Seasonal feasts in school settings create a "school ethos" of sharing, caring, and mutual respect. It is important to raise the profile of First Nations schools by showcasing innovative activities. Awards, incentives, and celebrating the achievements of teachers and students in a public way attracts enrolment. Alumni and student testimonials of how Beardy's & Okemasis' Cree Nation programs and courses are benefiting their lives are good for retention purposes.

Land-based education is the Cree way of teaching and learning. Cree peoples have their own Cree ontology, epistemology, methodologies, and pedagogical practices. Cree ontology is linked to how we see the world and our place in it. We see the world in an interdependent way. Everything is connected.

Cree epistemology is how education is perceived. We learn from humans as well as from the animal and plant nations that nurture our minds, bodies, and spirit. The animals and fish are significant to the Cree peoples, not only for sustenance but also how they fit into surrounding ecosystems in a spiritual and relational sense. Bridging Western science and Indigenous ways of knowing is important (Cajete, 2000).

Cree methodology uses diverse and rich methods to pass knowledge on to the younger generation, including hunting, trapping, fishing, and gathering activities. Students learn regular school subjects on the land, lakes, and rivers. Teachers develop multiple outlets of expression for students to share, apply, and demonstrate their knowledge in their own way. Storytelling methodology and story methods are ways of passing on knowledge and wisdom. Students learn Cree ways of knowing, cultural teachings, origin stories, traditional values, survival skills, food sovereignty, and self-sufficiency.

Cree pedagogy includes different Cree teaching methods and processes. In traditional times, the extended family members were the teachers. They have diverse knowledge and skill sets. Mentoring and the "See and Do" approach was a common way to sharpen skill sets. Sharing circles are one of the traditional processes used to share knowledge and traditional stories. Hunters also learn how to hunt by observing how animals and birds hunt on the land. Teachers combine teaching methods learned in teacher training and practices learned from community resource people.

There is a need to provide multiple supports for students of First Nations heritage. Understanding the social determinants of health and wellness is essential. Many are intergenerational survivors of residential schools, day schools, the Sixties Scoop, and child and family services without access to culture. School counsellors, mental health workers, psychologists, and educational psychologists should have a good solid background in historical trauma, its multidimensional impacts, and the skills needed for recovery.

Indigenous education is about focusing on strengths rather than deficits. Concentrate on inherent strengths and resilience within families and communities. Pride is developed by highlighting successes. Advances have been made in communities within a very short period of time. It's necessary to teach First Nations contributions in Canada, including "land and resources." Cree historians are valuable in Indigenous education. Cree professionals from various sectors are role models that can be invited into classrooms. They have stories to share about their careers, education and work experiences, and their ways of knowing.

Indigenous education requires strong community involvement. Beardy's and Okemasis' Cree Nation members are key players in developing a school system that reflects their culture, worldview, language, values, visions, and aspirations. First Nations youth make up the fastest growing population in Saskatchewan and thus drive the need to invest in closing education and employment gaps. We want all children to have the best education possible so they can succeed in life. The youth are the next generation of nation-builders.

The visibility of community members within First Nations schools is important. Community members are encouraged to work closely with teachers and principals. Education beyond the school environment includes parent champions and quality outreach activities. A First Nations Education Framework and Strategic Plan helps guide curriculum development, scope and sequence, and unit and lesson plans in elementary and high schools. Visionary direction aimed at community capacity building is the cornerstone of nation-rebuilding efforts.

Indigenous education requires Elder involvement. First Nation Elders and Knowledge Keepers are the carriers of culture, history, language, stories, and ways of knowing. The entrenchment of Elders in a school is done by developing a mandatory school policy for Elder involvement. Elder offices are becoming common at all levels of the education system (Michell, 2011). Traditional Elders work closely with school counsellors and mental health workers around traditional ceremonies, as well as individual and group counselling. Elders play an advisory role at the governance, administration, teaching, and support levels. They are invited to participate in school meetings. They set the tone for respectful interaction.

Land-based education is linked to the seasonal cycle. First Nations people did certain things at certain times of the year. Seasonal practices become the curriculum framework for land-based education. Youth are taught harvesting protocols and sustainable ways of thinking and being. We take what we need from the land and leave the rest. Students learn the "Ethic of Conservation." Traditional land users teach natural laws when they engage in hunting and gathering activities. In Cree belief system, the animals offer themselves so we can live. Tobacco is sprinkled on the ground to give thanks and sacred appreciation.

Land-based education is connected to food sovereignty and food security. Students learn how to be self-sufficient and independent. Community food sovereignty initiatives are recommended. Participants learn how to grow and harvest natural food. They learn how to gather edible plants and medicines from the land for health and wellness. Store-bought foods can be expensive; they can also be highly processed and unhealthy. A sedentary lifestyle and fast foods are linked to obesity, circularity diseases, diabetes, and other chronic illnesses (Samson & Pretty, 2006). Service projects such harvesting fresh fish, meat, and medicines allow students to learn the "Ethic of Reciprocity" by sharing and giving back to the community.

Land-based education is essential for Cree culture and language immersion. One must be immersed in the land in all of its seasonal facets in order to learn Cree culture and language. People won't be able to learn about Cree culture with books or from one-day workshops. Cree culture is a way of life that must be lived, experienced, shared, and applied. Cree language is best learned on the land where there is a stimulus of reference points from the natural world. There are immersion and experiential teaching methods available for teachers.

The land has everything we need to survive including what we need to learn. The land and waters nourish and feed our bodies, minds, spirit, and the way we think about the world and our place in it. The social ills we see in communities today, such as alcoholism, drugs, violence, suicides, and gangs, are symptoms of historical trauma, assimilation attempts, and a disconnection from land and culture. Survivors and intergenerational survivors require multiple supports and constructive expression outlets. Land-based education creates a sense of immersion, belonging, healing, and hope.

There is a heavy focus on land-based education across the country. For Cree people, land-based education is not a trend. Land-based education is necessary for culture and language survival. Teachers have been doing land-based education in different forms throughout the years. Ongoing teacher professional development opportunities are essential as theories and best practices emerge. Bringing together land-based teachers to share and learn from one another reinforces curriculum strength and outcomes.

Entrenching land-based approaches in different sectors will strengthen First Nations community foundations. The education sector is a good starting place as it filters through all other sectors: health, justice, policing, corrections, social work, mental health, and environment. An interagency hub approach can be implemented to help fulfill visionary community goals and pool resources together to deal with challenges. Reconciliation is a shared responsibility. There is respect for diverse cultures and knowledge systems.

Land-based approaches are important in Indigenous Awareness Training. We need to take people out on the land to share the beauty of who we are as First Nations people. We have Cree processes that reinforce balance and respect. Anti-racist and anti-oppressive professional development opportunities are important for judges, lawyers, police officers, corrections officers, doctors, nurses, teachers, mental health workers, and other service providers.

Land-based education is the future. Community resource people are diverse with diverse knowledge and skill sets. Community resource directories can be developed to ensure teachers have access to a pool of community members that are available for school activities and lessons. Cree Knowledge Keepers believe it is their sacred responsibility to pass on Cree ways of knowing to the younger generation. The school is a key site for Cree knowledge production and mobilization using community protocols and land-based approaches.

Teacher passion, motivation, creativity, and fun are ingredients in Indigenous education. Students need variety. The use of technology is a bonus to teaching and learning. Teacher incentives for those specializing in land-based education to strengthen culture and language are recommended. We want our youth to be exposed to meaningful learning experiences, rich content, hands-on activities, and diverse projects where they have opportunities to expand their knowledge base and transferable skill sets.

Land-based education reinforces gender equality. Out on the land, everyone shares roles and responsibilities. Students learn to support each other through teamwork and collaboration. In traditional times, men would leave for long periods of time on hunting excursions. Gender roles were blurred. Women hunted and killed big game like men. Two-spirited and gender-diverse peoples are highly valued. Everyone belongs in a community. The "Ethic of Hard Work and Equality" is promoted early in life. Students are taught to respect women who are the life givers of our nations.

Land-based education benefits children from all nations. There is value in learning from different knowledge perspectives. Learning is enriched. Taking care of the earth is a shared responsibility. Students are exposed to the perspectives of First Nations people who have had a strong relationship with the land for thousands of years. Cree teaching methods and processes used in land-based education are based on respect for people and the natural world. All humans must bond with the earth like our closest relative. It feels us as we walk on the surface. We can feel her pain from destructive human forces. We have a shared responsibility to take care of our life giver.

Teacher recruitment and retention is part of Indigenous education. High teacher turnover affects consistency in the delivery of the curriculum. Key areas linked to staff recruitment and retention include school policies, appropriate funding to run programs, support for teacher growth and teacher benefits, rate of pay, language incentives, and housing. There is a need for clear expectations, roles, and responsibilities based on school plans. Annual evaluations of teachers allow opportunities to celebrate milestone achievements in fulfilling school goals and strategic plans. Best practices and teacher testimonials are highlighted and showcased. Teachers' voices, perspectives, and recommendations are important in school operations. A "welcoming ceremony" can be developed for new teachers.

Land-based education coordinators are crucial. It is important to have a point person and "teacher champion" guided by the school's land-based education and curriculum development goals that will assist the principals and teachers in fulfilling annual strategic actions. This educator can act as a liaison between school and community. This person can also liaise and work with sports, recreation, and culture staff. The land-based education coordinator engages in ongoing background research on land-based education initiatives in other schools while showcasing best practices. The land-based education coordinator is a key player in assisting teachers with planning out land-based excursions, activities, and lesson plans.

Land-based education activities are developed so that students are engaging, thinking, observing, doing, and applying knowledge while actively learning their language. Land-based education allows students to explore the world around them using deep thinking skills and engaging in age-appropriate activities. Land-based educators often use thematic stations to show step-by-step ways of butchering animals. There is rigour and focus involved. Land-based curriculum development teams, teacher buddy systems, and teachers networking with other land-based educators builds knowledge and skill sets.

The land is alive in our Cree world. The land is both a teacher and healer. Spirit filters through the land and waters and the animal and plant nations. The land is a "community of teachers." Cree epistemology reinforces the belief that we learn not only from humans but also from the animals, plants, and wildlife that share our existence. Youth learn how to "read" and "converse with" the land, lakes, and rivers. Cree worldview is developed by becoming aware of how we are *spiritually connected* to everything around us.

Beardy's & Okemasis' Cree Nation has strong links to the land. Chief Beardy's Willow Plains Cree hunted and trapped throughout the Duck Lake area prior to signing Treaty 6 on August 28, 1876, at Fort Carlton. Beardy (Kahmeeyistoowaysit) was so named because of his black beard. He chose land for both himself and Chief Okemasis (Sayswaypus) west of Duck Lake and began building small log houses and cultivating gardens. After Beardy died in 1889, his reserve was without a chief until 1936.

The Beardy's & Okemasis' Cree Nation constitution is rooted in the lands Cree people occupy. The constitution outlines fundamental freedoms and rights. It reinforces the right of members to exist as distinct peoples with Cree laws, Cree governance, Cree-led regulations, and Cree-developed policies in all community sectors. It lays out the parameters of citizenship. It acknowledges treaties and treaty promises made by the British Crown. The constitution requires an articulated Beardy's and Okemasis' Cree Nation Education Act.

The constitution and legislative acts are necessary for the Cree functioning of the nation. At the signing of the treaties, a pipe ceremony was a common practice. Every aspect of the pipe is linked to the land with the Great Spirit as witness to the treaty. Treaty 6 is a sacred covenant. It is a legal document between two nations to live side by side without interfering in each other's life ways. Today, developing right relations is critical to restoring treaty balance in the aftermath of colonization and residential schools.

In conclusion, we have outlined some of the basic elements of land-based education, decolonization, and the indigenization of schooling. It is important to note Indigenous knowledge systems are not static. They evolve and transform as new research is introduced. Cree knowledge production is incredibly complex. One can never know all there is to know about Cree culture in a lifetime.

This article has limits; for example, we did not use Cree language terms to describe Indigenous land-based education. The United Nations Declaration on the Rights of Indigenous Peoples (UNDRIP) reinforces First Nations people's rights to develop their own education systems. The TRC calls to action in education also offer strong recommendations.

UNITED NATIONS DECLARATION ON THE RIGHTS OF INDIGENOUS PEOPLES

Article 14

1. Indigenous peoples have the right to establish and control their educational systems and institutions providing education in their own languages, in a manner appropriate to their cultural teaching and learning methods.

Article 13

1. Indigenous peoples have the right to revitalize, use, develop and transmit to future generations their histories, languages, oral traditions, philosophies, writing systems and literatures, and to designate and retain their own names for communities, places and persons.

Article 12

1. Indigenous peoples have the right to manifest, practise, develop and teach their spiritual and religious traditions, customs and ceremonies; the right to maintain, protect, and have access in privacy to their religious and cultural sites; the right to the use and control of their ceremonial objects; and the right to the repatriation of their human remains (United Nations, 2007).

TRUTH AND RECONCILIATION CALLS TO ACTION IN EDUCATION

62. We call upon the federal, provincial, and territorial governments, in consultation and collaboration with Survivors, Aboriginal peoples, and educators, to:

   i. Make age-appropriate curriculum on residential schools, Treaties, and Aboriginal peoples' historical and contemporary contributions to Canada a mandatory education requirement for Kindergarten to Grade Twelve students.
   ii. Provide the necessary funding to post-secondary institutions to educate teachers on how to integrate Indigenous knowledge and teaching methods into classrooms.
   iii. Provide the necessary funding to Aboriginal schools to utilize Indigenous knowledge and teaching methods in classrooms.
   iv. Establish senior-level positions in government at the assistant deputy minister level or higher dedicated to Aboriginal content in education (TRC, 2015).

> We Want to Create a Rich Land-based Learning Environment.
> The Next Generation of Nation Builders
> Will Be a
> Community of Visionaries and Knowledge Keepers
> Protectors of Cree Culture and Language
> and
> STEWARDS OF THE LAND

REFLECTION QUESTIONS

1. What are the meanings of land-based education from and within Indigenous perspectives?
2. How can we learn and practice these meanings in our everyday practice?
3. How are Indigenous worldviews and land-based education interconnected?
4. What are the benefits of Indigenous land-based education and programming?

SUGGESTED READINGS

- Battiste, M., & Henderson, S. (2021). Indigenous and trans-systemic knowledge systems (ᐃᑯᑕᐃᒡᓇᐱᐅᓐ ᓄᐅᑦᐊdgᐊ ᐊᑉd 'ᔑᐊᑉᐅᐅᑦᓴᑕᐸᐅᐅᓴᒐ ᓄᐅᑦᐊdgᐊ ᓐᑦᓐᓴᐦᓐ). *Engaged Scholar Journal, 7*(1), i–xix. https://doi.org/10.15402/esj.v7i1.70768
- Hoffman, K. M., Christianson, A. C., Dickson-Hoyle, S., Copes-Gerbitz, K., Nikolakis, W., Diabo, D. A., McLeod, R., Michell, H. J., Al Mamun, A., Zahara, A., Mauro, N., Gilchrist, J., Ross, R. M., & Daniels, L. D. (2022). The right to burn: Barriers and opportunities for Indigenous-led fire stewardship in Canada. *FACETS, 7*(1), 464–481.
- Michell, H. (2005). Nēhîthâwâk of Reindeer Lake, Canada: Worldview, epistemology and relationships with the natural world. *The Australian Journal of Indigenous Education, 34*, 33–43. https://doi.org/10.1017/S132601110000394X
- Michell, H., Hardlotte, B., & McLeod, R. (2021). Traditional ecological knowledge (TEK) of the Woodlands Cree and Denesuline Peoples of northern Saskatchewan, Canada: The land as teacher and healer. *Journal of Indigenous Wellbeing, 6*(1), 26–36.
- Parlee, B., Huntington, H., Berkes, F., Lantz, T., Andrew, L., Tsannie, J., Reece, C., Porter, C., Nicholson, V., Peter, S., Simmons, D., Michell, H., Lepine, M., Maclean, B., Ahkimnachie, K., King, L. J., Napoleon, A., Hogan, J., Lam, J., … Howlett, T. (2021). One-size does not fit all—A networked approach to community-based monitoring in large river basins. *Sustainability, 13*(13), 7400. https://doi.org/10.3390/su13137400

REFERENCES

Battiste, M., & Henderson, J. S. Y. (2000). *Protecting Indigenous knowledge and heritage: A global challenge*. Purich Publishing.

Cajete, G. (2000). *Native science: Natural laws of interdependence*. Clear Light Publishers.

King, T. (1990). Medicine River. *Wicazo Sa Review, 6*(2), 15–20. https://doi.org/10.2307/1409290

Michell, H. J. (2011). *Working with Elders and Indigenous knowledge systems: A reader and guide for places of higher learning.* J Charlton Publishing.

Michell, H. J. (2015). *Shattered spirits in the land of the little sticks: Contextualizing the impact of residential schools among the Woodland Cree.* J Charlton Publishing.

Michell, H. J. (2017). *Reconciliation from an Indigenous perspective: Weaving the web of life in the aftermath of residential schools.* J Charlton Publishing.

Michell, H. J. (2018). *Land-based education: Embracing the rhythms of the earth from an Indigenous perspective.* J Charlton Publishing.

Michell, H., Hardlotte, B., & McLeod, R. (2021). Traditional ecological knowledge (TEK) of the Woodland Cree and Denesuline Peoples of northern Saskatchewan, Canada: The land as teacher and healer. *Journal of Indigenous Well-being, 6*(1), 26–36.

Royal Commissions on Aboriginal Peoples. (1996). *Report of the Royal Commission on Aboriginal Peoples: Perspectives and realities* (Vol. 4). Canada Communication Group. http://data2.archives.ca/e/e448/e011188230-04.pdf

Samson, C., & Pretty, J. (2006). Environmental and health benefits of hunting lifestyles and diets for the Innu of Labrador. *Food Policy, 31*(6), 528–553. https://doi.org/10.1016/j.foodpol.2006.02.001

Truth and Reconciliation Commission of Canada. (2012). *They came for the children: Canada, Aboriginal Peoples, and residential schools.*

Truth and Reconciliation Commission of Canada. (2015). *Honoring the truth, reconciling for the future: Summary of the final report of the Truth and Reconciliation Commission of Canada.*

Tuck, E., McKenzie, M., & McCoy, K. (2014). Land education: Indigenous, post-colonial, and decolonizing perspectives on place and environmental education research. *Environmental Education Research, 20*(1), 1–23. https://doi.org/10.1080/13504622.2013.877708

United Nations. (2007). *United Nations Declaration on the Rights of Indigenous Peoples.* https://social.desa.un.org/issues/indigenous-peoples/united-nations-declaration-on-the-rights-of-indigenous-peoples

Wildcat, M., McDonald, M., Irlbacher-Fox, S., & Coulthard, G. (2014). Learning from the land: Indigenous land based pedagogy and decolonization. *Decolonization: Indigeneity, Education & Society, 3*(3), i–xv.

Wilson, P., & Wilson, S. (2010). *Land-based education.* Aboriginal Boreal Conservation Leaders. http://www.abcleaders.org/stories/634/dr-peggy-wilson-and-dr-stan-wilson

CHAPTER 4

The Pedagogy of Decolonization through a Paradigm Shift in Birth Work from an Indigenous Woman's Perspective

Kristie Billard

In this chapter, I use my experience to explain the need for anti-racist community building through a return to Indigenous midwifery. I first explain the various terms like decolonization, reconciliation, colonial Canada, and the influence of Western ideals. I use this to highlight the need for change in the education and healthcare systems that discount and vilify Indigenous land-based knowledge and oral histories. Second, I explain the significance of acknowledging Indigenous heritage, having grown up in Treaty 7 without ties to a First Nations community, never being taught the history of my people, and experiencing intolerance and racism in education systems in Calgary, Alberta. Third, I explain how I am working to decolonize my knowledge, learning my history through the words of my ancestors and questioning colonial accounts of historical fact. Fourth, by discussing responsibilities for change, I propose a need for institutions to create alternate routes to meet Western educational needs, including pedagogy for Indigenous midwives that recognizes First Nations knowledge. Fifth, I explain why Indigenous birthing bodies need access to midwifery care, the importance of midwifery in the health of a community, and the systems preventing access to care. Finally, I share my thoughts on responsibilities for reconciliation on the part of Canada, specifically in Treaty 7 Territory.

I am grateful for the recognition and reverence of allies and researchers who deeply connect to the plight of Indigenous communities worldwide. I wish to address the education system's colonial structure that teaches us the ways of Indigenous people through the writings of Indigenous and non-Indigenous academics. It is not lost on me that these institutions teach traditional Indigenous knowledge and oral history in a way that would have never happened in the past. In my journey, I follow Elders' and knowledge keepers' teachings to lead my cultural training. With this in mind, I have tried to use oral histories and teachings from as many Indigenous academics and Elders as possible for this chapter and opted for much of my referencing to be conversations or videos of Indigenous Elders and women speaking instead of solely written papers and articles. Part of my decolonization journey is recognizing the vast difference between simply reading about Indigenous knowledge and obtaining it directly by building relationships with Indigenous people who have lived experience.

RESPONSIBILITIES FOR DECOLONIZATION

My understanding of decolonization has changed considerably in my 43 years. As an Indigenous woman of colour raised by a Canadian/European family, my understanding and need for decolonization were central in reconciling my Indigenous lineage and colonial upbringing in Canada. This chapter discusses my decolonization journey, which has guided my path to becoming an Indigenous birth worker. I discuss my heritage and the hurdle acknowledging it represented for me in overcoming bias, stereotypes, racism, and prejudice encountered in the colonial systems of education, healthcare, and the discourse of Canadian society. I have embraced decolonization as a necessity for engaging in a respectful, ethical discourse to reconnect with my culture and exist within a society built on the elimination of our people. Indigenous decolonization is vital to challenging the dominant Eurocentric perspective, which originated in Western Europe and was brought over by colonialists.

Decolonial stories told by Indigenous peoples about the First Nations' relations with Canada are different from stories told by the newcomers wanting land and resources. Learning Indigenous perspectives and the inconsistencies between colonial narratives and Indigenous oral histories empowered me to search for the truth concerning my people and the need for reconciliation in colonial society. Reconciliation is a path to enlightenment for Western systems; Canada needs to enter into a relational pluralism, attempting to understand and establish a link to Indigenous peoples' ways of life without trying to dominate (Schouls, 2002). Reconciliation is a Catholic term (Wilson, 2016) and a path that seems easier than conciliation, which would require Canadian governments to address colonialism (Anti-racist scholar and activist from Treaty 6 Territory and one of the founders of the Idle No More movement, Dr. Sheelah McLean, personal communication, January 23, 2021). Conciliation is the first step for the Canadian government and the Christian church to correct history and move towards equality for the Indigenous and non-Indigenous to live in Treaty on this land.

SIGNIFICANCE OF ACKNOWLEDGEMENT

When I was young, my worldview was clouded by how others projected my heritage on me. I was never white-passing but grew up in a mainly white, Western European family. My mother and grandparents, third-generation Canadians of Scottish, Irish, and American descent, raised me. My father of origin is Indigenous, his mother First Nations from the Tsuut'ina Nation bordering Calgary and his father of Caribbean descent, hailing from Maryland in the United States. I struggled with identity as neither the Indigenous nor non-Indigenous communities fully accepted me. My grandmother married a non-Indigenous Black man and was enfranchised; her children were considered half-breeds within her community and treated as *others*. I was never introduced to the reserve or Indigenous ways by my father or grandmother. The lack of representation within white society and culture, school, peers, and community reminded me daily that I did not belong.

There was a diverse group of kids growing up in Calgary in the 1980s, with many families of first-generation Canadian children from around the world. First Nations children within my quadrant of urban Calgary were a minority. Canada had a reputation as a multicultural society, frequently offered as a juxtaposition to the United States, where persecution for culture, religion, and beliefs often occurred. However, the intolerance shown to this country's Indigenous peoples did not exude a multiculturalist ideal. In the province of Alberta, with no exposure to Tsuut'ina or the other Treaty 7 nations' knowledge or beliefs, all I had was a white worldview. These worldviews taught me about where I came from, what my Indigenous family was like, what I was like, and why I should feel shame for who we were.

Throughout my years in public school, conventional education taught me nothing about Canada's relationship with Indigenous people. The basis of social studies texts were highlights of colonial successes, and the celebration of Canada's centennial was bereft of Indigenous involvement. The minor details of Indigenous people were just footnotes containing erroneous accounts of land surrender (Calgary Public Library, 2020). The minuscule content did not highlight Indigenous knowledge, ways of life, beliefs, connection to the land, traditional healing and being, or the relationship with animals, water, and plants (Hart, 2010). The stereotypes, prejudice, and racial slurs heard in society and in homes were not assuaged by truths heard in schools or higher institutions; those truths were not being told. Dr. Verna St. Denis (an Indigenous anti-racist scholar) argues that reconciliation needs an anti-racist movement in urban education; schools have a history of ignoring racism, which will continue to happen without drastic change (personal communication, January 23, 2021). As one of few Indigenous students, I was a target of discrimination and long-held biases; as a result, my lineage was not something I shared openly. Everyday society, including all types of institutions, had never offered me a positive image of my people. It was not until I started seeking my truths and embracing my heritage, learning it through the eyes of Elders and other Indigenous people, whom I engaged with and learned from, that I understood the strength and pain of my ancestors. I am proud of my Indigenous heritage now; I approach my path with traits I admire in my ancestors: honour, peace, equality, humility, and always humour. Learning about my heritage has given me purpose and a voice; it has revealed a path where I once was lost.

COLONIAL CANADA AND WESTERN IDEALS

Western colonials wrote their narratives, painting themselves as an evolved society based on their written laws, language, and history; in contrast, Indigenous societies held oral history as a cornerstone of teaching, and colonials used this difference to try to prove our primitive ways (Athabasca University Wolfe, 1977). However, based on our knowledge transfer system, Indigenous people survived on this land for centuries before colonization. First Nations cultures' underlying ideologies are sharing in peace, and one spoon, one bowl, where everyone takes and gets what they need (TreeTV/N2K Need to Know, 2016). These Indigenous tenets kept our communities safe and birthed the next generations. Indigenous people's inability to recognize the fundamentally different worldview they held in contrast to colonialists created a context in which colonials claimed dominion over Indigenous people (Hart, 2010). Colonial systems of governance where power and oppression reigned perpetuated the ill-treatment of First Nation communities for centuries.

In the book *21 Things You May Not Know about the Indian Act*, Bob Joseph (2018) highlights how the *Indian Act* debilitated the ways of Indigenous knowledge transfer within First Nations communities in Canada. The Act declared language, ceremony, and traditional clothing illegal, and to facilitate more significant control over Indigenous people, they were confined to reserves and made wards of the state. First Nations were treated as incapacitated adults in need of the state to watch over them (The Agenda | TVO Today, 2018). Denying access to traditional hunting, gathering, and fishing territories disabled First Nations from feeding their families (Desjardins & Monderie, 2012). For 150 years, First Nations children were removed from their communities and taken to residential schools, systems rampant with physical, emotional, and sexual abuse (Wolochatiuk, 2012). The school system deliberately separated children so Elders could not teach Indigenous youth their traditional ways, breaking the link of knowledge to the next generation.

Colonial society did not revere their women as the Indigenous community did; women traditionally held a place of importance for creating life and having important tasks that kept the family alive (TreeTV/N2K Need to Know, 2016). Indigenous nations abided by a land-rights system tied to the matriarchal bloodlines; the patriarchal treaties deliberately discluded women to stop these land transfers. The new patriarchal society the British created for the Indigenous undermined the power that women held. The *Indian Act*, which the government still abides by today, was built from this system meant to exclude women and undermine their voices. The *Indian Act* relegated women to less than , and declared them undeserving of rights, land, and power. The only feminine terms within the Act pertained to control over their marriage; childbirth; sexual conduct; exclusion from band business, including voting; and the inability to inherit the land (Lawrence, 2004). Removing rituals pertaining to birth was a deliberate act of control that removed power from the women in the community. Colonial government systems have marginalized, oppressed, and tried to assimilate or kill off the Indigenous people of Canada (TreeTV/N2K Need to Know, 2016). Rather than sharing in peace as the First Nations had agreed to in treaties, the government chose to wage a genocidal war lasting 500 years in order to gain land and resources without conforming to Indigenous ideals (Palmater, 2014). Our strength lies in empowering women to do the work our ancestors did; we need to take that back.

The pedagogy of colonialism runs deep; it is not just what they teach or exclude from the education system. It is a symptom of long-ingrained values and beliefs taught by people uneducated in Indigenous ways, with learned biases from colonial systems. It is affirmed in laws, practices, and institutions that do not recognize

Indigenous rights and knowledge. Learning Indigenous perspectives on treaties and oral versions passed through Indigenous Elders challenges the Western account and its English words (Calgary Public Library, 2020). Oral traditions claim different terms and promises from the treaties (Calgary Public Library, 2020). The refusal of Canadian government-derived systems to legitimize Indigenous oral traditions and traditional knowledge as reliable accounts of history allows them to continue to inhabit and pillage this land. British written versions have the First Nations giving away land, but First Nations' land knowledge and traditions say the land is not theirs to give; they are only stewards of the earth. Indigenous traditions and knowledge view Earth as a mother, an entity all its own (Desjardins & Monderie, 2012). The entire government system is devised based on a version of the treaty that does not bear our own words or ideals of sharing in peace and only plow deep (Mantyka-Pringle et al., 2015). The Canadian government refuses to address the wrongs done through colonization and the genocide committed because doing so would threaten their claims to the land, the resources within it and most importantly, the capital that comes from it; these capitalist gains are a significant barrier to the critical step of truth (Palmater, 2014). Admission of wrongdoing in terms of colonialism may complicate claims to this land (Tuck & Yang, 2012) and keep sovereignty from First Nations (Boutilier, 2017).

The healthcare and educational institutions' foundations are colonial ideas that perpetuated the theft of our land and genocide against our people. Since their inception, these same colonial institutions have not changed the core values and beliefs that perpetuated the genocide against us. There has not been a big enough paradigm shift in the ways of doing things to say that they can now be part of the solution. Learning of my people's oppression and the unfairness within our history was what I needed to move from a place of shame towards a path of decolonization.

DECOLONIZATION IS RELEARNING

I have worked hard to unlearn the colonial ideologies and disregard the dominant Canadian worldview towards First Nations people. Anti-racist and decolonial colour settler scholar Dr. Ranjan Datta's (2018) definition of decolonization, includes "an ongoing process of becoming, unlearning, and relearning" (p. 2). There is an overrepresentation of First Nations experiencing addictions, homelessness, jail, and the foster care system. For Canadians unfamiliar with the trauma of colonization and the ripple it has caused throughout every generation of Indigenous people, it can be hard to differentiate between the trauma and the people. The colonial government systems are responsible for Indigenous people's disproportionate socioeconomic status in urban settings as well as for creating biases and stereotypes against them (Hubbard, 2004). There is a disconnect between what Westerners see and the intergenerational trauma which is the root of this suffering. The systems of government operating today are born from colonialism and continually perpetuate the trauma through the *Indian Act* and laws that were born to assimilate. Colonialism penetrates every area of a First Nation person's life, from how they think of themselves and their communities to their treatment within Canadian social systems, which include education and healthcare. When Tk'emlúps te Secwépemc found unmarked children's graves on their residential school grounds in May of 2021 (Sterritt & Dickson, 2021), the sheer number made the world notice. It felt like a shift in the dominant opinion of Canadians, part of the process of becoming aware. The many other discoveries that came after the initial one on various other former residential school sites will hopefully lead to unlearning and relearning by Canadians about the truth of the genocidal treatment of Indigenous children in Canada.

Decolonization guides my newfound purpose of supporting Indigenous women in the sacred ritual of birth and looking after the needs of our women and children in the coming generations. I want to empower Indigenous women with the reverence they were held in before within First Nations communities and reignite the veneration we had for children. Indigenous communities prioritized children and focused their goals, teachings, and traditions on seven generations ahead. Indigenous women traditionally gave birth using midwives; now, generations later, Indigenous women are being denied care by midwives. Our women deserve the right to go through this sacred ceremony in a way that is not medicalized and institutionalized. Sarain Fox calls her act of having children as an Indigenous person a political act, "if we don't have babies, the colonizers win, and that's what they want" (2020). Helping women raise and protect their children is the opposite of genocide; it is a way to heal and further an Indigenous revolution (Fox, 2020). We do not need more shame and judgment, or the fear of losing our children to birth alerts and scoops due to a lack of understanding and colonial standards which are based on values that allowed mass genocide. Indigenous people have long been targeted with abuse and racism in healthcare systems. Instances of Indigenous people not seeking healthcare at all based on past experiences leads to worse health outcomes. Seeking it has sometimes led to death due to ingrained bias. People who understand Indigenous people's experiences and want to look after their kin need access to education and training. Giving birth with relational care involves community and continuity in healthcare workers without unconscious bias; Indigenous birthing bodies and babies need to be offered this kind of care.

As someone who has worked in healthcare for 22 years, the post-pandemic healthcare scene and the lack of healthcare workers in every sector is something I have never seen before. We are on the verge of a mass generational retirement; however, education systems in Alberta are not taking in more students, and tuition is rising, becoming yet another barrier to Indigenous students. Indigenous women already receive less in terms of healthcare and have worse maternal–fetal outcomes than any other group in Canada (Sheppard et al., 2017). In a system already failing our Indigenous people, reconciliation looks like alternate paths for Indigenous people to get paid to look after our own.

RESPONSIBILITY FOR AWARENESS

My wish to be a midwife includes using a practical birth justice paradigm and returning to Indigenous epistemologies within women's health and child-centred care (Tabobondung, n.d.). I wish to learn from the teachings of other Indigenous healers and Indigenous women who caught babies and passed on knowledge through generations for thousands of years. I seek decolonial pedagogy, knowledge gained from traditional Indigenous teachings from communities and women who cared for women and babies for generations before the onslaught of Western European civilization to North America. Midwifery used to be an apprenticeship, the knowledge passed through women trained from a young age for their skill and interest. This education has been lost to us, put away for a time when we might use traditional knowledge openly. Unfortunately, the people who hold this knowledge are fewer and fewer. Like the languages that are going extinct, this too needs a revival. There are very few trained Indigenous midwives in Alberta serving Indigenous communities. Very few Indigenous women have a chance to give birth at home on reserve with the community, in birth centres or hospitals with caregivers who do not have biases and ingrained racism. One of my mentors, Métis midwife Jessica Swain, says asking women to give birth requires the same intimacy and hormone release required to achieve orgasm (personal communication, October 2022); this vulnerability can be unattainable in institutions with a history of forced and coerced sterilization of Indigenous women (Mercredi, 2021). Asking Indigenous populations to give birth in institutions with long histories of abuse and ill-treatment without proper relational care is not reconciliation. Our people do not need more colonial values; they need people whom they trust and who care about and nurture their emotional, physical, psychological, and spiritual selves through pregnancy and postpartum. Relationships, like community, should be built over several cups of tea (Alycia Two Bears, Indigenous birth worker, personal communication, November 2021); relational care is not part of the care models for Indigenous birthing bodies in Alberta. Bringing birth back has enormous cultural significance and ripple effects in all areas of community health (National Council of Indigenous Midwives, n.d.). One way to start healing our communities is by returning to the birth rituals we had before colonization and nurturing the next generation's parents.

The recent spike in the desire for midwifery after it became subsidized in Alberta in 2008 proves that birthing bodies want midwifery care. I had my three children in the care of midwives, two of them before subsidization. The cap on midwives in the province of Alberta creates a massive demand for midwives and education; more than 300 people apply for the 12 seats in the Bachelor of Midwifery course at a university in Alberta each year. The degree program, since 2011, has not offered more than 12 seats due to provincial caps on graduates and available practicum placement (Berenyi, 2016). This university bases course admittance on a 4.0 grade point average and a high score on a for-profit test that "predicts future success in medical school" and tests things like your capacity to understand ethics, equity, and professionalism (Casper, 2022). Casper tests these "soft skills" through fast-paced short-answer questions that are known to favour a white, middle-class upbringing and have problematic colonial values (Moemeni et al., 2018). Participants never know their score, ranking, where they went wrong, how to improve, or whether they did great; the advice on the site is to "work on yourself" if you want a better score. The test is lacking in cultural sensitivity, and as someone who has taken it three times, it only adds to the shame of once again not living up to the standards colonials have set. Vine Deloria Jr. (Athabasca University Wolfe, 1977) explained Indigenous knowledge as understanding the interconnectedness of nature, human life, and time; they consider all aspects of people, emotions, and society. This Western university system bases a midwife's potential success on two numbers on a page, scores gained in other Western institutions that embrace compliance to a Western-based hierarchy of values and a test built on Eurocentric pedagogy and middle-class white values. This university in Alberta purports to save two seats for self-identifying Indigenous people, a nod to reconciliation. Numbers have never been released about how many Indigenous women have completed the program or how many are working in community or with community. The graduates tend to serve predominantly white, middle-class women within the cities of Calgary and Edmonton or other provinces. Women in rural, remote, and vulnerable communities need better access to midwifery care (Berenyi, 2016).

RESPONSIBILITIES FOR RECONCILIATION

Reconciliation is access for Indigenous birthing bodies to trained, knowledgeable, culturally sensitive, trauma-informed Indigenous midwives who can take the governing body's tests within their province for certification. Traditional midwifery practice has become institutionalized; people practised it for thousands of years on their land before colonization. Descendants of Indigenous midwives no longer have access to it or a way to learn it (Vega, 2018). The practice of midwifery and ceremony of birth "along with their land, women and children, in a direct attempt to stop the exchange of knowledge and culture that had allowed us to help conduct this ceremony of birth to generations, since time began" was taken from the First Nations in North America (C. Couchie, personal communication, June 2022). Now institutions are selling it back to us, but also gatekeeping the education required to pass the exams for the governing body of midwifery in our territories. The pedagogy within the communities of Indigenous people in the past included teaching those who showed interest, those who showed skill, and those who wished to serve their communities. Now people who want to serve their communities, and urban Indigenous women without communities, cannot because the education required for provincial licensing is not inclusive. I take issue with the gatekeeping within Western education systems with colonial epistemologies initially built to assimilate or eradicate Indigenous people.

The National Aboriginal Council of Midwifery (NACM) in Ontario, whose goal is one Indigenous midwife in every Indigenous community, has worked to create alternate education routes for Indigenous people to become midwives and practice (National Council of Indigenous Midwives, n.d.). The pay, however, is not the same as a midwife who goes to a colonial institution and serves the mainly white urban population. These midwives in Ontario and Atlantic Canada who can practise exempt from the regulated health professions want so badly to follow this path and serve their people but are often reliant on funding that is not always sustainable (Narine, 2022). The amount of skill and knowledge to deliver an Indigenous baby is more than your average midwife. Serving Indigenous populations requires cultural awareness, sensitivity, and trauma-informed relational care. Besides this university in Alberta, five other universities within Canada have a midwifery degree program. The United States and other places worldwide offer one but also require bridging programs when you return to Canada. I want to serve on my land with my people in Alberta; there is a need, I have seen it, and there is a considerable gap not being filled by the health professionals here. The decolonial opposite of genocide is allowing our Indigenous birthing people access to midwives. Colonial education systems need mandates within the provinces that create and fill positions on reserves and urban centres to care for Indigenous families. Birth needs to be repatriated to Indigenous people through educational routes and pay equity.

CONCLUSION

Understanding Canada's colonial legacy is critical to understanding decolonization and reconciliation (Dr. Datta, personal communication, March 2, 2021). Without the background knowledge of the crippling injustices, marginalization, oppression, and genocide faced by Indigenous people—perpetrated by settlers and colonialists and carried on by the Government of Canada over the last 500 years—reconciliation cannot happen. On my journey thus far, I have met Elders and Indigenous people who have created a desire within me to be as honourable as my ancestors. Regardless of the disadvantages Indigenous people have faced because of the government's versions of treaties, our ancestors have always honoured them (Calgary Public Library, 2020). Through my decolonization journey, I am creating a greater connection to my people and land, as I have learned the value of where I come from and community. I have learned the strength of culture and its underlying ideologies, worldview, and natural systems of knowledge that have carried us through since time immemorial. I am only at the precipice of knowledge about such diverse people with a complicated history of dealing with issues that have come up since first contact with Western colonialists. I am responsible for seeking answers from reputable Elders and knowledge keepers and taking information with respect and acceptance. I am responsible for engaging in my community, attending forums, and listening to issues that affect Indigenous people in Canada. When I acquire knowledge, it is my responsibility to share it as I have learned from Elders because knowledge is not ours to keep; we are just humble guides passing it along. I have learned from Elders a relational gift of respect that opens doors and hearts, and ears to others' stories and truths. Through respect and protocol, I hope to learn from Indigenous communities how to guide birthing back into an Indigenous framework for the Indigenous women that I serve. I will endeavour to build working relationships between healthcare systems and Treaty 7 people. Repatriation of our land and resources seems far off, but the ability to birth our children without fear and racism and regenerate our families into healthy units is attainable. In building an equitable Canada, the government, healthcare, and educational institutions must work together to improve access to Indigenous people's needs and to help us build back what we have lost; it will be at this point that reconciliation genuinely works.

REFLECTION QUESTIONS

1. What is your family history? Where are your people from? Is your ancestry tied to the land?
2. Do you know the territory you live in now and the history of the people who lived there?
3. How can you acknowledge colonization and work towards a fairer Canada in your chosen career?

SUGGESTED READINGS

- Kim Anderson: Cree Métis, well-known book *A Recognition of Being: Reconstructing Native Womanhood*. Reading Anderson's words in an edited book was one of the turning points in my life; she made sense of Indigenous women's struggles and how they pertain to our relationship with the land.
- Bonita Lawrence: Mi'kmaw, well-known book *"Real" Indians and Others: Mixed-Blood Urban Native People and Indigenous Nationhood*. Lawrence researches and writes about how deeply ingrained the oppression of Indigenous peoples is in our justice and social systems through her understanding of colonization and the *Indian Act*.
- Listen to Elders. They are a significant wealth of knowledge. Be grateful for the stories and wisdom they share with you.

REFERENCES

Athabasca University Wolfe. (1977). *Civilization and isolation with Vine Deloria Jr.* [Audio].

Berenyi, V. (2016). *Call the midwife!* Mount Royal University. Retrieved April 18, 2022, from https://www.mtroyal.ca/Summit/midwife.htm

Boutilier, S. (2017). Free, prior, and informed consent and reconciliation in Canada: Proposals to implement Articles 19 and 32 of the UN Declaration on the Rights of Indigenous People. *Western Journal of Legal Studies, 7*(1).

Calgary Public Library. (2020, September 30). *Treaty day: The making of Treaty 7* [Video]. YouTube. https://www.youtube.com/watch?v=HgUCUser3xY

Casper. (2022, March 8). *What Is Casper?* Acuity Insights. Retrieved April 18, 2022, from https://takealtus.com/casper

Datta, R. (2018). Decolonizing both researcher and research and its effectiveness in Indigneous research. *Research Ethics, 14*(2), 1–24. https://doi.org/10.1177/1747016117733296

Desjardins, R., & Monderie, R. (Directors). (2012). *The invisible nation* [Film]. National Film Board of Canada.

Fox, S. (Director). (2020). *Inendi* [Film]. Land Back Studios.

Hart, M. A. (2010). Indigenous worldviews, knowledge, and research: The development of an Indigenous research paradigm. *Journal of Indigenous Voices in Social Work, 1*(1A), 1–16.

Hubbard, T. (Director). (2004). *Two worlds colliding* [Film]. National Film Board of Canada.

Joseph, B. (2018, April 10). *21 things you may not know about the Indian Act: Helping Canadians make reconciliation with Indigenous peoples a reality*. Indigenous Relations Press.

Lawrence, B. (2004). *"Real" Indians and others: Mixed-blood urban Native peoples and Indigenous nationhood*. University of Nebraska Press.

Mantyka-Pringle, C. S., Westman, C. N., Kythreotis, A. P., & Schindler, D. W. (2015). Honouring Indigenous treaty rights for climate justice. *Nature Climate Change, 5*, 798–801. https://doi.org/10.1038/nclimate2714

Mercredi, M., & Fire Keepers. (2021). *Sacred bundles unborn*. FriesenPress.

Moemeni, B., Paradis, K., Truong, J., Wafa, K., Frishtack, H., Prufer, L., Arsovski, A., & Nissan, R. (2018). *BeMo's ultimate guide to CASPer test prep: How to increase your CASPer SIM score by 23% using the proven strategies they may not want you to know*. BeMo Academic Consulting.

Narine, S. (2022, May 13). No need to wait for government regulations to have Indigenous midwifery in communities. *Toronto Star*. https://www.thestar.com/news/canada/2022/05/13/no-need-to-wait-for-government-regulations-to-have-indigenous-midwifery-in-communities.html

National Council of Indigenous Midwives (NCIM). (n.d.). *Reconciliation, regulation & risk*. https://indigenousmidwifery.ca/reconciliation-regulation-risk/

Palmater, P. (2014). Genocide, Indian policy, and legislated elimination of Indians in Canada. *Aboriginal Policy Studies, 3*(3). https://doi.org/10.5663/aps.v3i3.22225

Schouls, T. A. (2002). *Shifting boundaries: Aboriginal identity, pluralist theory, and the politics of self-government in Canada*. UBC Press.

Sheppard, A. J., Shapiro, G. D., Bushnik, T., Wilkins, R., Perry, S., Kaufman, J. S., Kramer, M. S., & Yang, S. (2017, November 15). *Birth outcomes among First Nations, Inuit and Métis populations*. Statistics Canada. https://www150.statcan.gc.ca/n1/pub/82-003-x/2017011/article/54886-eng.htm

Sterritt, A., & Dickson, C. (2021, July 15). "This is heavy truth": Tk'emlúps te Secwépemc chief says more to be done to identify unmarked graves. *CBC*. https://www.cbc.ca/news/canada/british-columbia/kamloops-residential-school-findings-1.6084185

Tabobondung, R. (n.d.). A story of Indigenous birth justice. *MICE Magazine.* https://micemagazine.ca/issue-two/story-indigenous-birth-justice

The Agenda | TVO Today. (2018, May 07). *The Indian Act explained* [Video]. YouTube. https://www.youtube.com/watch?v=OhBrq7Ez-rQ

TreeTV/N2K Need to Know. (2016, September 16). *Oren Lyons on the Indigenous view of the world* [Video]. YouTube. https://www.youtube.com/watch?v=kbwSwUMNyPU

Tuck, E., & Yang, K. W. (2012). Decolonization is not a metaphor. *Decolonization: Indigeneity, Education & Society, 1*(1), 1–40.

Vega, R. A. (2018, April 6). How natural birth became inaccessible to the poor. *SAPIENS.* Retrieved April 18, 2022, from https://www.sapiens.org/biology/indigenous-midwives-mexico

Wilson, B. R. (2016). *Religion in secular society: Fifty years on.* Oxford University Press.

Wolochatiuk, T. (Director). (2012). *We were children* [Film]. National Film Board of Canada.

CHAPTER 5

An Indigenous Journey: From a Colonized Mindset to Decolonized Dreams

Ryan Whitford

Throughout this chapter, I wanted to take the reader on my personal journey of decolonizing my mindset. In the last several years I have undertaken a journey to gain a better understanding of myself, my heritage, and my identity as an Indigenous person; I learned that my mind has been ingrained with a settler-colonized lifestyle. With the journey that I will be taking the reader on, I want the reader to reflect and find a path forward to decolonize their own mindset, and I want the reader to see that anyone can grow from their experiences and move forward on a steady path in life.

The reader can call what I wrote many different things like objectives or learning experiences, but I want the reader to know that everything I will be writing going forward about my life involves speaking my truth. For me, speaking my truth and writing about my experiences have been extremely therapeutic, and I have learned so much, not only about how I see myself but about how I carry myself around others. I hope the stories I wrote will help lead the Indigenous community when times are dark and the proverbial settler walls are closing in. Storytelling is a huge part of every Indigenous community, and my story needs to be passed down for decolonization to continue, much like many other Indigenous stories.

I want this to also be used by all Canadians to gain a better grasp on how their mind is colonized and the path forward to live a decolonized lifestyle. The stories have benefited me by lifting a weight that I have carried on my shoulders for years, while letting me look through an Indigenous lens like I was supposed to. I leave my heart on the following pages and I want the reader to pick my heart up and mend it back together with their own learnings from what I wrote.

CHALLENGES IN COLONIZATION

Waves crash against the shore as a turbulent wind struggles to carry a ship, heavily manned with British colonizers, to find new land on the Canadian Indians' shores. Sand splits in a divide as the ship comes to a stop on the shore. A neat, compact row of men descends from the plank of the boat to the island. In the distance, the captain of the boat sees a foreign, dark-skinned–looking creature in the dense foliage of trees. The captain approaches the wild creature with his army of men and the boat's priest. Upon further inspection, the creature turns out to be a man of a completely different skin colour than the captain and his men. Holding up a cross to the dark-skinned men, the priest begins to say the Lord's Prayer in hopes of taming the beast. Confused, the dark-skinned man stares at the army. One of the men in the back whispers to the man in front of him, "This dark man seems inept; this is our new home." Like a nasty game of telephone, the words make their way up to the captain. The captain looks at the dark-skinned man and smiles.

Was that not a beautiful story of how the British first met an Indigenous man? That was a made-up tale, but I am sure it is not far to the truth. The truth is that the British thought that they could take land from humans who were different from them. What were the British doing there? Colonizing! What else was there for white men to do in the 1800s? Colonization is felt all around us from political policies to racial discrimination. I, like many Canadians, never really understood colonization, nor did I take it seriously until I started to understand who I was and what my heritage is. I am an Indigenous/French male and not until I became sober did I realize that colonization was fully ingrained into my inner being.

Throughout this chapter, the reader will take a journey through my mind, focusing on my identity and the process of decolonizing my mindset. This is a journey that I needed to take and one that I will be on for the rest of my life. My experiences with colonization might be tough for some to read; I am not sorry for this. It has been equally hard for me to write some of this as it is for you to read it. We are in this together, and I hope my words will bring you a new way of thinking.

INDIGENOUS IDENTITY: AM I INDIGENOUS ENOUGH?

My relationship with being Indigenous has always been a complicated force that I have yet to master an understanding of. I have struggled to find mental significance in showing Indigenous pride when I am so conflicted with being half white and half Indigenous. *Who am I to wear Indigenous clothing when I am only half? Who am I to listen to the beautiful beat of the drums at a Powwow when I am only half?* I have reflected on these questions for years of my life and have drawn a conclusion that I can no longer avoid. I have fallen into a colonial mindset. I often worry about what people will think of me and how I will look to settler people; I am often nervous that I will be judged by settler people based on my own Indigeneity.[1] I need to decolonize myself and my mind. Drain the colonized fluid from my brain and fill it back up with Indigenous knowledge.

If you have not come to the conclusion yet, I am Indigenous. My father is Cree and Métis, and my mother is French. When I was younger, I was not able to admit that I was Indigenous until I became sober. Being more than six years sober, I have learned to represent my Indigeneity the best way I can: by learning. Every so often I get a crushing feeling that sneaks into my head, yelling in the back of my mind: Am I Indigenous enough? What a sick thought to have; I can see that I am Indigenous from the colour of my skin. The length of my hair, the clothes I wear, and the way I hold my head up are all indications that I am Indigenous.

I have struggled with my own Indigeneity for most of my life. In high school I would often joke that if something went wrong, it was because I was native. I was never comfortable with being Indigenous for various reasons. For instance, I went to a white school and grew up in a white neighbourhood[2]; I never had a lot of interaction with Indigenous people. I was always the tanned kid in school and when people would guess my nationality, I would always get Mexican or Greek. Growing up as a tanned kid in a white neighbourhood is quite easy when nobody knows that you are Indigenous. Maybe in the back of my mind I knew it would be easier for me to not admit that I was an Indian kid so white people would accept me. Throughout my teens, I acted "white." I would get uncomfortable when someone would bring up that I was Indigenous and downplay it or avoid the topic altogether, in fear that I would be looked at differently because the secret would be out. This is what colonization had already done to me at a very young age. My formative years were spent downplaying that I was Indian. It seemed like the settlers' demand for assimilation had worked.

My relationship with my own Indigeneity and Indigenous people around me has always seemed to be fractured throughout my life. As I continued to learn more and more about my heritage and identity as a whole, I started researching more about my people, soaking in every book I could read and asking my dad about his and our family's history. I cannot help having that pesky thought eating away at the back of my mind asking if I am Indigenous enough to be practising what I am learning, or if other people find me to be Indigenous enough to learn and grow from their teachings. A thick cloud of shame and embarrassment hangs over my head when I feel like other Indigenous people do not look at me as one of them. I sink deeper into my thoughts as I feel like a fake. I am not full-blooded; I do not have a status card. That does not define my Indigeneity, but I continue to have this yelling in the back of my mind that I will not be seen as Indigenous because of that.

If you close your eyes for a second, imagine yourself having your arms pulled violently by two beings. One is the devil, and one is an angel, but you do not know which side is which. This is how I feel about being Indigenous enough for myself and for my people. I would like to reflect on a poem I wrote about my conflict with my Indigeneity.

AM I INDIGENOUS ENOUGH?

I am Indigenous enough to be followed around a store.
I am not Indigenous enough to be eyed when I go on a reserve.
I am Indigenous enough to be asked to speak for all Indigenous people.
I am not Indigenous enough in the eyes of the government.
I am Indigenous enough to be looked at like I am exotic.
I am not Indigenous enough to be fully shunned by white people.
I am Indigenous enough to fit the alcoholic stereotype.
I am not Indigenous enough to be treated like one.
I am Indigenous enough to be called racist names like chug or asked if my last name (Whitford) came from my parents having sex in a white Ford.
I am not Indigenous enough to understand the full hurt of this until it was too late.
I am Indigenous enough to struggle with being Indigenous in the white world.
I am not Indigenous enough to struggle with being Indigenous in a white world.

MYSELF BEING COLONIZED

My life is colonized; I cannot beat around the bush or sugarcoat how I live my life. I am a mixed-race Indigenous male who has conformed to the settler lifestyle. It is much easier to conform to a lifestyle that white society has ingrained into me and my people for decades. I want to take a minute to reflect on what a lifestyle truly is. *Oxford Learner's Dictionaries* (2023) defines lifestyle as "the way in which a person or a group of people lives." Lifestyle is the way you or I define how we wake up and where we rest our heads every night. That word defines who we are for our whole life and can be changed.

Racism is all around us; any person of colour experiences racism daily. Racism does not always come as a slur said to someone; rather it can be a microaggression towards their race or clothing. It is difficult to believe that still to this day, we have socially acceptable forms of racism. I reflect a lot on the racism around me, regardless of whether it was directed at me or someone else. I see racism often when I go shopping alone or with my son. I get followed around either by security or a sales associate when I go shopping. I assume they see an Indigenous male and automatically think I am going to steal something. I have never stolen anything. I always pay for my items when I go out shopping and even point out if I get undercharged. It pains me to reflect on this. My son is white presenting. As hard as it is for me to admit, I am happy that he is whiter than me because he will not have to experience the racism that I have experienced in my lifetime. He will never get called Indian, "chug," or other disparaging racial slurs.

Disparaging racial slurs towards Indigenous people of Canada continue to be used, even as movements like Black Lives Matter and Stop Asian Hate have seeped into the nation's veins and ingrained anti-racist sentiments in the younger generations. I was born and raised in Alberta, Canada. Alberta is known for oil production, people driving lifted trucks, and the Rocky Mountains. Another thing Alberta is known for is its white residents being racist towards the Indigenous community. From Alberta hospitals rating Indigenous patients as less urgent than non-Indigenous people (Yourex-West, 2022) to a scholarly institution creating a toxic environment for Indigenous people by employing a teacher who actively dismisses Indigenous suffering, Alberta seems to be quite comfortable with open displays of racism towards Indigenous residents.

Being born and raised in Alberta, I have seen racism towards myself and other races through my eyes. Whenever someone says that Alberta is not that racist, I always replay a memory of my former boss giving me tickets to a Drake concert and saying, "here is your fucking [N-word] Drake tickets." Or when I was working at the Calgary Stampede for a Canadian mobile company and a manager asked why I was early. I said, "My meeting was just down the street." He replied, "OH! You can't handle your firewater." I could go on and on about racist remarks I have heard throughout my life, but then this essay would not leave you feeling uplifted. Before I continue, I want to admit that I have used racial slurs and made disparaging remarks towards my people. I have learned from these experiences and now understand the power that words can hold.

Words hold a lot of power when we say them to anyone. Words can convey love, hate, anger, happiness, and many more emotions. I have explained in my stories above how words have hurt a lot of people. Harmful words and actions have turned my people against each other. All too often Indigenous people look down on someone who is not full-blooded; this type of judgment was settler-introduced when the term "blood quantum" was ingrained into our heads. Blood quantum is a term that was used by the government to determine if a First Nation person is Indigenous enough to get a status card. Blood quantum was designed to slowly eradicate Indigenous people. I think blood quantum has been pushed on us for so long that we have now begun to question our own people's heritage and look down on people who are half or a quarter Indigenous.

Clearly this is one of the damaging effects colonization has had on me. As I continued to be successfully ingrained into colonization, I started running away from the troubles in my life and my alcohol addiction started to leak out of my pores and wreak havoc on everything around me. I coddled my addiction like it was my first-born child. I could not keep it hidden anymore; my path of destruction started. My inner house was burning, and I had nothing to extinguish it. The more I drank, the more I could stuff my problems and troubles down while acting like nothing was bothering me. I feel that the white people around me loved that I was a drunken Indian. I fit their stereotype; I was their drunken Indian for them to laugh at.

The story of the drunken Indian has been told since alcohol was first introduced to my people. Colonization brought alcohol to the tribes and turmoil started. Following the ban on alcohol throughout reserves in 1985, a section of the *Indian Act* was amended to give reserves the right to regulate alcohol within their own territories. Canada has dry reserves (no alcohol) and reserves that allow alcohol, further pushing the myth of the alcohol-intolerant Indian. Still, at the time I share my stories, I feel that a lot of settler people continue to view Indigenous people as lazy drunks who cannot handle their "firewater." The stereotype that Indigenous people are all drunks is not true; "35% of Indigenous people are abstinent from alcohol—one out of three Indigenous people does not use alcohol" (CBC, 2017). The preconceived notions settler society has about my people are wrong. Even though my people have a high percentage of abstinence from alcohol, settler society still labels us all as "drunken Indians."

Having become the "drunken Indian," as settler society has ever-so-nicely labelled Indigenous people, I had no other choice (other than losing everything

I had) than to get sober. I broke the curse of my family. My grandmother was an alcoholic and my father was an alcoholic. Alcoholism is a sick tradition that was passed down to one of the children in my family. The intergenerational trauma from my great-grandmother and grandmother has been felt for several generations. The trauma stems from the residential school system that both women had to attend. You should know by now the horrible atrocities that happened within each residential school's walls; if by chance you do not, I implore you to do some research on Canadian residential schools.

Residential schools will always be a horrible part of Canadian history. Indigenous people still feel the effects. Intergenerational trauma is the outcome that has trickled down from the generation who went to residential schools to their children. My Kokum (grandmother) went to St. Bruno's residential school in Joussard, Alberta. She never talked about attending residential school, but she suffered trauma from attending. I will not try to guess what happened to her, but I do know she became an alcoholic from the trauma she experienced. She wanted to drown her sadness and trauma in a bottle of alcohol. With this, my father is an alcoholic, and I am an alcoholic. The intergenerational trauma from residential schools is very apparent in my family; I am the one to break the cycle of addiction with my child. I want to stop this cycle of trauma and hurt that subjects my family to a hellish lifestyle that is hard to escape.

Colonization has messed up a lot of moments in my life. How do I break free of the proverbial shackles of colonization that have been placed on my ankles, slowing my growth since birth? I think, first, I need to focus on myself. Decolonizing is a powerful yet arduous task that takes years and extreme mental fortitude. If I can change my mindset, then everything else should fall into place.

DECOLONIZING MY MINDSET AS SELF-DETERMINATION

Decolonizing my mindset has proven to be more difficult than I could ever have imagined. One step in this process is my need for a better understanding of how I am seen by settler society. H. K. Trask's *The Colour of Violence* (2004) has helped me have a better understanding of how coloured people (myself included) are perceived. "We are ghettoized by a hierarchy in which people of colour, and particularly Indigenous people, occupy the bottom strata and in which white people occupy the top" (p. 14). Settler society has always imposed their belief that they are more important than we (Indigenous people) are.

What Trask masterfully penned truly gives me the empowerment to decolonize myself. I need to uplift my people and not look at us as the bottom of the colonial racial totem pole. I need to usher in what my ancestors have tried to pass down for generations: that we are strong and resilient people who can withstand anything. The resilience that Indigenous people have, the resilience that I see all around from my Indigenous people, helps me when I struggle with decolonizing my mind.

Settler society, time and time again, continues to develop on sacred land that was once a teaching ground for Indigenous people across Turtle Island. An Indigenous Elder and Knowledge Keeper from Treaty 7 Territory, William Singer III, led an Indigenous land walk for Mount Royal University students through Nose Hill Park in Calgary, Alberta. He led us through scary teachings such as the act of laying down tobacco while giving thanks to the land and showing respect to the land we walk on (personal communication, March 17, 2022). In my reflective learning, I closed my eyes and envisioned what it would be like without the cityscape of skyscrapers and cracked-up concrete roads. I envisioned beautiful rolling hills where we could hear the wind rustling through the long grass. There was not a soul in sight. The air was fresh, clean, and unpolluted. As I opened my eyes, I saw what had been done to what was once a peaceful, rolling land of free-flowing air, and I could not help but feel a sense of sadness. Indigenous people have once again had something extremely important to them taken away by colonization. My biggest takeaway from Singer's (2022) walk was that I must be one with the land and appreciate what we still have. I must cherish and love every step that I take when I am on the land. I must love the plants that grow around my feet, and give back whatever I take away. An invaluable lesson was taught to me that day. A lesson that I will hold close to my heart until the day I die.

As an Indigenous person, I am constantly learning lessons, be it from my wife, my son, or the world around me. I soak in every moment as an opportunity to grow and work on myself. One of the most powerful growing experiences I have faced as an Indigenous person was quitting alcohol and drugs. I did not want to be another stereotype that settler society pins on Indigenous people. "See, we are right, there is another Indian who can't handle his liquor" is a thought I often have when I tell settler people I am sober. Becoming sober flourished my Indigeneity and helped me understand what it is to be an Indigenous male growing up in a colonized society.

Combining being sober and being Indigenous are true forms of decolonizing my mind. Not only my mind but also my body. I moved away from the awful stereotype that plagues my people and proved to settler society that I can rise above the crutch I once needed to function. I am empowered by this to be what settlers fear the most: A sober, educated Indian.

Education has taken me a very long time to embrace. I never really took school seriously until the age of 33. I coasted by, managing to just pass my courses in high school. As I got older and started to see how important education was, not only to myself but to my people, I started to take a more serious approach to education. I have now been in university for two semesters as of writing this. The education system for Indigenous people seems to have been put in place to appease settler society.

I look at the courses that I would like to take in school. I am extremely passionate about Indigenous people and their rights. Yearning to learn my people's language (Cree First Nation), I find that it is not offered at the school I attend. We have an Indigenous centre for Indigenous students and faculty. The school offers university-level Indigenous courses; some are taught by Indigenous people and some not. The school has Indigenous ceremonies and reflects on Indigenous holidays. All of this is in play and the school does not have any Indigenous language courses. If I were asked what my thoughts on this are, I would have to say, "it seems like a slap in the face; the school seems to be showboating."

As a mature student knowing my path to get into my program and what is required of me, I see younger Indigenous students not able to cope with the pressures of university. In my first semester, I had an Intro to Indigenous Studies course which had approximately 10 Indigenous students. On the final day of class, I was the only Indigenous student left. Personally, I feel that younger Indigenous students are not being properly set up to attend a colonized institution. Schools need to do more to make sure these students know what they are getting themselves into, have a path to follow, and are set up for success.

Every person needs a path to follow, but very few have mastered the path they have chosen. Autumn Peltier is one of these few who have mastered their path. She is a water protector from Wiikwemkoong First Nation on Manitoulin Island. Peltier was born to protect the water and land (CBC News, 2018). Reflecting on this and seeing how Autumn masterfully lives out her purpose, I ask myself as an Indigenous father, "What is my path? What is my purpose?"

Weaving these questions together, I can shift my focus to the future and say that my path in life is to help people. I have always been drawn to helping people who are in need. My heart bleeds when I read another story about a missing and/or murdered Indigenous woman. Tears fall from my eyes when I see one of my people being followed around a store and called racist names, being stereotyped as a thief. I am beginning to pave my path as an Indigenous male and father; much like Autumn Peltier, I know where I am needed and what I need to protect.

Protection is often taken for granted in settler society. Whether it's from the police or the government, these forms of protection work in the favour of settlers. Protection for young Indigenous children by settler society is at an all-time low. The suicide epidemic on reserves is being brought to the nation's attention with nothing more than a "thoughts and prayers"-style response from settlers. Therefore, I am going into social work. I want to help Indigenous kids find a path forward and not feel so alone. I will not singlehandedly solve the suicide epidemic, but I want to give it my all and help as much as I can.

Children are the way of the future. In a 2013 article, Mahi lays out a plan to see Kalihi children succeed in a colonial world. He also suggested the importance of connecting with children. I can relate my learning with Mahi's perspectives. For instance, I am a father of a little toddler; I have watched him grow into his own personality, and I connect with him on so many levels. I sit back sometimes and think, "What if I was never in his life like my father was?" while also thinking of how Indigenous males are stereotyped as being absent fathers. It pains me to even think about not being with my son and watching his milestones. I am breaking the stereotype of the absent father and, more importantly, raising him to see through an Indigenous lens.

I was taught in my first Indigenous studies course to see the world through an Indigenous lens. Indigenous educator and Powwow dancer Karen Pheasant-Neganigwane is the teacher who taught me to look at life through an Indigenous lens; in one of her other courses I took, the course assigned a chapter that she wrote in an essay collection entitled *Global Citizenship, Commonwealth and Uncommon Citizenships*. "Dancing for Change" was the title of the chapter and what struck me the most was the question she started the essay off with: "What is it you fear?" (Pheasant-Neganigwane, 2018). What a complex question to answer. I have asked myself this many times in my life and for the last six years, my answer has been, *"I do not want my son to turn out like me."* This is very hard for me to put out into the world. I fear my son will turn out to be an alcoholic who does not get his life together until he is close to 30. I fear my son will be judged based on the colour of his skin like I have been. I fear my son will not be loved by his father as I wasn't. I have a lot of fears for my child, but if I continue to pave a way that brings both of us to see through an Indigenous lens and raise him with a decolonized mind, I think I can assist with alleviating these fears.

I have many fears that will live with me until the day I meet the Creator. Learning to live past these fears and be more apologetic to myself has taken a long time to understand. I apologize to myself for being so harsh and for not understanding who I wanted to be, and I give thanks to the people around me for accepting my apology for the life I used to live as a drunk and a drug user. Apologies can make a world of change in people's lives, much like when the Australian government made a formal apology to the Indigenous people of Australia. This was a monumental move from the Australian government due to how unfairly Indigenous people in Australia are treated.

Stephen Harper's conservative government apologized to Canada's Indigenous people in 2008. This was a thinly-veiled attempt to gain Indigenous trust. As Indigenous Canadians continue to be taken advantage of by the government, one should ask, *"Why to give an apology when you do not mean it?"* That question is something I ponder whenever I am about to apologize to someone. I reflect on whether I am being sincere with my apology, proving to myself that I am trying to rid myself of a colonized apology structure, rather than saying sorry just to make myself feel better. My mindset changes each time I reflect on an apology.

Woodland Cree Elder Joseph Naytowhow (2022) asked in an Indigenous studies course, "Who are we?" He brought the question to the students by also asking us if we had learned anything from our grandparents. Closing my eyes and seeing my Kokum (my grandmother), I cannot help but smile as I remember the one thing she taught me: to love unconditionally. She always had a smile on her face, no matter how hard life was for her. She was an alcoholic, much like myself and my father. She had her "moment of clarity" when she was told she could not see her grandchildren until she stopped drinking.

My Kokum lived a hard life; she was often treated as a "dirty Indian" by the community she lived around. Regardless of how she was treated, she always continued to smile and look at the positives. The night she passed away, I was deep asleep. I was dreaming that I was standing on a vacant street with several brick buildings around me. As I looked around, I looked up to the sky and saw her smiling down at me. She said, "Hold the family down." I awoke to my phone ringing at 5:30 a.m. It was my dad, and he told me that my Kokum had died. This experience is one I will always cherish with my Kokum. My Kokum was a prime example of someone who lived with a decolonized mindset trying to navigate a colonized world.

Decolonizing one's mindset is a difficult task to take on. It comes with a lot of self-doubt and uncertainty about who I am and what I need to do to succeed. As I continue to peel away each layer of my colonized mind as if it were a stale onion only good at the centre, I learn more knowledge to move forward, not only by being a leader in my life but also by stepping aside when it is needed. My future is the only one I can control, but I hope people will notice that I am making a change and they will follow suit to decolonize their own and society's mindsets.

CONCLUSION

I started with a colonized mindset, and I was not truly able to reflect on who I was as a person until I had a dynamic shift in the conscious lens through which I see the world. Colonization started with and continues to perpetuate a harsh physical and mental climate for the colonized, further putting a divide between the colonizers and the people who were colonized. The divide will continue until we start seeing through a decolonized lens, improving how colonized people are treated. How do we do that? I implore you to start your research now and actively try to work on bridging the divide together.

My mind is changing and will continue to change until my last breath. I have never factored colonization into my development as a person until I started to accept my faults and want to change them. I was the stereotypical drunken Indian who had no direction in life, much like how settler society still views my people. I have erased settlers' pigeonholing of Indigenous people from my mental computer and uploaded a new version of decolonization, which involves uplifting Indigenous people and respecting myself. In the introduction, I wrote that this was a journey for me; I hope your journey starts here and does not end. Working on ourselves to be the best we can be is a task that neither you nor I should take for granted, so I will let us start with decolonizing. As you read my final words, I want you to reflect on this question: *What have you done to decolonize your mind?*

NOTES

1. I define *Indigeneity* as ingraining Indigenous culture and traditions into my everyday life. Living and breathing my Indigenous life.
2. White: the colour and lifestyle of the people I grew up around. I ingrained myself into the white lifestyle, which was the only culture that was around me.

REFLECTION QUESTIONS

1. Can you talk about your relationships that have helped you think about how to engage in decolonization?
2. How do you understand the relationships of settlers, non-Indigenous peoples, and Indigenous peoples?
3. Can you talk about experiences in your organizing where you have felt that your group or you as an individual were acting in a manner that maintained colonial relations?

4. What types of relationships do you see as being decolonizing?
5. Can you talk about successes and failures you've had in trying to decolonize your mindset?
6. Are there any models of organizing society differently that you hold as possible examples?

SUGGESTED READINGS

- Ahmed, S. (2012). *On being included: Racism and diversity in institutional life.* Duke University Press.
- Arday, J., Belluigi, D. Z., & Thomas, D. (2020). Attempting to break the chain: Reimaging inclusive pedagogy and decolonising the curriculum with the academy. *Educational Philosophy and Theory, 53*(3), 298–313. https://doi.org/10.1080/00131857.2020.1773257
- Arday, J., & Mirza, H. S. (Eds.). (2018). *Dismantling race in higher education: Racism, whiteness and decolonising the academy.* Palgrave Macmillan.
- Benitez, M. (2010). Racialized rhetoric, racialized bodies, racialized spaces: Politicizing how race and racism are experienced in higher education. *Iowa State Conference on Race and Ethnicity, 11*(1). https://www.iastatedigitalpress.com/iscore/article/id/10088/
- Bhopal, K. (2017). Addressing racial inequalities in higher education: Equity, inclusion and social justice. *Ethnic and Racial Studies, 40*(13), 2293–2299. https://doi.org/10.1080/01419870.2017.1344267
- Bhopal, K. (2018). *White privilege: The myth of a post-racial society.* Policy Press.
- Dale-Rivas, H. (Ed). (2019). *The white elephant in the room: Ideas for reducing racial inequalities in higher education.* Higher Education Policy Institute. https://www.hepi.ac.uk/wp-content/uploads/2019/09/HEPI_The-white-elephant-in-the-room_Report-120-FINAL-EMBAROED-19.09.19.pdf
- DiAngelo, R. (2018). *White fragility: Why it's so hard for white people to talk about racism.* Beacon Press.

REFERENCES

CBC Books. (2017, June 28). Chantal Fiola on why you should read Firewater: How alcohol is killing my people (and yours). *CBC.* https://www.cbc.ca/books/chantal-fiola-on-why-you-should-read-firewater-how-alcohol-is-killing-my-people-and-yours-1.4181898

CBC News: The National. (2018, March 21). *The teen fighting to protect Canada's water—meet Autumn Peltier* [Video]. YouTube. https://youtu.be/xqdE_7OZaqE

Mahi, D. (2013). The children of Kalihi. *Reclaiming Children and Youth, 22*(1), 50–54.

Naytowhow, J. (2022, March 28). *Land-based learning* [Google Drive Video]. Sturgeon Lake First Nation Band.

Oxford Learner's Dictionaries. (2023). Lifestyle. In *Oxford Learner's Dictionaries.* Retrieved September 25, 2023, from https://www.oxfordlearnersdictionaries.com/us/definition/english/lifestyle

Pheasant-Neganigwane, K. J. (2018). Dancing for change. In L. Shultz & T. Pillay (Eds.), *Global citizenship, common wealth and uncommon citizenships* (pp. 141–157). Brill Sense.

Singer W. (2022, March 17). *Indigenous-led land walk for the Indigenous Land-based Learning Course.* Mount Royal University.

Trask, H. K. (2004). The colour of violence. *Social Justice, 31*(4), 8–16.

Yourex-West, H. (2022, January 19). Evidence of racism against Indigenous patients is growing: Is a reckoning in Canadian health care overdue? *Global News.* https://globalnews.ca/news/8523488/evidence-of-racism-against-indigenous-patients-is-growing-is-a-reckoning-in-canadian-health-care-overdue/

CHAPTER 6

Spiralling In to Spiral Out: Teaching in a Land-Based Mohawk Immersion School

Gabrielle Yakotennikonhrare Doreen

> "By working back, students and teachers can begin moving towards decolonizing understandings of community and to think about what non-colonial relations might look like both in theory and practice. Here we can see that a land education approach requires that students understand themselves fully within the context of place."
> (Calderon, 2014, p. 28)

INTRODUCTION

Indigenous Land-based education is important for indigenizing and decolonizing education. Indigenization upholds and builds on Indigenous knowledge, theories, and philosophies (Allard-Tremblay, 2022), while simultaneously rejuvenating Indigenous praxis. The objective of decolonization is to critically engage with and deconstruct systems that impair or suppress Indigenous ways of being, knowing, and doing (Allard-Tremblay, 2022) in order to initiate healing processes and repair broken relations caused by colonialism. Radu et al. (2014) express that "decolonization means caring and loving for one another and invigorating the body with the effort of surviving on the land" (p. 101). Decolonization in education means healing from the residential and Indian day school systems. For over a century, tens of thousands of Indigenous children were removed from their homes and communities and were forced and/or coerced to attend Indian residential schools.

According to the Truth and Reconciliation Commission (2015), "The federal government's determination to have as cheap an Indian policy as possible, coupled with the church's drive to enrol and convert as many children as possible, meant that the schools were sites of hunger, overwork, danger and disease, limited education, and, in tens of thousands of cases, physical, sexual, and psychological abuse and neglect" (p. 131).

Early in my *Kanien'ké:ha* (Mohawk language) learning process, I had the opportunity to listen to Tom Porter speak in Kanatsiohareke[1] (the place of the cleaning pot). He told us how his great uncle was sent to Carlisle Indian Boarding School and eventually ran away. Tom went on to talk about how the residential school system removed us from our culture, language, and connection to land. He then proposed that what we needed was a complete opposite of that system to reteach what was taken away (Tom Porter, personal communication, spring 2009). This chapter highlights my experience as a *Kanien'ké:ha* primary immersion teacher, working to rebuild an education program that invokes pride in Indigenous identity, and healing historical trauma by facilitating relationships with and of land through language and cultural learning.

The main objectives of this chapter are to explain Indigenous Land-based education; to provide core elements of Rotinonhsonníh (Haudenosaunee) Land-based education; to advocate the importance of Indigenous languages; and to highlight the benefits of project-based learning as reclaiming Indigenous praxis. In this chapter, I first introduce myself culturally, professionally, and academically. I will then provide a definition of Indigenous Land-based education; following that, I briefly describe the pillars of Rotinonhsonníh Land-based education. I will then explain the physical aspects of *Kawenna'ón:we Yonterihwaienstáhkhwa* (original words school) before discussing experiences relating to Rotinonhsonníh Land-based education to demonstrate how spiralling in to spiral out evoked meaning-making and knowledge creation, both academically and culturally.

POSITIONALITY

Iakotennikonhrare iontsyá'ts, Kanien'kehá:ka niwakonhontsò:ten. Wakenyàhton. Kenhetke nitiwaké:non. They call me Iakotennikonhrare, which means *she takes care of them*. I am Mohawk, turtle clan. I'm from Tyendinaga Mohawk Territory.

I was born in Burlington, Ontario. My dad, Amzy Doreen, is Mohawk, wolf clan. My mom, Alberta Doreen nee Ryan, is part Welsh and part Scottish, Lamont clan. I fall under Bill C-31 Indian status because my paternal grandfather

Amzy Doreen Sr. was enfranchised and when he and my paternal grandmother Ada Doreen nee Maracle married, our family lost status. When my grandfather passed, my grandmother began relearning her mother tongue. I was 10 when she started teaching me *Kanien'ké:ha*. I was 12 when we regained our status and 14 when my father was able to obtain a certificate of possession on reserve land. I moved home, to Tyendinaga, when I was 15 and started to learn more about culture through singing, dancing and travelling with the Peacemaker's Drum. I started my own family in my early twenties. Raising four children, earning a diploma in early childhood education and working in childcare programs, I found myself wanting to speak *Kanien'ké:ha*.

I attended *Shatiwennakarats* (they elevate the words) adult Mohawk immersion program from 2008–2010. The program was co-offered by *Tsi Tyónnheht Onkwawén:na*[2] (keeping the words alive), First Nations Technical Institute (FNTI), and Trent University. When I attended the adult immersion program, many women of my cohort had young children, including myself. It was decided by *Tsi Tyónnheht Onkwawén:na* that a language nest would be offered congruently so that our children could learn to speak *Kanien'ké:ha* at the same time. In 2011, our children were growing out of *Totahne* (at grandma's house) language nest. A small independent school was created so that *Totahne* children could continue with their language acquisition. After finishing the language program and earning a Bachelor of Arts degree in Indigenous Studies, I began teaching at *Kawenna'ón:we* in 2013. At this time, I was also taking courses at Six Nations Polytechnic through Queen's University to earn a Bachelor of Education degree.

Ever since I was re-placed in community, at 15, it has always been important to me to immerse myself in *Onkwehonwe'néha* (ways of original peoples). Rotinonhsonníh are often referred to as a matrilineal society; having a non-Indigenous mother, I didn't have a clan. Learning about who I am as a *Kanienke'hàka* (person of the flint nation) has been a lifelong learning journey and commitment to community that eventually lead to being named in ceremony under the turtle clan. I have spent many years reflecting on and learning from the creation story, *Ohén:ton Karihwatéhkwen* (words before all matters), cycle of ceremonies, *Kaienerakó:wa* (the great law of peace) and wampum theories, as well as learning language and land-based craft, song, dance, and gardening. I applied these elements in my own teaching practice at *Kawenna'ón:we*.

My personal teaching and learning philosophy is spiralling in to spiral out. Spiralling into Indigenous ways of knowing, values, histories, stories, ceremony, and land relations to spiral out, bringing back into existence a strong sense of Indigenous identity, thinking in Indigenous languages, and cultural understandings needed to navigate and guide our present way of life. Shortly before starting my teaching career, I experienced spiralling in through a dream. Shawanda (2020) expresses that "our dreams are part of our methods as we co-create with universe and the Ancestors" (p. 38). They are valued sources of knowledge that challenge conventional Western knowledge held in academic institutions (Shawanda, 2020). Shawanda goes on to create a reference guide for citing dream knowledge.

I dreamt I was teaching *Kanien'ké:ha* in an elementary school setting and my grandma led me to different classes. The first class she showed me was indoors with desks in rows. The students were not engaged and appeared hollow. She then showed me a class outside, sitting under a tree. The students were speaking, laughing, being kids, and learning. Before the dream ended, she told me, "You have to get them outside" (personal communication, 2011). Little did I know the impact that message would have on my future teaching and learning practices.

INDIGENOUS LAND-BASED EDUCATION

Indigenous Land-based education is not just taking the students outside and teaching them about language and culture. It's about developing and engaging in relations with land and on land holistically (Wildcat et al., 2014). Indigenous Land-based education is relational, contextualized in and of the land, water, and cosmos (Virtanen, 2022). As noted by Datta (2018), "Indigenous peoples inherently include land-based knowledge in their practice because land stresses the importance of the holistic connection of all living beings (i.e. relationships of humans to humans, to animals, to plants, to the elements, to the spiritual world and to the cosmos)" (pp. 54–55). What Indigenous Land-based education means to me as an *Onkwehón:we* (original person) is going to be different than what it means for others, because the land, waters, and cosmos we originate from are diverse. "As indigenous people, our cultures are shaped by knowledge and ways of knowing that are connected to land" (Wilson & Laing, 2018, p. 136). How Indigenous peoples view the world, how we know what is true, as well as our values on how to live a good life is diverse as the land we originate from. Indigenous Land-based education recognizes the importance of origin stories and songs as oral transmissions of knowledges. Our stories are connected to land (Corntassel, 2009) and "carry Indigenous philosophies, epistemologies, and theories within their narratives" (Sium & Ritskes, 2013, p. 5). Indigenous languages enhance and deepen cultural understanding, not just by speaking *Onkwehon:we'neha* (the way of the original people) but thinking in *Onkwehon:we'neha*. "The language tells us who we are" (Doreen & Porter, as cited in Maracle, 2002, p. 402). Corresponding with language, Indigenous Land-based education re-stories and reconceptualizes place and time (Smith, 2021; Tuck & McKenzie, 2015) and reaffirms the Indigenous presence on and with land throughout history, present, and future. Reaffirming Indigenous presence on land must include Indigenous queer folk. Queering Indigenous Land-based education, described by Alex Wilson et al. (2021), involves "reconstructive practices" (p. 224) that "undo colonial gender and sexuality constructs, while simultaneously strengthening the bond to land" (p. 228). In Rotinonhsonníh worldview, land is gendered as relational beings, represented as kindred spirits of creation. Gendering land in this sense reaffirms "the kinship systems in which the more-than-human world is protected through ethics of relational accountability" (Spillet, 2021, p. 24). Land, as original Mother of creation, provides for us with a home, sustenance, and wellness. Indigenous Land-based education reconnects us to natural food and medicine systems. Applying respect, relevancy, reciprocity, and responsibility (Kirkness & Barnhardt, 1991) in Indigenous Land-based education engenders relational accountability to land and to the human and more than-human beings we share this home with.

When developing a Rotinonhsonníh Land-based education program at *Kawenna'ón:we*, seven key elements of Rotinonhsonníh knowledge creation and meaning-making began to emerge. The creation story, *Ohén:ton Karihwatéhkwen*; cycle of ceremonies, *Kaienerakó:wa*; wampum theories; Land-based practices including craft, story, songs, and dreams; and finally, worldview informed by language were elements of Rotinonhsonníh culture that we spiralled into to bring out ancient wisdom and new knowledge.

As a child living in Hamilton, Ontario, I was first exposed to Rotinonhsonníh stories through the book *Tyendinaga Tales*. In her introduction, Rustige (1998) explains that "older residents were unanimous in explaining that in the past the perpetuation of Mohawk tales and language was discouraged in the reserve school and elsewhere because it was considered a sign of 'backwardness'" (p. xiv). Reading the stories and looking at the pictures, it didn't feel backwards to me. It felt right, correct, true, and genuine. I wanted to learn more and have since dedicated my life to learning *Kanien'ké:ha*, stories, songs, ceremonies, and practices. I've been fortunate that creation has supported my learning and has created opportunities and people to learn from. I have a reciprocal responsibility to share and teach others, so that our way of life, our way of knowing and doing is never viewed as unacceptable or backwards ever again. With this responsibility, I share the following elements that shape Rotinonhsonníh Land-based education.

Elements of Rotinonhsonníh Land-Based Education: Creation Story

The creation story starts off by explaining that this world was covered in water. The only occupants were water beings and birds. Another world exists in the sky. In sky world, there was a celestial tree with a variety of fruit and flowers. A pregnant woman craved the roots of the tree to make tea. Her husband, the tree's caretaker, knew it was wrong to damage the tree, but he relented and uprooted it to reveal a deep, dark hole. As the woman reached for the roots, she fell into the hole. She fell for a long time and eventually geese saw her descending. They formed a V and caught her on their wings. On the waters' surface, a turtle saw what was happening and directed the birds to land on its back. Once on the turtle's back, sky woman explained how she needed earth to survive. The water beings held a meeting. It was remembered that earth could be found at the bottom of the ocean, so they all took turns to retrieve it. All failed, until the muskrat tried. After being gone a long time, the muskrat finally surfaced with a bit of earth in its paws. Sky woman took the earth and placed it on the turtle's back and began to dance in the direction of the sun. As she shuffled her feet, the turtle's back grew large enough for her to live on. Sky woman eventually gave birth to a young woman. This young woman grew quickly and one day she was visited by a spiritual being from sky world. The sight of the spiritual being made her faint. The spiritual being placed two arrows on her stomach. One arrow was sharp, and the other dull. Her mother began to suspect her daughter was pregnant as the days went by. The daughter was carrying twins, but even in utero the twins began to quarrel. When it was time to be born, the right-handed twin headed towards the birth canal, but the left-handed twin wanted to be born first, so when he saw a light coming from above he tried to escape through his mother's mouth and nose. The opening was too small, so he pushed his way out his mother's armpit. The mother died giving birth to the twins. Not sure what to do with her body, the grandmother covered it with earth. From the mother's body grew original foods and medicines. Tobacco grew from her head, strawberries grew from her heart, and potatoes grew from her toes. Corn, beans, and squash grew from her breasts, stomach, and fingers.

The sky woman, now grandmother, was horrified and in her grief mixed the two babies up. She blamed the right-handed twin for killing her daughter and favoured the left-handed chid. As children, the twins were named Sapling (right-handed twin) and Flint (left-handed twin); Sapling's name changes to *Tharonhià:kon* (he is holding the sky) later in the story. The twins had the ability to create life on earth. Sapling would create small game as Flint would create predators. Sapling created flowers and edible fruit, while Flint created thorns and poison berries. Finally, after the world was created, Sapling created a human figure from clay and after baking it in the fire, he breathed three times into it to make it come alive. When he finished creating humans, he instructed them to remain thankful, for everything on earth is to help sustain them. Even though Flint created harmful, destructive beings, there was balance on the earth. The thorns protected the flowers. The predators prevented overpopulation. Flint also tried to create humans but was unsuccessful, so instead he created creatures that would destroy human beings. Sapling took Flint's creatures and barricaded them in a cave. Not wanting humans to be hurt, Sapling wouldn't allow his brother to create any more beings. Angry, Flint challenged his brother to be the one to oversee all of creation.

The first challenge was *kaientowá:nen* (a big field) game. This is a game of chance. In this game, fruit pits are burnt on one side so that they are half dark and half light. The fruit pits are placed in a bowl and shook by each player. The player who turns up all the pits of the same colour wins the round. Flint and Sapling played all morning but come noon, no winner was declared. It was then decided that a game of lacrosse would be played by the brothers to determine who would mind creation. Again, the brothers played an even match. Finally, they agreed to battle it out, each choosing a weapon. But before they fought, they agreed to fight fair. Flint brought a stick to fight with, while Sapling, who was determined to win for the good of all creation, brought a sharp deer antler. Flint's stick did not do much harm, and he was defeated easily. The grandmother was angry that Sapling cheated and came between the brothers. They tugged and fought over her. Sapling gripped her upper body while Flint pulled at her legs. Her body ripped in half. Her head flew into the sky, while her body landed in the ocean. Flint pleaded with Sapling to have mercy on him. Sapling recognized his brother's strength and agreed that minding creation could be a shared responsibility. Flint would forever be with his grandmother, the moon, and mind the earth in darkness, and Sapling would mind creation during the daytime.

This short version of the creation story has many teachings such as the importance of balance and conflict resolution. It is an important aspect of Rotinonhsonníh Land-based education as it explains how we are loved and related to the natural world, water, and cosmos. "As the last beings Teharoniawakon created, humans are and remain dependent on all other beings, and whether those beings offer their lives for our nutrition or their sentience for our thinking and imagining, ancient reciprocities continue." (Sheridan & Longboat, 2006, p. 366). The Rotinonhsonníh creation story reminds us of our responsibility to be appreciative and in awe of the natural world.

Elements of Rotinonhsonníh Land-Based Education: Ohén:ton Karihwatéhkwen

The *Ohén:ton Karihwatéhkwen* is one way Rotinonhsonníh were instructed to give our love greetings and appreciation for the gift of life. At the time of creation, when the first humans made from clay were shown all the land, water, and sky beings we share this earth with and are related to. When we give our love, greetings, and appreciation, it is taught that we say it from heart. We start with the people and then from the earth we move up; acknowledging the waters and water beings, roots, grasses, and medicines; we continue with the bugs, fruits, and cultivated foods; next comes the wild animals and trees. Then we give acknowledgement to the sky dwellers. The birds, four winds, thunders, sun, moon, and stars. Finally, we give thanks to the one who created our bodies. *Ohén:ton Karihwatéhkwen* is to be said first thing in the morning and every time people gather, be it for a celebration, a ceremony, or a meeting. It is said that we are inviting the natural world into the space with us, and that any business, celebration, or ceremony should be conducted with the good of all creation in mind. The *Ohén:ton Karihwatéhkwen* is not a prayer, but an act of reciprocity and acknowledgement. Respected Elder Otsi'tsakén:ra Patton of Kahnawà:ke explains, "We don't pray, we don't have to ask the Creator for anything because he already gave it to us. All the Creator ever did, we give thanks for and appreciate what we have and that's really what these words are about" (Patton et al., 2021, p. 2). Collectively listening to the words and putting our minds together to give our love, appreciation, and gratitude is powerful energy that invokes meaning into the day, ceremony, or meeting. It makes the business real. In regards to Rotinonhsonníh Land-based education, the *Ohén:ton Karihwatéhkwen* is important as it is an act of reciprocity and relationality. Recognizing that creation sustains us, the cycle of ceremonies is another aspect of Rotinonhsonníh Land-based education.

Elements of Rotinonhsonníh Land-Based Education: Cycle of Ceremonies

Revolving from the natural cycle of sustenance, celebration and gratitude is given to the natural world with speeches, tobacco offering, song, dance, and food. Beginning with mid-winter, we celebrate and give thanks for another year. The next ceremony we celebrate is the opening of the trees, in order to safely collect the first medicine, maple water. Towards the end of maple season, we give thanks for the trees and recognize the maple as the leader. In the spring, we give thanks for medicines and seeds. The peach stone game is played to decide who wins the responsibilities to ensure planting is done. In early summer, we celebrate the strawberries as they are the first wild berries to be gathered. Later in the summer, we have ceremony for green beans and raspberries. Towards the end of summer, the green corn is ready and we celebrate through ceremony. This is the stage of growth when white flint corn can be eaten uncooked, straight off the cob. In the fall, just before hunting season, it is harvest time. This is when we give our love greetings and appreciation for all the cultivated foods. Ceremonies that indirectly relate to perpetuation of food and medicine renewal celebrate the arrival and departure of the thunders, Grandfather Ratori (haduwi) medicine society, and Okiwe (ceremony for ancestors). Other ceremonies involve medicine, but these ceremonies are more personal in nature. Teaching through the ceremonial cycle of the Rotinonhsonníh, students become more connected to land. Over time they learn how to recognize and predict seasonal changes, where and when natural foods grow, and how to plant, protect, and prepare cultivated foods. Most importantly, students learn that the natural food cycle is a gift of creation and that we need to be mindful of our actions in order for that gift to continue. Otsi'tsakén:ra Patton goes on to explain, "Food is life and we give thanks to the food life and because we give thanks to the food life, then, life continues, right? If there was no more food left, what would life be for us?" (Patton et al., 2021, p. 5).

Elements of Rotinonhsonníh Land-Based Education: Peacemaker and *Kaienerakó:wa*

The next element of Rotinonhsonníh Land-based education we taught from was the story of the Peacemaker and *Kaienera'kó:wa*. The origin story of the *Kaienera'kó:wa* and the Peacemaker is highly revered and takes days to recite. Many spiritual people from around the world consider Tyendinaga, or Kenhteke, a significant spiritual location. The Peacemaker is a central figure in Rotinonhsonníh history. At a time of war between nations and within communities, a mother had decided to remove herself from society and raise her daughter alone, away from conflict. She raised her child, *oherò:kon* (under the husk). As a young woman, the daughter was visited in the night by the spirit of the west wind and she became pregnant. The mother didn't understand her daughter's pregnancy and when the child was born, the now grandmother attempted to kill the child. She tried drowning him twice under the icy waters, but each time she returned to the lodge, the baby was fast asleep in his mother's arms. Then the grandmother made a fire and took the sleeping child to throw him in the flames, but again, when she returned to the lodge the baby was in his mother's arms. After the third attempt to get rid of the child, the grandmother was visited in a dream. Creator informed her that the child was sent to bring a message of reasoning to the people. The baby would grow quickly into a young man, and one day, he would have to leave in a stone canoe to travel and spread the message of *kaienerá:kowa* (great goodness). The Peacemaker was told to teach the people how to reason by using *kanikonrí:io* (a good mind), so that there would be *skén:nen* (peace) and we would have *kasasténshera* (strength and unity). A sign that his message was and is still accepted is acknowledged every spring, during maple season. If a tree is tapped and the sap runs clear, the message of peace and reasoning lives on. If the sap runs red, we are in for some troubled times.

The Peacemaker story continues with the Peacemaker meeting Aienwatha. Aienwatha was an Onondaga chief, whose wife and daughters died as a result of evil misdoings by Atotarho. In grief, Aienwatha left Onondaga after the death of his family and headed east, towards the Mohawk Nation. On his travel, he comes to a marshy lake. As he crosses the lake, the ducks and geese begin to flap their wings with great force. As they fly off, they lift the water with them. On the lake bottom, Aienwatha notices small shells and begins to collect them. He continues his journey, stringing the shells and expressing words of condolence to himself. The words of condolence speak of wiping his vision and tears so that he can see clearly again, drinking fresh water so that the lump in his throat would be removed, and cleaning out his out his ears so that he can hear again. Aienwatha and the Peacemaker finally meet and the Peacemaker repeats the words of condolence back to Aienwatha, using the shell-beaded string. Having the burden lifted, Aienwatha is able to travel with the Peacemaker and help spread the message of *skén:nen, kasasténshera, and kanikonhri:io*.

Elements of Rotinonhsonníh Land-Based Education: Wampum Theories

The first wampum used for ceremony appeared in the formation of the Great Law of Peace, with the condolence of Aienwatha. "According to tradition wampum was introduced to the Iroquois by Hiawatha at the time of the founding of the League of the Five Nations. Hiawatha decreed and regulated its use." (Tehanetorens, 1972, p. 3). Wampum, or *onekórha* (shell), and wampum belts (*atia'tenha*) are relational and sentient. The principles and events in wampum are alive and passed down from the experiences of our ancestors. They remind us how to be good people and of the agreements we made with each other and the natural world. Each belt or string is its own theory. Kovach (2016) describes Indigenous theory as "a particular theoretical orientation with specific attributes and characteristics" (p. 100).

They may provide principles on how to be a good relative, such as the dish with one spoon, or recalling a relational agreement, such as the George Washington belt, or both, such as the Two Row Wampum. Wampum made from shells and the words and intent we put in them are alive. Wampum are often referred to as trade beads, mnemonic devices, and currency, but rarely as theory. From a Rotinonhsonníh perspective, wampum are precious and important and held with high regard, for they hold within them our theories, our collective consciousness, and our agreements with each other and creation on how to live a good life. From governance to grief, wampum theories articulated in different wampum strings and belts are applicable in all social domains, including education. Wampum theories are culturally appropriate foundational approaches to Rotinonhsonníh Land-based education.

KAWENNA'ÓN:WE IONTERIHWAIENSTÁHKHWA: ORIGINAL WORDS SCHOOL

Teaching in *Kanien'ké:ha*, from creation stories, *Ohén:ton Karihwatéhkwen*, cycle of ceremonies, Peacemaker's journey, and wampum theories invokes spiralling in to spiral out, and provides an alternative to the marginalization of Indigenous ways of knowing and learning in mainstream education (Bowra et al., 2021). By centring Rotinonhsonníh ways of knowing and land-based practices in education, *Kanienke'hàka* students begin to better understand their relationship as one with land, self, families, communities, and nations, ensuring the continuance of *Onkwehon:we'neha* in a contemporary society.

Kawenna'ón:we is a small private Mohawk immersion school in my home community of Tyendinaga Mohawk Territory. We had anywhere from 10 to 15 students at a time. I taught grades two to four. Being a small private school meant we had little funding but a lot of room for creativity, and we were encouraged to teach through a Rotinonhsonníh lens. The first school was housed in an office/conference space at FNTI. There was a large conference room that served as the main classroom. A smaller, former office room served as a secondary classroom space for the older children. We also had a small kitchenette. In another office space, we created a longhouse room for when we opened the day and sang Rotinonhsonníh social songs. The walls were faux-painted to look like logs, and we hung braids of corn and *kastowas* (traditional head piece). Benches were placed around the perimeter of the room. On the bench by the window, we kept a basket of rattles and a water drum. There was an office for administration and a photocopier. The building was located at the community airport, which once served as a military base. Within walking distance is the Bay of Quinte and its tributary creeks and streams, as well as marshlands and hardwoods. Most notably is Eagle Hill, where it is said the Peacemaker was born. I taught at this location from 2012–2013.

In the beginning, it was decided that our school would run on a 12-month cycle, without a prolonged summer break, because the focus of our school was language and cultural acquisition and there was a concern that the students would lose language over the summer. We ran eight sessions that were five weeks each, alternating one- and two-week breaks between each session. We taught the Ontario overall curriculum expectations but wanted those education expectations to be taught within Rotinonhsonníh epistemology and pedagogy. One of the first things we did was photocopy and cut out the expectations for each subject and each grade we taught. We then laid out eight Bristol boards for each session, two for each season. We mapped out the cycle of ceremonies and *Ohén:ton Karihwatéhkwen* on the boards before matching them up with the overall curriculum expectation. For example, in the winter we celebrate the new year, the sun, moon, and stars, as well as people, families, and ancestors. We also celebrate stories and dreams. The overall curriculum expectations paired with the winter teaching block included understanding earth and space systems for science, and geometry and spatial sense for math. It was important for me to ensure that what was happening in the classroom reflected what was happening in the natural world. When I was a student teacher, I was tasked with teaching a unit on the plant cycle in November. I questioned why we were teaching this unit now when the plants were getting ready to sleep for the winter, and I was told it was the next unit in the book.

Daily Routine

Our daily routine started with the *Ohén:ton Karihwatéhkwen* in the longhouse room. The children coming from *Totahne* language nest were very proficient in this practice. We used hand gestures, walks outside, drawings, and felt boards to support students with little to no *Kanien'ké:ha*. Everyone took turns and contributed to the opening.

Every morning after the *Ohén:ton Karihwatéhkwen*, we sang and danced social songs. Sitting around the benches, we would pass the water drum around to give everyone an opportunity. If someone didn't feel comfortable to lead the song, they had the option to pass. I usually passed, but one day, I had found the courage to lead a song. I don't know why but I was so nervous. I knew the songs but felt enormous pressure to lead sing. I have a hard time keeping a steady beat. The students were compassionate, encouraging, and supportive. One student offered to model the beat for me and I found my voice and sang the song. After, they all hugged me as I cried tears of joy and relief. That was a *kasasténshera* (strength and unity) moment for me. As educators, we put pressure on ourselves to know everything, but it's okay to be human and to be vulnerable. We are learning together with our students. We all have strengths and weaknesses. For some students, math and reading is really hard, but singing comes naturally. It's good to ensure different learning opportunities throughout the day so that all children feel valued.

After singing, we would have a short recess. Coming back from recess, we split into two groups: kindergarten and grade one, and grades two to four. We taught math until lunch. We were fortunate to have math textbooks translated in *Kanien'ké:ha*, as well as a word list of math-related terms to teach from. Because of our small budget, we had to get creative with manipulatives. We purchased flat glass marbles from the dollar store and used painted rocks as counters. One math manipulative I found handy and culturally connected to wampum and our base ten counting system was the 100-bead string. One hundred pony beads were strung in a pattern of 10 in one colour and 10 of the second colour. This manipulative worked well to teach the children the *Kanien'ké:ha* counting system. The alternating colours helped the students see the language used for counting. Holding the beaded strings and remembering the meaning of each bead as their fingers glided down the string also introduced the students to the action associated with reading wampum.

After lunch, I would take my group of older students outside to explore the woods, marshes, and creeks. We took notice of seasonal changes, insect and animal habitats, identifying trees by the leaves, and noted these observations in journals. Most of all, I wanted the kids to learn through play and to connect with land and each other on their terms. They would help each other cross log bridges and climb up icy slopes. They laughed, screamed, and sometimes cried, but they learned a lot about the natural world and about each other. I had two students who didn't get along very well because they had different personalities. One student thrived with change. He enjoyed different activities and unexpected moments. He hated to sit for too long. Getting outside to learn was his favourite part of the day. The other student liked structure. He needed to know in advance what to expect. Exploring the outdoors was stressful for him. These differences made it hard for these two students to get along, so we talked about it. How each one felt about going out to learn and staying in to learn. They eventually came to an understanding of *kanikonhri:io* and *skén:nen*. They began to empathize with each other and appreciate the learning environment they were uncomfortable with because it was comfortable for the other person.

In the winter months, we would work on projects, such as baking, moccasin or cornhusk doll making, beading, decorating paddles to stir mid-winter ashes, and string art. Every year I tried to incorporate a multi-subject, project-based learning activity with Rotinonhsonníh material culture. Aside from learning math and literacy skills, they learned practical skills such as sewing, beading, wood work, wood burning, leather work, reading a recipe, and preparing foods and medicines. In a small classroom setting of six to eight students, you can give them the attention they need to build those skills. It was hectic as I was constantly threading needles, tying knots, watching over them as they used hot glue guns, wood burners, hammers, scissors, and small kitchen knives but they learned safety, concentration, and to use tools for their intended purposes. *Kanien'ké:ha* is a verb-based language. Together, we learned a lot of vocabulary when talking about what we were doing as we were doing it. Aside from language and skill development, this was also a good time to introduce symbols and metaphors in our culture, such as sky domes, celestial trees, the clans, and more. When I reflect on culturally responsive project-based learning, I am reminded of my own childhood, learning by doing with my grandmother, aunties, and parents. I was rarely told that I was too young or of the wrong gender when I wanted to help bake or sew or fix something.

We alternated the last part of the day for gym and art. We were fortunate that we had access to the FNTI gym and some equipment in the building next door. It was a treat to go and play in the gym. Gym class usually consisted of a warm-up, a group game using equipment, and a cool-down. Once we built up a routine and repertoire of games, the students began to have more agency in deciding what they wanted to do in the gym. Every June, our sister community, Kahnawà:ke, hosts the Races for Health event. In the spring, we would start our training sessions. We made a makeshift track using pylons in the front yard. First, we started out walking; the next week we would alternate running and walking until eventually we got to running the track three times. We focused on reaching personal goals and encouraging one another over competition. The real fun and prize was the opportunity to go on a trip with parents, families.

Art time was open-ended as we tried to emphasize process over product. The situation of having a small budget, as most art supplies were either donated or purchased by myself and coworkers, fostered creativity. One issue that came up often was the use of others' ideas. During these incidents, we reminded the students that it's good to learn from one another, to share ideas, and to know that their idea was so good it inspired someone else to try it, modelling Indigenous knowledges are held in common for and by the people.

We decided to attend ceremonies with our students so that they could hear and gain an understanding of ceremonial languages. The ceremonies our school attended included mid-winter, maple, seeds and medicines, thunders, strawberry, and harvest. Ceremonies can be held anywhere from one to four days. It was optional that parents went with their children to ceremonies. We prepared our students by going over what to expect the week before ceremony was to take place. We shared with them language, songs, and dances they were going to hear, so they would know what to do and when. Come the day of the ceremony it was easy to mind and care for them, because they knew their role and responsibility in that place and time. When it was time to listen, they not only listened but understood what was being said. When it was time to dance, they danced; when it was time to sing, they sang; and when it was time to eat, they ate. It's not the responsibility of children to put through ceremony, but it's reassuring knowing that if these children stay connected to who they are, ceremonies will be able to continue for another 50 or 60 years.

At the end of June, we would host a moving up ceremony. Inviting families and community members, we celebrated all students moving to the next level in their education. A special mention went out to those who would move out of our Grade 4 program and into the federal school on the territory, as well as students that would move from the junior room to the senior room, and also *Totahne* children who would move from the language nest to *Kawenna'ón:we*. Also celebrated at this time were the adult learners in the *Shatiwennakaratats* adult immersion program. A feast was catered; students were gifted with certificates and presents; we then ended the evening with a social in their honour. The first year we had about 20 children and 20 adult students doing the work to revitalize language and culture.

Although we taught year-round, September was the start of the school year. After our first full cycle of teaching blocks, one of the students came back to school in September, very proud to show me his back-to-school supplies. Instead of a backpack, he had a traditional black ash pack basket. Inside his pack basket, he had a medicine pouch, a braid of sweet grass, and his rattle. At eight years old, he was prepared to learn what was important to him, *Onkwehon:we'neha*.

New Location

We moved to a new location in the community library building in January 2014. This building was on a large, open field. The woods, marshes, creeks, and Eagle Hill were no longer within walking distance. We also lost access to the gym, but our program director was able to access funding for climbing equipment, raised planters, and swings. We eventually purchased a class set of archery equipment as well. Inside the building, we had a large communal room, two small classrooms, a kitchen, a curriculum storage room, and a couple of offices used for administration. We used one of the smaller classrooms as a literacy and science room, and the other small classroom was a math room. The communal room was used for the *Ohén:ton Karihwatéhkwen*, art, and singing. The kitchen was large enough for a big kitchen table, and the students were able to eat together. Accessing funding for healthy meals, our program director was able to hire a cook who also helped in the classrooms.

The students adjusted well to the move. In the spring of that year, I began to have them train for Races for Health. We walked and ran the perimeter of the large, open field. The field was flanked by roads on the three sides and was not fenced. I had the older group of six- to nine-year-olds and made sure to keep my eye on them. They respected the boundaries and it was freeing to not be fenced in. The more we walked around the field, the more we began to appreciate and enjoy the practice. We continued this practice every day and began to notice seasonal changes of the land. They noticed where the strawberries grew, where the best mud holes appeared after the rain, how pinecones busted open after the rain, where animal tracks led to a den, and where the ice formed when the field froze up. They waved to the delivery truck driver that passed every day, and he would honk the horn for them. The big, empty field wasn't so empty anymore.

One day, we had a large box of donated art supplies, and inside were various beads of all different kinds of shapes and sizes. This gave me an idea to make *Ohén:ton Karihwatéhkwen* bracelets. By now the students could recite their own personalized versions of the address, but sometimes they would forget one or two beings in the natural world. I thought the bracelets would be a good memory tool. After they made their bracelets, it was my break and their play time. I came back and heard one student speaking into his wrist. "Hello birds, I'll come out in just a bit." I looked around the room and another student had her bracelet up to her ear, listening to a message from the trees. These beaded mnemonic devices were telecommunicators. I was impressed, not only by their imagination, but by their open and free relationship with the natural world.

That year a new clan chief was installed by the Grand Council in Six Nations. I took the opportunity in our social studies class to study the names and positions of the 50 chiefs within the confederacy. Separating the chief names by each nation of *Kanien'kehá:ka* (people of the flint or Mohawk), *Oneniote'á:ka* (people of the standing stone or Oneida), *Ononta'kehá:ka* (people of the hills or Onondaga),

Kaion'kehá:ka (people of the swamp or Cayuga), and *Shotinontowane'á:ka* (people of the great hill or Seneca). We took a few minutes each day to go over the names with corresponding pictographs. I did a bit of research and found how corn kernels were laid out to practice the roianer (chief) roll call. Hewitt & Fenton (1945) reference Cayuga Chief Abram Charles's notebook, citing, "The arrangement of dots to represent these groups in Chief Charles's notebook, moreover, follows a design for laying down kernels of corn that he and other Iroquois ritualists employed when instructing Eulogy singers in the Roll Call of chiefs and in teaching their relationships" (p. 305).

The week I started using corn as placeholders for the names, one of my students came to school all excited. He said he had a dream of being in longhouse with the chiefs. He spoke to them and told them he knew them. When they spoke back to him, they spoke in their own language. They told him that he needed to dance for them to believe that he knew and understood them. He said he danced his hardest and they believed him. The student was so excited telling me that in his dream he could understand five languages of the Rotinonhsonníh chiefs. It used to be common for people, especially orators and messengers, to speak several languages of the confederacy. What a treat for that young person to have experienced that sense of knowing.

At the new location, I began implementing a land-as-classroom approach to my teaching. One winter day, I took the students outside and began making a large picture with my footprints. Soon they were creating their own pictures. One student in particular created a 20-by 40-foot picture inspired by the creation story, depicting a turtle with a celestial tree on it. I was impressed with his ability to think big! Another day, I took them outside for math. We were learning about three-dimensional shapes and had a box of fillable shapes to measure volume. We used these manipulatives as molds for snow and the children made sculptures. In *Kanien'ké:ha*, they were able to describe the shapes they used and use prepositional phrases to describe how the shapes were placed. Another way I implemented land as classroom, while instructing math, was by using sticks, pebbles, and leaves as base 10 counters. The leaves represented hundreds, sticks were tens, and pebbles were ones. We made a game of it with the counters and wipe-off boards. One of my students, who struggled with remembering number values in written form, caught on very quickly. By learning math concepts with the natural elements, he was able to make the connection between value and written form. His math skills and confidence in math began to improve.

One practice that I began to implement every September was commitment strings. Students would bead a string representing the Rotinonhsonníh values of *skén:nen, kanikonhri:ío,* and *kasasténshera* that I expected they demonstrate while learning. The next set of beads represented learning barriers such as divorce, change within the house, death, and so on. After learning barriers, we talked about learning supports and strung beads to represent people, pets, or places that supported and loved them. The most important bead on the string was the "YOU" bead, a special bead that represented themselves. One of the students, who I'd taught for three years, had experienced the loss of his mother when he was a toddler. Every year he placed a bead that represented her on his string as a barrier to learning, visually expressing that it was hard to learn through grief. In September of my last year of teaching, he placed the bead that represented her in his support section. He told us that he accepted her passing and felt that she was supporting him from sky world.

By April of 2017, I was ready for change, as I had worked with children for nearly 20 years, and accepted a university-teaching position. I am appreciative of my time teaching at *Kawenna'ón:we* for I had the freedom to learn about and develop my practice in Indigenous Land-based education. I haven't had much opportunity to check back with students but from social media posts, I've learned they are all now teenagers, some applying to college. A couple of students were Grade 8 valedictorians. One student is playing on an elite baseball team and another is a community-respected hunter and cultural knowledge holder. I am proud of them all. I am currently on the board of directors for *Tsi Tyónnheht Onkwawén:na* as a means to continue to be involved in and support culture and language in Kenhteke (Tyendinaga). We are currently working on building a permanent location for our language programs.

CONCLUSION

Indigenous Land-based education is not a definitive end result but a process and a movement to reclaim and heal relational Indigenous ways of knowing and doing with and of the land. By spiralling into Indigenous practice and theory, Indigenous Land-based education facilitates decolonization and Indigenization by spiralling out genuine contextual knowledge and meaning-making. In this chapter I have briefly spiralled into the Rotinonhsonníh creation story, *Ohén:ton Karihwatéhkwen,* cycle of ceremonies, the formation of the *Kaienerakó:wa* through the story of the Peacemaker, theories embedded in wampum, as well as language and land-based practices and handiwork to better understand and spiral out Rotinonhsonníh Land-based pedagogy in education as an antithesis of Indian residential and day schools. This chapter demonstrates how teaching through stories and cultural practices creates cooperative and relational programming, valuing children's individual gifts while reviving Indigenous languages. Recognizing that not every education program can dedicate as much cultural knowledge to their program as we did at *Kawenna'ón:we*, it is important for readers who are educators, parents, and students to understand the importance of Indigenous Land-based pedagogy to Indigenous identity and decolonization. I share my teaching experience at *Kawenna'ón:we* as a means of uplifting, inspiring, and acknowledging work being done to create a better existence for future generations, for the land and all our relations.

NOTES

1. Not-for-profit community in upper New York re-established in 1993 by Tom Porter.
2. Culture and language centre in Tyendinaga, established in 2000.

REFLECTION QUESTIONS

1. As a child, when did you feel most connected or one with creation?
2. In this chapter, Rotinonhsonníh theories and philosophies were introduced through stories, language, and practices as elements of Rotinonhsonníh Land-based education. Why is it important to consider nation-specific, cultural knowledge when planning or participating in Indigenous Land-based education programs?
3. The *Ohén:ton Karihwatéhkwen* reminds us to give our love, greetings, and appreciation to all of our relations. Why is this important in education and what actions can accompany these words?
4. How does Indigenous Land-based education differ from outdoor education?
5. Using the information provided in this chapter, your experiences, and cultural knowledge, what would your dream school or education program look like?

SUGGESTED READINGS

- Hill, S. M. (2017). *The clay we are made of: Haudenosaunee land tenure on the Grand River*. University of Manitoba Press.

- Porter, T. (2008). *And grandma said... Iroquois teachings, as passed down through the oral tradition*. Xlibris.
- Simpson, L. B. (2017). *As we have always done: Indigenous freedom through radical resistance*. University of Minnesota Press.
- Styres, S. D. (2017). *Pathways for remembering and recognizing Indigenous thought in education: Philosophies of iethi'nihstenha ohwentsia'kekha (land)*. University of Toronto Press.

REFERENCES

Allard-Tremblay, Y. (2022). The Two Row Wampum: Decolonizing and indigenizing democratic autonomy. *Polity, 54*(2), 225–249.

Bowra, A., Mashford-Pringle, A., & Poland, B. (2021). Indigenous learning on Turtle Island: A review of the literature on land-based learning. *The Canadian Geographer/Le Géographe canadien, 65*(2), 132–140.

Calderon, D. (2014). Speaking back to Manifest Destinies: A land-education approach to critical curriculum inquiry. *Environmental Education Research, 20*(1), 24–36.

Corntassel, J. (2009). Indigenous storytelling, truth-telling, and community approaches to reconciliation. *English Studies in Canada, 35*(1), 137–159

Datta, R. K. (2018). Rethinking environmental science education from Indigenous knowledge perspectives: An experience with a Dene First Nation community. *Environmental Education Research, 24*(1), 50–66.

Hewitt, J. N. B., & Fenton, W. N. (1945). Some mnemonic pictographs relating to the Iroquois condolence council. *Journal of the Washington Academy of Sciences, 35*(10), 301–315.

Kirkness, V. J., & Barnhardt, R. (1991). First Nations and higher education: The four R's—Respect, relevance, reciprocity, responsibility. *Journal of American Indian Education, 30*(3), 1–15.

Kovach, M. (2016). Thinking through theory: Contemplating Indigenous situated research and policy. In N. K. Denzin & M. D. Giardina (Eds.), *Qualitative inquiry outside the academy* (pp. 92–106). Routledge.

Maracle, B. J. (2002). Adult Mohawk language immersion programming. *McGill Journal of Education, 37*(3), 387–404.

Patton, O. C., Ibarra-Lemay, A., & White, L. (2021). Ohén:ton Karihwatéhkwen and Kanien'kehá:ka teachings of gratitude and connection. *Genealogy, 5*(3), 81. https://doi.org/10.3390/genealogy5030081

Radu, I., House, L. M., & Pashagumskum, E. (2014). Land, life, and knowledge in Chisasibi: Intergenerational healing in the bush. *Decolonization: Indigeneity, Education & Society, 3*(3), 86–105.

Rustige, R. (Ed.). (1998). *Tyendinaga tales*. McGill-Queen's University Press.

Sium, A., & Ritskes, E. (2013). Speaking truth to power: Indigenous storytelling as an act of living resistance. *Decolonization: Indigeneity, Education & Society, 2*(1), i–x.

Sheridan, J., & Longboat, R. (2006). The Haudenosaunee imagination and the ecology of the sacred. *Space and Culture, 9*(4), 365–381. https://doi.org/10.1177/1206331206292503

Smith, L. T. (2021). *Decolonizing methodologies: Research and Indigenous Peoples*. Bloomsbury Publishing.

Shawanda, A. (2020). Baawaajige: Exploring dreams as academic references. *Turtle Island Journal of Indigenous Health, 1*(1), 37–47.

Spillett, T. (2021). Gender, land, and place: Considering gender within land-based and place-based learning. *Journal for the Study of Religion, Nature and Culture, 15*(1), 11–31. https://doi.org/10.1558/jsrnc.39094

Tehanetorens. (1972). *Wampum belts*. Iroquois Publications.

Truth and Reconciliation Commission of Canada. (2015). *Canada's residential schools: The history, part 1: Origins to 1939* (Vol. 1). McGill-Queen's University Press.

Tuck, E., & McKenzie, M. (2015). *Place in research: Theory, methodology, and methods*. Routledge.

Virtanen, P. K. (2022). Relational epistemology and Amazonian land-based education: Learning the ideas of intra-dependency in the central Purus River. *Anthropology & Education Quarterly, 53*(4), 341–356. https://doi.org/10.1111/aeq.12421

Wildcat, M., McDonald, M., Irlbacher-Fox, S., & Coulthard, G. (2014). Learning from the land: Indigenous land based pedagogy and decolonization. *Decolonization: Indigeneity, Education & Society, 3*(3), i–xv.

Wilson, A., & Laing, M. (2018). Queering Indigenous education. In L. T. Smith, E. Tuck, K. W. Yang (Eds.), *Indigenous and decolonizing studies in education* (pp. 131–145). Routledge.

Wilson, A., Murray, J., Loutitt, S., & Scott, R. N. S. (2021). Queering Indigenous land-based education. In J. Russell (Eds.), *Queer ecopedagogies: Explorations in nature, sexuality, and education* (pp. 219–231). Springer.

PART II

RACIALIZED IMMIGRANT WOMEN AND CHILDREN COMMUNITY REFLECTIONS ON DECOLONIZATION IN PRACTICE

Many colour settler scholars argue that many colour settlers, including racialized immigrants' women communities, have failed to address colonial forces affecting Indigenous peoples in settler nations, identifying people of colour as settlers who benefit from Indigenous dispossession. This part aims to offer a response to this debate that is informed by decolonial theories and seeks to decolonize our practices.

1. **Jebunnessa Chapola** as a racialized colour settler woman shares her decolonial reflections on how learning Indigenous meanings of land acknowledgement has been a critical benefit to creating her belongingness with the land and people.
2. **Priyanka Mahey** discusses why taking responsibility to build a decolonial community plays an important role in leading anticolonial environments of change.
3. **Jasmin Bhawra** shares her research focusing on how decolonizing digital citizen science can drive self-governance of historically colonized populations via data sovereignty.
4. **Prarthona Datta and Prokriti Datta** (two sisters) share their learning experiences focusing on how land-based learning from an Indigenist perspective helped them understand who they are as second-generation colour settlers on this Indigenous land and their responsibilities to the land and people.

CHAPTER 7

Learning the Importance of Indigenous Meanings of Land Acknowledgement: A Racialized Colour Settler Woman's Decolonial Reflection

Jebunnessa Chapola

This chapter explores the importance of learning the Indigenous meaning of Land[1] in shaping who I am in this Indigenous territory currently known as Canada. From my 12 years of lived experiences as an insider of the newcomer immigrant community in Canada, I have observed that many settler people of colour live in this country without knowing its colonial history, the stories of Indigenous peoples, and the meaning of Land through Indigenous ways of knowing, in part because they do not have access to Indigenous knowledge. As a racialized settler woman, I have learned through Saskatoon community garden activities that it is essential to understand the Indigenous way of understandings of Land acknowledgements to begin a meaningful decolonial journey. It took me more than a decade as a newcomer to realize my responsibility to learn about Indigenous peoples, their histories, and their cultures in order to develop an understanding of building decolonial communities through Indigenous understandings of Land and creating relationships between cross-cultural settlers and Indigenous communities.

My relational decolonial autoethnographic research[2] has helped me learn how to take responsibility for building meaningful relationships between Indigenous and non-Indigenous communities and to understand the Indigenous meaning of Land in Saskatoon, Canada. At the same time, I have co-learned over 10 years that the community garden's educational initiatives and gender-inclusive approaches can enhance the livelihoods of BIPOC[3] settlers, refugee women, and their families. In my life experience, the University of Saskatchewan campus community gardens have been a place to connect people and build relationships between Indigenous and non-Indigenous communities. It is also a place to strengthen community capacity, improve self-determination among cross-cultural newcomer communities, and learn Indigenous ways of understanding Land.

I have organized this chapter by drawing upon my lived experiences, collaborative community co-learning, and working with many cross-cultural gardeners from all walks of life. I draw from my decolonial, autoethnographic transformative learning reflections captured in my commonplace (reflective learning) books.[4] I have explored my learning experiences with community educators, scholars, leaders, activists, artists, environmentalists, feminists, children and youth (ages 2–30), Indigenous Elders, Knowledge Keepers, and cross-cultural gardeners, primarily from the University of Saskatchewan campus family residences. In addition to reviewing my commonplace books, I have used my learning reflections, my more recent memories, a student newspaper article from *The Sheaf* on our community garden, and interviews with *The Sheaf* and the CBC to contextualize my experiences. I have also used the community garden funders' yearly reports to compile my learnings. My goal in analyzing these learning reflections is to frame racialized settler women's empowerment and responsibilities to engage with community learning spaces and Indigenous knowledges in order to know more deeply how decolonization and reconciliation are vital to reforming our relationships with one another and with the Land, which sustains us.

SITUATING SELF

As a doctoral student during the COVID pandemic I took a year off from working and taking the lead in community garden activities outside of the home in order to focus, read, write, research, think, and reflect on my last 10 years of community gardening activities and learnings. During the early years of my life in Canada, around 2010, I engaged in community events voluntarily, without thinking deeply about any specific benefit. I aimed to keep my leadership skills alive and get to know people around my community. Year after year, I gravitated to the community garden for my own and my family's survival, and I observed that people mostly appreciate the harvest, as well as one another's community relationships. Still, very few people were aware of the other invisible benefits I found in the community garden. I learned by doing and discovered an opportunity to engage collaboratively with community members invested in making social changes. Therefore, I began to undertake various initiatives, including art activities for the children, anti-racist workshops, Indigenous Elders' talks, environmental and feminist talks, educational movie nights, and presentations on the benefits of gardeners respecting the Land. It was a great experience, learning and practising local leadership through awareness-raising events for international students and newcomer immigrant gardeners. In bringing gardeners and community guests together, cooking, providing rides to people, managing child care, mentoring newcomer women in meeting their various needs, helping them to connect with community garden information, collecting seeds and saplings for the gardeners, and arranging distribution, I began to develop my place in the cross-cultural gardeners' community as a hub to build relationships. I started to make friends among Indigenous and cross-cultural communities through this small piece of Land.

It was challenging as a racialized settler woman to lead community garden activities with an unknown shared piece of Land and an unknown community of people, all with various ideologies and mindsets. It took courage to take a leading role with this community garden for an entire decade. I have learned how to empower myself and my family members through the community garden Land, speak up for social justice, develop my leadership skills, and build relationships among Indigenous and racialized settler communities in Canada's Treaty 6 Territory.

The community garden project is a powerful way of building relationships among Indigenous and non-Indigenous communities, as well as among children and community youth. It connects with neighbourhoods, enriches experiences, and inspires us to learn about new ways of knowing, co-learning, and re-learning. In the last 10 years, I have experienced firsthand how people are changing their communities through the power of community gardening, relating to one another through a small piece of Land. Our community garden is a place for relational networking, connecting with community needs, and creating belongingness within this new Indigenous Land. It is a beautiful place to share cross-cultural stories, learn about Indigenous science and worldviews about the Land, share interdisciplinary knowledge, and enjoy natural beauty and spirituality. This garden fosters a positive environment to watch children play as they grow peacefully with nature. This garden has created an approach to allyship and welcoming space for 2SLGBTQIA+[5] people through its anti-racist and decolonizing educational activities. I have seen through my gardening activities that youth are beginning to learn about Canadian history and understand the deeper meanings of Land, decolonization, and reconciliation. Below, I will discuss how I have taken the responsibility to understand the meaning of Land acknowledgements through experiential learning in my leadership role supporting community garden activities.

MY DECOLONIAL JOURNEY TO UNDERSTAND THE INDIGENOUS MEANINGS OF LAND

My anti-racist, postcolonial, social justice, critical pedagogy, transnational, intersectional, decolonial feminist education grew through formal and informal Saskatoon community events and my doctoral training at the University of Saskatchewan. Situating myself has profound importance in learning about the Indigenous meaning of Land acknowledgements. My doctoral research helped train me to understand the meaning of relationality and my responsibility to this Indigenous Land and its original people.

I want to acknowledge that I grew up with colonial ways of knowing because I was born in a colonial Land with many social privileges as a majority Muslim or mainstream woman in Bangladesh (my home country), equivalent to being "white" in Canada. I received formal and informal colonial education from Bangladesh, Sweden, Norway, the United States, and Canada through my educational background in sociology, social work, and gender and development. My upbringing and socialization processes happened within the colonial mentality of national education systems (social, political, educational, and economic). My decolonial journey started recently, after my formal and informal anti-racist and critical decolonial feminist educational journey began, in 2014 at the University of Saskatchewan, the Colleges of Arts and Science, the College of Education events, the Aboriginal Student Center, CFCR Community Radio, and our community garden. However, I learned about sociology and feminism long before, during my undergraduate education in Bangladesh.

The formal anti-racist education with Indigenous scholar Dr. Verna St. Denis at the University of Saskatchewan and my direct engagement with many social justice movements through the college of education and our women's centre gave me a voice and awareness to adopt a decolonial feminist position for the first time. This social justice education helped me speak back against the social stigmatization of my interfaith married (Hindu–Muslim) life, share my untold child abuse story, disclose my ongoing racist sufferings, and raise our children without any traditional religious identity. My anti-racist, anti-oppressive learning engagements with the campus Building Bridges program[6] and the Aboriginal Students' Centre also gave me the power to teach my children and community members about Land-based education, decolonial and anti-racist education, and spirituality, instead of introducing my children to any conventional colonialist religions, and to say it publicly without hiding. I got engaged with the Land directly through community gardens around 2011 in Saskatoon and started to share that I do not follow any colonialist religions for my children and myself. I began to learn how to practice Indigenous spirituality from my Indigenous relations who shared their approaches to social justice. I started to learn how to respect Indigenous people's views, rituals, and relationships with the Land.

From my social justice education, I have learned that intention and a learning spirit are the key determining factors in meaningful engagements with Land acknowledgements. As stated in Wark (2021), these "box-ticking exercises, [are] strictly symbolic gestures, and moves to settler innocence. They have also been accused of lacking critical thought regarding their purposes and attempts to rewrite Indigenous and settler-colonial history" (p. 195). I have observed that Land acknowledgements are indeed used in events as a checkmark, in sorry-not-sorry protocols that mock Indigenous peoples and perpetuate the dismissal of Indigenous cultural losses. As Huntington (2021) argues, "If I am willing to acknowledge that I live and work on Indigenous lands and waters, I must be prepared to back my words with actions and attitudes that match" (p. 5). "When Indigenous peoples acknowledge one another, it is a cultural and political practice fundamentally tied to nationhood" (Wark, 2021, p. 193). Settler Land acknowledgements do not hold the same intention or respect for others and the Land; instead, they dishonour the entire Indigenous community and their diverse histories when they are pro-forma.

My understanding is that Land acknowledgements require critical thought involving social location, situated knowledges, intersectionalities, and accountabilities. Wark (2021) states that without genuine understanding based on an open mind, "Land acknowledgements are rhetorical devices that reference a mythical fabrication of Indigenousness that is consistent with settler dreams of benevolence and innocence" (p. 192). I also learned from the community garden workshops with Indigenous Elders, scholars, and Knowledge Keepers that the Land that we stand on, benefit from, and live on has been occupied, managed, and governed since time immemorial by sovereign Indigenous peoples. I have always felt welcomed and liked the warmth of these kinds of humble words, traditional knowledge, and friendships. My heart melted when I heard Dwayne Lasas, an Indigenous Cree musician, call me his relative. He said that in Indigenous culture they respect all their relations and consider all the newcomers to be relatives.

DECOLONIZING MAINSTREAM RELIGIOUS PRACTICE

During my community garden engagements, I have observed and heard that many gardeners and learners are not ready to personalize Land acknowledgements because of their colonialist educations, upbringings, and conflicts arising from religious beliefs and practices. As a mainstream Muslim woman who grew up with a monotheistic theological ideology in Bangladesh, my understanding of the ethnopsychology of Muslim community members shapes my experiential learning about Land acknowledgements. Muslims begin all their actions in the name of *Allah* by saying "*Bismillahir Rahmanir Raheem*," which means the Most Merciful, the Most Benevolent, to remember that everything is for His sake, in hopes of being rewarded and blessed by *Allah*. By saying *Bismillah*, Muslims invite and welcome blessings and the help of *Allah* (SWT) to make their lives easy and good. *Allah Subhanahu Wa Ta'ala* (SWT) is an honorific phrase used by Muslims to praise *Allah* whenever they mention the name of God and as a show of respect to Him. I was taught from childhood through formal schooling, community, and family that only *Allah* owns and created heaven, earth, Lands, oceans, rivers, the sky, rocks, clouds, and mountains. He (*Allah*) solely takes care of everything in this universe's human and non-human environments. As one of the Abrahamic religions, there is a considerable affinity with Judeo-Christian monotheisms as well.

By learning Indigenous meanings of Land acknowledgements, there is a fundamental difference between colonial religious understanding of Land and Indigenous meanings of Land. For instance, in Canada I learned that Indigenous people take care of Land, which is different from my own religious upbringing and knowledge. On top of that, I grew up learning that Islam does not allow critical questions about the superpower of *Allah*, because that would be *Shirk*, which means a comparison of *Allah* with other deities or anything else is considered a sin. The *Qur'an* (Islamic scripture) stresses that *Allah* does not share His powers with any partner, his creations, or idols (*sharik*). Thus, Islamic ideology contradicts other religious theologies, panentheistic or animistic worldviews. For Muslims, *Tawhid* is the basis of religion, most precisely expressed in the formula, "*La ilaha illallah*," which means there is no God but *Allah*. All praise and thanks are due to *Allah* alone, the One, the All-High and All-Merciful. *Allah* is believed to be omnipotent as He is the creator of the universe. All of heaven and earth are His. He is the Highest and Most Exalted (Al Baqara: 255)[7]. Allah is omnipresent, omniscient, and omnipotent. He (*Allah*) knows what humans do not know. Animism, however, affirms a spirit or consciousness within all things, including inanimate objects, plants, and animals. As a Muslim, I was told that *Allah* is everywhere; however, the unconscious forces and entities (rocks, Land, water, mountains, plants, the sun and moon, the arts) do not have spirits or lives. On the contrary, I have learned from the Indigenous Elders that all non-human beings have a life, and we need to respect rocks, fire, trees, water, and animals.

In Buddhism, there is a reference to the Buddha consciousness within all things. Hinduism acknowledges consciousness within all things, but Islam disagrees by positioning Land, water, and rocks as *Allah's* creations. Therefore, in practising Islam, I have experienced some intercultural incommensurability. Most monotheistic religions elevate humans and their masculine duties and do not practice Indigenous approaches to relationality. This creates a context of the struggle for hegemonic power, particularly when combined with state nationalisms. However, by initiating reconciliation practices with Land acknowledgements, which some moderate Muslims have accepted, extremist Islamicists are challenged by the possibilities of gentle, non-dominating power, invested in the mutual flourishing of all beings and lifeways. Still, some who join in Land acknowledgements may bear silent reservations among Muslims living in Canada as a targeted religious minority.

In daily conversations with Muslims, I have learned that Muslim gardeners may not be comfortable with Land acknowledgements that seem to conflict with their Islamic faith; for example, a gardener, a doctoral candidate in Bioinformatics and Computer Science, explains his views about Land acknowledgements below:

> Yes, Land acknowledgment conflicts with my Muslim faith. My Islamic faith taught me to acknowledge and worship only the Creator, Allah. I should not associate with or worship any other things besides Allah. Allah has created everything (Land, water, mountains, human, non-human things, etc.). As humans, it is our responsibility to take care of all living and non-living things. According to my Islamic faith, first, I should show respect and honour to our creator for the blessings he provided to us. As a Bangladeshi Muslim, I love to feel the creator's gifts by providing us with fertile Land. I pray to the Almighty Allah for the people which He created. Allah takes care of everything, and in His creation, humans take good care of this Land and He helps us use it and benefit from it, which I am thankful for. (personal communication, 2016)

He adds that

> Faith conflicts could be minimized by understanding the situation from a neutral point of view. For example, if everybody tries to help each other wholeheartedly, irrespective of their faiths, colours, or customs, they can come to a common ground. They can choose the good customs of different religions and practices among themselves, if that does not hurt the core beliefs of their faith. According to my faith, I should respect and honour our creator Allah for His blessings to us. But, at the same time, we should be respectful of other religious people and customs.

From 10 years of community garden activities, I have learned that many gardeners and learners are not ready to personalize Land acknowledgements because of their colonial mentality, past learnings, and moral superiority which they learn from religious ideologies and many restrictions. They are not prepared to engage fully in the decolonial re-learning and unlearning processes. Many community gardeners raised the question of why newcomers need to acknowledge this Land as Indigenous. Following settler logic, they argue that newcomers' ancestors were not colonizers, so as racialized settlers with their own challenges, why would they need to learn about this Indigenous Land and Canada's colonial history? From this experience, I understand that Land acknowledgement is the first step to understanding the reconciliation process, essential for all Canadians. It teaches us how we can accept and treat each other as human beings, non-violently, seeing ourselves as one among many living creatures, a respectful way to situate our lives in relation to the histories that brought us all here and think about what kind of relationships and communities we want to build for the next generations. I like how Indigenous scholar Dr. Alex Wilson (2015) speaks of the "Land as our body" because "we came from Land, and we will go back to Land again." I appreciate what becomes possible when the premise of reconciliation recognizes the Elders' teachings that "Land is not for owning, Land is for sharing."

In contrast, *Allah* is seen to own the Land and doesn't want to share His power and credit as a creator of the universe. That dominating power, which informs all of the Abrahamic and other monotheistic religions, becomes problematic and vulnerable to capitalism, which encloses the Land as property and relentlessly resists practices of sharing, except for the extraction of accelerant energies like fossil fuels, under harsh state regimes. Indigenous knowledges help to deconstruct these objectifying practices of ownership, building on Land acknowledgements and ethical relationship development. I feel good about my Indigenous, anti-racist, social justice, and decolonial education, which has shaped me into a new person today. I support Land acknowledgements and relation-building towards reconciliation from the core of my heart.

MY LEARNING REFLECTIONS ABOUT LAND ACKNOWLEDGEMENTS

Land acknowledgement is the first step in understanding who I am as a racialized settler woman in this Indigenous Land. I have observed and learned from a decade of community engagement that many settlers live in Canada without building any meaningful relationship with the Land and its original peoples for many systemic, social, and interpersonal reasons. As Wark (2021) argues, the damage of scripted Land acknowledgements is simply emphasizing symbolic gestures to "[maintain] the status quo" (p. 195). Therefore, where I have had the opportunity to learn about Indigenous histories, cultures, and sacrifices, I want to make my Land acknowledgements by heart, not anything scripted. I want to acknowledge the Indigenous Land first, because I have benefited from my exposure to Indigenous worldviews, Lands, waters, natural living ecosystems, and relationships with Canada's original Indigenous individuals and people; decolonizing approaches have influenced my learnings. The University of Saskatchewan campus, where I did most of my doctoral research, is located on Treaty 6 Territory and the homeland of the Métis. I pay my respects and gratitude to the First Nations and Métis ancestors of this place and reaffirm our living relationships with one another in the present and with the Land that sustains us all.

I also would like to recognize that I have been living and working remotely during the global COVID-19 pandemic on the traditional territories of the Blackfoot and the people of the Treaty 7 region in Southern Alberta, which is home to the Siksika, the Piikani, the Kainai, the Tsuut'ina, and the Stoney Nakoda First Nations, including Chiniki, Bearspaw, and Goodstoney First Nation. Mount Royal University, Calgary, where I am writing, teaching, and residing, is situated on Land adjacent to where the Bow meets the Elbow River. The traditional Blackfoot name of this place is "Mohkinstsis," now called the City of Calgary. Calgary is also home to the Métis Nation of Alberta, Region III. These acknowledgements introduce my active commitments to learning about decolonization and reconciliation as an academic, making relationships with the Land and treaty peoples working to recover better ways of supporting each other and decolonizing our relationships with one another.

In my learning journey for my doctoral research, I have come to respect the histories and heritages of Indigenous communities and those who have taken care of this Land, like a mother or other unpaid caregivers. I have learned that Indigenous communities have treated this Land as a part of their bodies and spiritual existence. Still, the violent installment of imperialist Land ownership informs our shared painful histories. I care about the enduring relationships between Indigenous peoples and their traditional territories, how they share the Land with newcomers and offer friendship less shackled to imperialist class, race, and gender models. As guest in this Indigenous Land, I need to understand the colonial history of Canada and the aspirations of Indigenous peoples who continue to live here and shape our shared futures. As its beneficiaries, it is the responsibility of new arrivals in this Land to learn the dynamics of settler colonialism to begin undoing its harms.

As a racialized newcomer settler woman, I am invested in mutual flourishing with Indigenous peoples and Lands, emphasizing gentler and more sustainable approaches to power and knowledge. I have learned from community activities that Land acknowledgements help foster individual and collective actions supporting shared social responsibilities to eliminate ongoing colonialism and racial, social, and environmental injustices. They uplift Indigenous views and minoritized voices seeking redress. My personal experience is that Land acknowledgements teach rootedness, responsibility, decolonization, and strong accountabilities. However, they require mindfulness and committed effort to learn and take responsibility for that learning.

I acknowledge the many First Nations, Métis, and Inuit whose footsteps have marked these Lands for centuries. When I arrived in Canada, I did not know about Indigenous peoples and the practices of Land acknowledgements, which were not practised when I lived in Bangladesh, Sweden, Norway, or the United States. I also recognize that the Lands on the University of Saskatchewan campuses are situated in the traditional territories of diverse Indigenous peoples. I lived on Treaty 6 Territory for 10 years, respected the histories and cultures of the First Nations and Métis ancestors of the Land, and reaffirmed our relationships as a corrective practice in challenging prevailing knowledge politics. I believe nothing will change in this world unless we listen to each other's stories gently, passionately, and respectfully by taking responsibility for mutual care.

I have learned from many community members that a Land acknowledgement is a formal and sincere declaration that aims to recognize Indigenous people as stewards of the Land we reside upon. It invites people to be good and responsible guests. I realized from the beginning that such practices of respect are empowering for me, internally. They help me develop proper relationships with the peoples and places upon whose Lands I remain an uninvited guest, even when I am locally welcomed into Indigenous ceremonies and other cultural teaching spaces.

In the beginning, I used to wonder about the significance of Land acknowledgements for racialized newcomer settler immigrants like me. As a newcomer in Canada, I observed Indigenous languages, cultures, and practices from the beginning of my arrival and settlement process in Saskatoon. I had working experiences with Indigenous Bangladeshi people back home. Gradually, I learned the Indigenous practice of acknowledging the Land and territories we live or work on. I also have observed how many events start with an Indigenous prayer, smudging, Land acknowledgements, and relationship building, which lifts participants physically, spiritually, and morally. The prayer is open to all races, nations, faiths, and genders. Because Land is sacred to Indigenous peoples, I realize that inviting an Indigenous person to do a Land acknowledgement exposes oppressive colonial histories and their consequences, including attempted cultural genocide. It situates our shared lived experiences within ongoing neo-colonialism. Land acknowledgements honour the injustices that target North America's original peoples, signalling that there is an untold story that informs narrow understandings of how this country was created. That history resituates each event, classroom discussion, and context into which racialized setter families arrive, somewhere beyond the nation-state.

A Land acknowledgement is a statement that formally recognizes and respects the Indigenous peoples of a place, offering to build relationships. Since the word "Indigenous" is a general term that refers to the first inhabitants of a region, a Land acknowledgement is a public recognition intended to raise awareness about the enduring relationship between Indigenous peoples and their territories. Indigenous communities have lived in and moved through this Land for hundreds of generations, and Indigenous peoples from many nations make their home in this region today. We newcomers, settlers, and all non-Indigenous people have a responsibility to join in recognizing and honouring Indigenous ancestors, descendants, Elders, and all other members of their communities.

I have learned by heart that Land acknowledgements help settlers from many countries of origin listen to Indigenous oral, personal, and experiential stories compassionately, to speak back humbly, with curiosity, committing to learning to act more justly. I gradually also learned from Indigenous community educators and Knowledge Keepers that when Indigenous peoples visit other Indigenous peoples, they acknowledge their territories and say that they are visitors to that new territory. For example, I heard a story from Indigenous Elder Joseph Naytowhow at the community radio studio. He says,

> When your people came here, like when you arrived here, we would call you Omantiok, which means we don't know how long you will be here as a guest. You come and go temporarily here, so we called you Oh Omantiok; look, these are the people that have come from another community or another country, and we don't know how long they will be here, but by saying that, we still acknowledge that you exist; you are a visitor. But we don't know who you are. When you will go back further. When you will be in a relationship and become my relatives like my brother, my sister, I don't know. Still, it's always based on whether I have to get to know your heart or your soul. I have to learn to trust you; that's

acknowledgement; you have to trust the people who arrived here. You get to know them, but initially, we call them Oh Omantiok; you know they're just passing through, which means that you're just a guest. And until such time, communities around here who originally lived here welcome you and say Omianto. Then you develop a relationship gradually, getting to know each other. (CFCR Saskatoon Community Radio Studio, personal communication, October 19, 2019)

Therefore, I am still an *Omantiok*, which means visitor and uninvited guest in this Land, since I came willingly from other parts of the world to pursue my interests. As a guest or newcomer, it is my responsibility and a gesture of courtesy to respect this Land and its original peoples. Then we can share our histories and cultures, adapting to their stories and practices out of respect. I also learned from Indigenous scholars and activists that the Land provides a way of being and knowing that belongs to Indigenous peoples; they are the caretakers of this Land, generation after generation.

As a racialized newcomer settler woman, I learned that Land acknowledgements are an initial way to recognize and respect the original peoples of the territory upon which our university and community garden are situated. I also learned from Indigenous educators that there is a tradition of knowing, teaching, and learning on this Land that goes beyond the history of settler education. Acknowledgements that encourage observance of land rights in everyday life are thus a means of creating awareness about the continuing Indigenous presence in these Lands, obscured by colonialist erasures through the abyssal thinking that grounds prevailing knowledge politics. Since I grew up with a colonial education system in Bangladesh and Europe, Land acknowledgements gave me a new way to engage with meaningful practices of decolonizing my everyday routines. It took a little while to get used to shifting my daily rituals and to understand the deeper meaning of seeking to do so as a racialized settler newcomer woman. Over the years, I have learned that Land acknowledgements are a way to share space with Indigenous peoples by weaving Indigenous protocols into different organizations and community procedures. Land acknowledgements prompt us to think about relationships between Indigenous peoples, the uninvited settler visitors to this Land, and our various colonialist institutions.

To build mutually respectful relationships, acknowledging the Land is essential for reconciliation. After spending a decade in Canada, I have learned that relationship building and maintaining relationships with love and care is at the heart of Indigenous education. Land acknowledgements are the first step of this relationship-building process. I feel stronger when I deeply listen and learn together. It is always an excellent opportunity to be connected with Indigenous Elders, educators, Knowledge Keepers, friends, and community members from across Canada. Land acknowledgements have enriched my understanding of Indigenous insights, allowing me to learn about or share Indigenous education practices repeatedly, a beginning oral tradition I have carried into my community radio show.

I love relationship building through Land acknowledgements from my heart, and I hope to apply this acquired knowledge to my homeland, community, and life. I want to pass on these learnings to my children and the next generations I meet around the neighbourhoods I inhabit. I started to meet, listen to, and learn to love Indigenous people because of their welcoming acceptance, gentle behaviour, and holistic and non-discriminatory worldviews. Through my efforts to take Land acknowledgements seriously, I believe that building a relationship with the Land is essential for rootless, Landless migrant people like me. If we can make a relationship with the Land and Indigenous peoples by resisting corporate consumerism, excessive consumption, hyper-competition, constant comparison, conformity, and new forms of colonialism, we can learn from the histories of colonialism that inform our migrations, recognizing the many involuntary sacrifices of innocent Indigenous children, women, families, and communities that inform the creation and maintenance of settler spaces.

Land acknowledgement and relationship building are tools to disrupt settler colonialism and a continuous reminder that this Land has been colonized. I also learned that it challenges the myth of *terra nullius*, which means "the Land of no one." Colonizers/settlers used to think the Land was empty if they did not encounter others like themselves; Indigenous people had been living there for thousands of years and did not count in this doctrine of religious racism. Land acknowledgement practices remind us of these foundational distortions of truth and of the generosity of Indigenous peoples sharing the Land with uninvited settlers. Newcomers and established settlers have much to learn about our responsibilities from Land acknowledgements. Not simply a token gesture, Land acknowledgement practices can become more meaningful if settlers and newcomers are willing to learn, unlearn, re-learn, and take the responsibility to exercise accountability and respect for the Land and to work to reconcile the effects of Canada's oppressive history.

Participating in community gardening activities has provided me with valuable lessons in terms of personal growth, intellectual and social development, as well as fostering relationships with diverse communities and Indigenous peoples. Therefore, I have learned that building relationships is my/our responsibility, to learn about the meaning of Land, decolonization, reconciliation, honouring, and acknowledging Indigenous treaties. As a racialized newcomer settler woman, it is my responsibility to learn and talk about reconciliation and treaties or unceded Lands, depending on what territory we live in.

I have learned from the community garden activities and from Indigenous scholar Dr. Alex Wilson, who has often explained that Land-based education reflects gender fluidity. If a person is not respecting gender fluidity and queerness, then they are not practising Land-based education. This is a vital issue to raise because many Indigenous stories, practices, and ceremonies have been influenced by white supremacy and heteropatriarchy. Therefore, Indigenous people created gendered protocols influenced by these invasive norms. If gender fluidity is not accepted in these protocols, Wilson suggests stepping back and inquiring whether this is how Indigenous ancestors practised their lives. Land-based education is inclusive and does not perpetuate any exclusionary practices.

Through connecting to Indigenous Two-Spirit friends, Elders, and Knowledge Keepers around various community events, I was able to start to decolonize my thinking. Their knowledge and social positioning helped me to stop thinking about the world through binary lenses. By questioning my colonial ways of knowing and decolonizing my worldview, I was able to deconstruct my colonial learnings about gender and sexualities. Without receiving this decolonial and non-binary understanding from Land-based education, I would not be comfortable as an academic and a guest of this Indigenous Land. Through my various community engagements and community gardening work over the past 10 years, I have discovered how I am responsible for educating myself and sharing this knowledge with my children, friends, and community members. I am also committed to doing the work of standing next to Indigenous peoples to make sure that reconciliation happens according to their rights and needs, making sure that I understand and practice Land acknowledgements, in the best ways, right from my heart.

NOTES

1. Throughout this chapter, I have capitalized "Land" to express respect for the Land, and its constituent waters, insects, plants, animals, and all living and non-living beings and forces. As a racialized settler, it is my responsibility to take a political stand for Indigenous Land rights.
2. There are many layers of injustices built into patriarchal, colonial, and nationalist systems in relation to gender, race, class, sexual orientation, age, and ability. I have spent more than 10 years unpacking how these are intertwined and could become

resources for building solidarities. Decolonial relational autoethnography assists me in situating my own lived experiences, personal agency, and collective community empowerment in the processes of developing relationships and building solidarities with and among racialized settlers, Indigenous people, and white Canadian settler communities in ways that are accountable to intersectional reconciliation.

3. Black, Indigenous and people of colour (BIPOC).
4. Commonplace book is a reflective learning book. I have maintained a series of commonplace books on community garden activities for three years. They focus on two main areas: first, my Indigenous Land-based learning and Indigenous and colonialist histories in Canada with Indigenous Elders and, second, cross-cultural activities (relationship building, children's art workshops, food sharing, newcomer women's challenges, and leadership).
5. 2SLGBTQIA+ refers to Two-Spirit, Lesbian, Gay, Bisexual, Transgender, Queer, Intersex, and Asexual people.
6. Building Bridges is a partnership between the International Student and Study Abroad Centre and the Aboriginal Students' Centre on the University of Saskatchewan campus. Founded in 2013 by student assistants Davida Bentham and Janelle Pewapsconias, the program was initially known as *Sapo Nistohtamowin*, which is the Plains Cree word for learning through understanding stories. It offers yearlong anti-racist education, trips to Wanuskewin Heritage Park (a cultural and historical centre for the First Nations) for the whole campus community with a focus on Indigenous, international and non-Indigenous relations, and cultural understanding. Building Bridges is a safe place to dispel myths, to ask questions without any hesitation, to discover commonalities and respectfully understand each other's cultural differences, to unpack misunderstandings about Indigenous people, and to build cultural bridges. (*The Sheaf*, 2015)
7. Al Quran, Surah Al Baqara: 255

REFLECTION QUESTIONS

1. What does Land mean to you?
2. How can you take responsibility for your place in this Indigenous Land?
3. How do you work to decolonize your binary thinking, colonial upbringing, and everyday learnings?
4. Land acknowledgements cannot be tokenized; how can you play a role in ensuring that you support meaningful Land acknowledgements?

SUGGESTED READINGS

- Ali, A. H. (2015). *Heretic: Why Islam needs a reformation now.* Harper.
- Datta, R (2013). A relational theoretical framework and meanings of land, nature, and sustainability for research with Indigenous communities. *Local Environment: The International Journal of Justice and Sustainability, 20*(1), 102–113. https://doi.org/10.1080/13549839.2013.818957
- Fatah, T (2008). *Chasing a mirage: The tragic illusion of an Islamic state.* Wiley.
- Malik, J. (1996). *The colonialization of Islam: Dissolution of traditional institutions in Pakistan.* Manohar Publications.
- Thorpe, J. (2005). Indigeneity and transnationality? An interview with Bonita Lawrence. *Women & Environments International Magazine, 68/69*, 6–8.
- Tuck, E., & Yang, K. W. (2012). Decolonization is not a metaphor. *Decolonization: Indigeneity, Education & Society, 1*(1), 1–40.
- Wild About Saskatoon. (2021). *The land feeds us: Indigenous food sovereignty and Prairie cities* [Video]. YouTube. https://www.youtube.com/watch?v=-AgVepIJKgI

REFERENCES

Huntington, H. P. (2021). What do land acknowledgments acknowledge? *Environment: Science and Policy for Sustainable Development, 63*(4), 31–35. https://doi.org/10.1080/00139157.2021.1924579

Wark, J. (2021). Land acknowledgements in the academy: Refusing the settler myth. *Curriculum Inquiry, 51*(2), 191–209. https://doi.org/10.1080/03626784.2021.1889924

Wilson, A. (2015). Our coming in stories: Cree identity, body sovereignty and gender self-determination. *Journal of Global Indigeneity, 1*(1), 1–5.

CHAPTER 8

Responsibility to Build a Decolonial Community: From a Colour Settler Woman's Perspective

Priyanka Mahey

INTRODUCTION

To explore the meaning of decolonization and reconciliation, it is important to recognize that they are a byproduct of colonization, the practice in which minority communities were and are displaced by Western colonies seeking economic and political superiority. To begin the process of decolonization and reconciliation, we must collaborate with Indigenous communities. By doing so, we are attempting to deconstruct the power dynamic. To help situate ourselves in inclusive ways, I suggest ways in which we can participate in the community such as taking Indigenous studies courses, utilizing land-based approaches, and finding ways to educate ourselves in meaningful ways. Indigenous history, culture, traditions, and practices are relevant in understanding how we can decolonize our Western practices (Datta, 2022). We are conditioned to adapt to the notion of inferior and superior, often putting people of colour at the bottom of the hierarchy (Nielson, 2020). Once we believe in the notion of inferior and superior, we adapt to an institutionalized way of living, where we begin to neglect the lived realties of others. When such occurs, we believe that we are separate from one another and that the histories of Indigenous communities are inaccurate or irrelevant. However, to dismantle social conditionings, we must be willing to learn and unlearn (Datta, 2022). The process of learning and unlearning requires us to dismantle the system that the institutions are built upon. In this chapter, I discuss how reconciliation and decolonization play a role in leading anticolonial environments of change.

Since colonization is the process of removing Indigenous peoples from their land, Wildcat et al. (2014) argue that to decolonize, "there must be forms of education that reconnect Indigenous peoples to land and the social relations, knowledges, and languages that arise from that land" (p. 1). For me, reconciliation and decolonization are the ability to admit one's wrongs and to take accountability for the wrongs committed. This process is not about making yourself look good; rather, it is the ability to admit and unlearn those biases that have affected others. An example of this would be creating an environment where everyone would be welcome to speak about their experiences. By sharing space with people lower on the social hierarchy, it allows individuals to see how institutional their thinking is. When we open our minds to the concept of decolonization, we are telling ourselves to look at the world through more than one lens, instead of a universal one. A single lens would be known as the Western viewpoint or Western rhetoric. Therefore, to outline the importance of decolonization and reconciliation, in this chapter, I have shared my identity as a colour settler in Canada. To discuss my positionality as a colour settler, I discuss who I am, where I come from, what a land acknowledgement means, and how my own cultural, traditional, and historical teachings reflect who I am. The second theme that I discuss in this chapter is responsibilities for decolonization. Here, I introduce more thoroughly the concept of learning, unlearning, and relearning history. This means finding proper resources to gather information such as asking questions and learning about important Canadian history. To explain how I have been learning, unlearning, and relearning, I talk about my learning reflections from Indigenous Elders, my active participation in learning about Indigenous cultures, and most importantly, how I play a role in the process of decolonization. Finally, throughout this chapter, I share my learning stories about responsibilities for reconciliation. This is an important aspect for me as it helps describe and articulate the importance of our role in this settler society and decolonial community building.

SITUATING MYSELF

As a colour settler, my identity has been shaped quite differently with several cultural backgrounds. My family history originates in India, but I also have roots in Canada, which I call home. Having a dual identity is hard and at times makes it hard to identify who I am and what my role is in decolonization. Colonization is such a heavy topic, and it is one that many youths like me do not understand or have difficulty facing. I think it is important to recognize that colonization is not an individual matter, but a collective one. My family comes from Punjab, India, home to many communities and religions—more specifically, the Sikh, Muslim, and Hindu communities. With that said, these communities influenced the way I learned things. Some of the things I was taught growing up reinstated the narrative that those who did not follow the same practices as us were not devote or sane. Likewise, when we look at Canadian culture and history, we tend to separate into groups. The problem in such situations is that we begin to identify as a commodity, a material object meant to attain wealth. When such happens, we ignore the lived realities and inequalities that are present because we are not the group being directly affected. As sociologists, we are taught to look at how our socialization is reflected through capitalism—the exchange process. Due to this, we abstain from stepping out of our social category in fear of being demonized and/or rejected. Thus, everyone is forced to remain a slave to the system.

Living in Canada, we must understand and honour the history of those who came before us. We cannot ignore the history, culture, traditions, and teachings we receive. Most, if not all, of the teachings come from several Indigenous communities; therefore, it is important we understand what is being said. I learned from Indigenous scholar William Singer (personal communication, March 16, 2022) that everything we do has a purpose that is constructed through the environment. He states that the land leads the way for us in instances that we cannot use modern technology. Singer (2022) passed around licorice root and tobacco to explain how the root quenches thirst and how tobacco sends thoughts and prayers around to your loved ones. During this offering, we were told to give thanks and release the tobacco back into the land to continue the cycle of compassion and equality. This is to give back what we are taking. As William Singer explained, we must remind ourselves to give thanks for the teachings we gather and the natural resources the earth provides for us. Thus, land acknowledgements are a crucial part in decolonization. They express gratitude and seek to dismantle the myths settlers have set out about "finding" and "saving" Indigenous people. However, on the opposite side of the spectrum, land acknowledgements have been used performatively, for nothing more than a statement of fact. In the end, acknowledgements support the system as it is structured to support and benefit white people. Therefore, educating ourselves on such topics allows us to see through an unbiased lens.

Growing up in Calgary, I knew little about the history of Indigenous people and land acknowledgements. Public schools did not make an effort to explore the truth of residential schools, the Sixties Scoop, or the process of evangelization. Rather, schools glorified how settlers saved Indigenous peoples from themselves—thus, remaining in a colonial mindset.

Due to that, we are conditioned to believe and follow this narrative that Indigenous peoples and Europeans had a symbiotic relationship. In addition to that, people believed that Europeans helped Indigenous communities in innumerable ways. It wasn't until Grade 11 that I started hearing about territorial acknowledgements and their purpose and intent. They have become widespread in the last few years, but overall, they imprison Indigenous communities with false acknowledgements. Hence, a large portion of my learned culture was based on colonial narratives; I assumed and followed through with negative stereotypes, I categorized, and I separated myself as a superior being. However, through the process of learning and unlearning, I recognize that the society we live in is structured to teach based on colonial views.

This system is not meant for people of colour as it protects and serves European settlers. Likewise, in my home country of India, the colonial rule of Britain left an everlasting effect. The Sikh community was forced to assimilate, leaving behind their cultures, traditions, histories, and practices to adapt to Western culture. This narrative was taught to my sister and I during our trips to India. We were taught about the segregation that resulted due to colonization and how the 1947 partition caused many families to separate. My parents made it so that we learned the major colonial pieces in an anticolonial way. A way in which we could see the story as what it was, not what it was supposed to be. To be able to revitalize and to relearn our cultures, traditions, and languages, it is essential that we target the issues in the correct way. We cannot blame an individual for the wrongdoings of the community. We must unite and use holistic learning techniques such as learning from Elders, researching the assimilation laws, and using sources that employ an anticolonial lens. Nevertheless, do not expect people of colour to teach you about their histories. You must guide your own learning process.

RESPONSIBILITIES FOR DECOLONIZATION

Learning

Decolonization is finding ways we can create change. This means we must be active participants in change. It means allowing people of colour to speak for themselves; it means fighting to change the system, actively learning, and finally, it means wanting to better yourself to see everyone as an equal through their heritage, history, and cultures (Wildcat et al., 2014, pp. 1–9). That said, decolonizing our minds is not as simple as reading a book or advocating for change; it is a continuous fight that is often challenging because we have never needed to acknowledge or dismantle our privileges. Learning is a process that begins with dismantling our worldviews (Hart, 2010). Our worldviews define who we are and what we believe in. Thus, when we believe in something for so long, we assume unequivocally that it is true (Hart, 2010). Hence, the use of capital-T Truth. Capital-T Truth can be referred to as our own beliefs. Our beliefs reflect our experiences and the things we have learned from our friends, peers, colleagues, and teachers. For instance, Michael Anthony Hart (2010) discusses the barriers that arise within Western worldviews as compared to Indigenous worldviews (p. 2). Hart argues that when it comes to Indigenous worldviews,

> knowledge is holistic, cyclic, and dependent upon relationships and connections to living and non-living beings and entities. Second, there are many truths, and these truths are dependent upon individual experiences. Third, everything is alive. Fourth, all things are equal. Fifth, the land is sacred. Sixth, the relationship between people and the spiritual world is important. Seventh, human beings are the least important in the world. (p. 3)

This statement expresses the simplicity of a holistic approach. Indigenous worldviews explore more than one worldview compared to a Western one. To further elaborate, if we were to look at gender from a Western viewpoint, we would say there are men and women. In an Indigenous worldview, there are men, women, and Two-Spirit people. There are no limitations that bind individuals to a single social construction; people who are "different" are idolized as a creation from the higher being. In the traditional Western view, there is no in-between—you either have to be a man or a woman. In this respect, Indigenous communities honour and respect unity and equality. Western communities have built their worldviews on competition and power, which is the leading cause of separation between like groups. For instance, the education system in Canada uses Christian doctrine when educating youth (Wagamese, 1994). Due to this, people have formed certain biases about historical encounters and about how they perceive Indigenous history. If we were to look at Indigenous worldviews, according to Hart and his seven themes, knowledge is experiential—from the land, from the people, and from our ancestors (2010, p. 3).

When non-Indigenous communities learn about Indigenous history, it is often through a colonial lens. When this happens, it becomes complicated, simply because we are conditioned to follow a single worldview, a colonial one. Colonial challenges arise when we are distancing ourselves from the dominant ideology (Hart, 2010). We are separating ourselves from a single worldview into one that is looking at the land, our relationship to the land, and our relationship with others around us. This shift in ideology is the first movement towards learning about Indigenous history accurately. Accuracy does not mean learning from people outside the community—it means learning from Indigenous Elders, traditional stories, partaking in learning sessions, and most importantly, self-education. Indigenous history is a painful one, filled with sorrow and assimilation, but to learn it, we must be willing to find resources that help us learn. Asking questions is good, but when we become reliant on others to do the work for us, it makes it hard to dismantle structures. As soon as we turn willingness into coercion, we are no longer able to deconstruct biases and stereotypes because learning is no longer a choice. Hart (2010) also mentioned that the minute we expect someone to teach us, we are reverting back to a Western worldview. This has to do with the colonial narrative of taking without giving in return.

Taking responsibility is the first step in decolonization. One of the first steps I took to take responsibility was deconstructing my worldviews. I started by learning about basic Indigenous terminology. I was able to do this by taking Indigenous studies courses, reading books by Indigenous authors and Indigenous land-based books, and listening to direct teachings from Indigenous Elders and knowledge keepers. By learning about basic terminology, I was able to understand the legal connotation of Aboriginal and Indian, and how these terms were synonyms for "other" or "different." The term "Indian" holds legal recognition within the *Indian Act*, but presently we employ the more inclusive term "Indigenous" on a global scale. While "Indigenous" serves as a universal descriptor, for greater precision we also utilize terms like "Inuit," "Métis," "First Nations," and others to specifically acknowledge distinct Indigenous groups. Words used to define a community are always capitalized as a form of respect and honour (Indigenous Foundations, n.d.). As a colour settler scholar, Datta (2022) explains how terminology plays a key role in portraying Indigenous peoples. The term "Indigenous" captures respect whereas the terms "Indian" and "Aboriginal" were used to criminalize and vilify Indigenous groups. That being said, these terms are now outdated as they hold negative connotations. The learning process is not linear, making it a unique process. Depending on where we live and who we are, we need to situate ourselves and take responsibility in order to participate in the process of learning. So long as we try to understand Indigenous identities and our relationships to the land, it is a stepping stone to learning through more than one lens.

Relearning

The process of relearning does not occur until we have learned and unlearned (Datta, 2022). For instance, when we learn something, it becomes a part of our worldview (Hart, 2010). Deconstructing colonial networks means actively making the choice to unlearn negative stories. The process of learning, unlearning, and relearning daily becomes harder when it requires us to deconstruct our ways of life. When living a privileged life, we may have a hard time understanding the lived realities of minority communities because we are at the top of the social hierarchy (Galeano, 2001). However, Eduardo Galeano (2001) states that when we are relearning, we understand that there is a social hierarchy present and that we are all active members of that hierarchy (Galeano, 2001). I learned this framework in scholar Tracy Nielson's academic courses as she states that the inequalities in our world reflect who we are. Like Galeano, Nielson argues that to change the system we must reconsider what is deemed "normal" in society. This takes place over a lifetime and includes having discussions with Elders and knowledge keepers, learning traditional stories, and by seeking to learn about our relation to the land.

Elders and knowledge keepers hold high levels of prestige within Indigenous communities (Hele, 2021). Elders seek to spread their knowledge onto the next generation and have culturally specific meanings depending on the Indigenous group (Hele, 2021). Recently, I had the opportunity to engage in a presentation with guest speaker Dwayne Lasas as he talked about the process of relearning. Lasas took an anticolonial approach and integrated the importance of land, Indigenous knowledge, and Indigenous history. He discussed the medicine wheel and how humans are a part of the circle. Moreover, Lasas articulated how

> the wheel represents all races: the Black race, the Yellow race, the white race, and the Red race. The Black race is the keeper of the water and masters of emotion through song and dance; the Yellow race—the Asians, far east and the middle east are keepers of the air, they master the mental aspect of humans. This happens through breathing techniques and intense martial arts. The white race is the keeper of the fire, they utilize the physical attributes of the human race, and finally, the Red race is the keeper of the earth and walks with the spirit aspect—through drums, ceremony, language, and the center of it—the heart. (personal communication, February 3, 2022)

When looking at these characteristics, it is noticeable how Indigenous communities see the larger picture, a holistic one; one where everyone has set characteristics (Lasas, personal communication, February 3, 2022). For example, being a part of the yellow race, I know my ancestors were involved in mastering the mental aspect and using breathing techniques to calm the spirit. This has impacted me because this hands-on interaction connected me to the land I am on. Additionally, this teaching has become a practice in my life because it explores the narrative of intersectionality, uniqueness, and provides an anticolonial approach to history. That said, this contributes to the process of decolonization because we are actively looking for Indigenous ways of knowing.

When we look at the process of relearning, it does not mean dismissing our past teachings (Datta, 2022). We are building on those foundations, trying to deconstruct false or negative connotations with purposeful and factual information. Again, Lasas (personal communication, February 3, 2022) argues the importance of teamwork. He states that there is a possibility to put scientific knowledge and Indigenous knowledge together. By doing so, we are creating a new worldview that explores anticolonialism and decolonization. For example, Lasas used different animal sounds and Indigenous songs to show how when played on his ukulele, they were forms of communication. This provides a different approach for learning that includes modern and Indigenous ways of knowing.

Land-based educator Christine Fiddler (personal communication, 2022) discusses the importance of reclaiming Indigenous language and culture. She discusses how traditional oral stories help revitalize lost power. Fiddler reflects that stories have three functions: to share general narratives, to employ humour, and to use role modelling. Storytelling can be telling someone about your day, a memory in the past, or creating fictional stories (Fiddler, 2022). Stories can also be used to employ humour. Within several Indigenous communities, humour is used to interact with peers and family to lighten the mood. This is a way for Indigenous communities to reconnect with their lost culture and to create a form of solidarity amongst one another. For example, during a discussion I had with an Indigenous fellow, they mentioned how in Cree culture, the use of humour was very common. It is a lighthearted way of discussion that breaks the hegemonic way of living as it is a more holistic approach, where there is a fundamental balance between the physical, emotional, spiritual, and psychological realms. As a settler, I would not have known the significance of joking within the Indigenous community because of my Western ways of knowing. We are so industrialized and commercialized that we see only what the oppressor wishes us to see (Creese, 2019). We are taught that anything that does not fit white standards is incorrect and unfathomable. If we partake in other cultural practices, we are considered to be the devil's spawn because we see life through a lens that is different from the Western one. Capitalism seeks to encourage this; we are taught that collective thought is bad and individual thought is good (McWilliam & Nielsen, 2020). This process supports white settler colonialists, creating disadvantages for minority communities.

Similarly, the Punjabi dialect may appear more abrasive in contrast to Hindi, Urdu, or Farsi. However, when these languages are transcribed in writing, the unique nuances and expressions of the expression can become less evident. This is very similar to Western texts; academic work follows strict guidelines in order to conform to Western academic standards. However, with spoken languages, a sense of belonging and connection arises. This is because we are able to connect emotionally and spiritually to what is being said. This has changed my perspective because for the longest time, I refrained from speaking my mother's tongue. I did this because I felt I had to prove myself to my white counterparts. In fact, I would not bring traditional east Indian foods because I was afraid that the aroma would be "foul" smelling. However, I have learned to love my mother's tongue and the foods we eat. This ties back to Fiddler's discussion around identity and culture because as minorities we are using our culture as a mechanism to revitalize our power.

INDIGENOUS HISTORIES OF CANADA

Learning Challenges

It is never easy to unlearn our assumptions, biases, and racism largely because it is hidden away in what we call multiculturalism. For example, when I was in grade school, I had only learned about Indigenous peoples for a short period of time, that too through a colonial lens. We can say we want to unlearn certain narratives, but it becomes hard when the system is reiterating those false narratives (Galeano, 2001). We must ask ourselves questions about where we are, who this land belongs to, whether we are being respectful to the land, and how we can help those who are living on this land. These questions create a focus point on how to relearn topics we have been taught. Residential schools are a prime example of this, as the awareness of residential schools and their profound impact on Indigenous communities has only recently gained prominence among most Canadians. According to Paulette Regan (2010), the Truth and Reconciliation Commission (TRC) is set to ensure that non-Indigenous peoples "learn about and acknowledge what Indigenous peoples have suffered as a result of assimilation policy and actions" (p. 7). What many choose to ignore is that residential schools were tools used to assimilate children and emphasized "taking the Indian out of the Indian." This phrase was used in Canada during the early 1900s, in which settlers tried to evangelize as many Indigenous children as possible (Haig-Brown, 1988). Indigenous children were stripped of their names and were called by numbers, their hair would be cut to introduce them to "civilization," and they were no longer allowed to speak their native tongue (Haig-Brown, 1988). Furthermore, people steer away from the topic of residential schools because they fear being uncomfortable. The Canadian school systems have failed to shed light on the intergenerational trauma inflicted upon Indigenous peoples. Moreover, the school systems turned a blind eye towards the involvement of the Canadian government in removing Indigenous peoples from their homes and families. In late 2021, the government discovered thousands of unmarked graves from residential schools across Canada. These unmarked graves are a reminder of the trauma and assimilation Indigenous peoples have endured. They are a constant reminder that Canada is not multicultural and has played a part in the genocide of Indigenous peoples. Thus, it is our internal responsibility to educate ourselves on such important and serious issues. In fact, we cannot rely on the system to teach us anything because the system is meant for and created by white people (Galeano, 2001).

Canadian history is very Eurocentric and one-sided. It is important that we recognize Canada's relationship with Indigenous peoples because this is a deep-rooted intergenerational issue. The longer we turn a blind eye, the more ignorant we become. As settlers, we are going to face learning challenges and will have a hard time deconstructing our own privileges, but to reconstruct an equal and just society, we must be willing to educate ourselves (Galeano, 2001). The *Indian Act* is a legal document that is currently being used in Canada and displays several notions of ignorance and racism against Indigenous peoples (Cook, 2018, p. 1). People either have the wrong idea of the *Act* or do not care since it does not affect them. These laws may not affect us directly, but they do affect our neighbours, friends, colleagues, and so forth. If we choose to remain silent, we will remain a part of the cycle that continues to assimilate and separate Indigenous peoples from society.

What Can/Should I Do?

Having discussed the process of learning, unlearning, and relearning, we must be willing to apply that knowledge to real-life situations (Datta, 2022). The moment we recognize that we gain something from the system, we have a choice to use our privileges for the greater good. In Indigenous culture, the circle represents the process of equality—we all sit equally amongst one another (Lassas, personal communication, February 3, 2022). In comparison, the Western hierarchy measures individuals according to their status, wealth, and race (McWilliam & Nielsen, 2020). Understanding the two will help in the learning process as one makes us work together and the other makes us compete with one another.

If we are students, we can take the initiative to take Indigenous studies classes, advocate, and create groups to support the community. I began my journey of relearning by taking classes in Indigenous studies that involved international perspectives, classes on Canadian history about residential schools and the Sixties Scoop, and classes on modern-day Canadian treaties. These classes helped me learn about Indigenous culture, history, and colonization. They also taught me to become accountable for my actions and the decisions that have contributed to colonization. We are responsible for educating not only ourselves, but the people we live with. By helping our families, we are encouraging the process of community building. Moreover, we are taking steps to decolonize a collective-thinking process. For instance, I have a responsibility to check myself when I am saying things that are stereotypical, biased, and/or racist.

TRC CALLS TO ACTION: CONNECTING WITH MY LEARNING

It is important to recognize that we are all students in the practice of learning, and everyone is at a different level (McWilliam & Nielsen, 2020). Recently, I learned about the meaning and value behind land-based walks. Land-based walks connect us to the land individually, so they mean something different to everyone. Therefore, our response and meaning will differ according to our relationality. A land-based walk for me encapsulates the process of doing one's inner work as you can reflect on the past, present, and future by connecting to nature. In the past, my walks entailed focusing solely on myself and my needs; I only focused on the material and did not have appreciation for nature and its significance. However, after understanding what a land-based walk meant—my way of thinking and viewing the environment shifted. Therefore, by learning about the environment in a hands-on approach, I made different connections and observations.

Indigenous land-based educator Yakotennikonhrare Doreen (personal communication, March 24, 2022) in her works discussed the importance of unity and how we are all connected in everything we do. When we open our minds and our eyes to our surroundings, we understand the world slightly differently. The Elder, Doreen, mentioned that we have become Western creatures that assume the role of the leader as we divide the world in ways that divide us from nature. Additionally, Doreen argues that Indigenous knowledge is understood from the ecosystem and how everything in the system is related. To further elaborate, everything from the spirit to the animal, to the human, to the trees, to the mountains and so forth are all connected (personal communication, March 24, 2022). For me, it all comes down to active participation. We cannot learn the full extent of something or someone without applying that knowledge to a real-life situation. For me, land-based walks helped clarify and magnify what Indigenous worldviews and knowledge really mean.

I recognize that after participating in multiple land-based walks, I was able to use my knowledge as power. By power, I do not mean inferior or superior; it means that I was able to connect more with my knowledge because I was able to apply it to my everyday life. These land-based walks mean so much only when we allow ourselves to see from a perspective of education and healing. For example, I never took note of the emotional change or the duration of the walk and how that makes a difference in our social adaptation. Growing up, I would play outside because it was joyous—the grass was green and the fields were big. However, this narrative we created and had enjoyed was no longer what it used to be. We now have pipelines, buildings, and emissions because we do not reciprocate the welcome the earth has provided for us (personal communication with Indigenous Elder Dwayne Lasas, March 10, 2022). As mentioned in the Fish Story (National Centre for Collaboration in Indigenous Education, 2020), "the Dene take care of the fish, and the fish take care of the Dene." This statement lays out how we should be living, but because of colonization we believe the earth is indebted to us. The colonial narrative that the earth and its belongings are for our taking is a misconception. I have learned that Indigenous peoples give back what they take from the environment (National Centre for Collaboration in Indigenous Education, 2020). In my culture, we are taught never to waste food because we are aware of the plight of those who cannot afford to have a meal every day. For instance, we are taught only to take what we need and to give back if we have the opportunity, because we should not be selfish beings.

I hope to pass on this knowledge to others because it is a form of education that removes us from the writer/listener phase (Smith, 1999). In this case, we are listening to others to reform and heal ourselves rather than writing about what we are being taught. When we are writing papers, we use Western dialects and do not refrain from using culturally sensitive words. For example, historically, many Indigenous peoples and their communities were often overlooked or underrepresented in Western sources. (Smith, 1999). The association of such words with self-sustaining people is a way to assert dominance over that group. Therefore, the justice system often failed to incorporate the traditional perspectives of many Indigenous communities. Once we acknowledge that Indigenous peoples are self-sustaining and deserve their own governing systems, we step away from Western rhetoric that claims to protect all its people (Smith, 1999).

RESPONSIBILITIES FOR RECONCILIATION

Learning Awareness

According to Indigenous scholar Barbara Barnes, Indigenous communities were self-sustaining long before European contact (personal communication, May 2020). Indigenous communities across the world, particularly in Canada, had their own governing systems that flourished because the community did not partake in the Western social hierarchy (Datta, 2022). During precolonial times, Indigenous peoples had self-sustaining hunting and gathering techniques (Barnes et al., 2021). Anything that was hunted would be used completely, to ensure no waste was left behind (National Centre for Collaboration in Indigenous Education, 2020). Before colonization, Indigenous communities relied heavily on bison for food, weaponry, and traditional goods (clothing, shoes, etc.; Campbell, 1964). But when Europeans came and recognized that the community was self-sustaining, they killed off a large portion of bison—making the Indigenous community dependent (Campbell, 1964). Therefore, it is essential that we understand that Indigenous peoples were not uneducated or savage-like, they were a community that focused on naturalistic methods. They believed in giving back what they took, to maintain equilibrium (National Centre for Collaboration in Indigenous Education, 2020). I learned this material in my first-year university course which talked about Indigenous relations and how colonization destroyed Indigenous peoples' sovereignty. Being able to learn this material enables me to practice and participate in safe learning environments to break the cycle of racialization and stereotyping.

When considering the modern-day effects on Indigenous communities, Dawn Mahi (2013) discusses the disparities Indigenous children and families face because of colonization. Mahi argues that children are "stuck between two worlds, ashamed of their origin and are living examples of assimilation and colonization" (p. 50). Here, we can understand the effects of colonization on the lived realities of Indigenous communities. Indigenous children are unable to practise their culture, tradition, or language because they fear being outcasted (Mahi, 2013). Moreover, when comparing this to residential schools, one can see drastic similarities. In both residential schools and modern day communities, Indigenous children are separated from their Indigenous cultures and forced to live in a white, Eurocentric world, where they are unable to communicate or be themselves; it is the epitome of taking the Indian out of the Indian. Learning about Indigenous self-determination and resilience are factors that lead us towards reconciliation. Nevertheless, it is not an easy process, but it begins with understanding that Indigenous peoples across the world have self-sustaining lifestyles. Once we distance ourselves from Western worldviews, we gain a sense of liberation and become more closely connected to our land.

Indigenous Treaty Rights

According to Barnes et al. (2021), Indigenous peoples were mandated to live on reserves under the *Indian Act* and were compelled to assimilate into Western culture. That said, Indigenous scholar Andrew Bear Robe (personal communication, May 2021) mentions that the land Indigenous peoples called home was broken down into territories, signed through treaty agreements. The process of reconciliation and decolonizing our minds requires us to understand the relationship we have with the land and why. In the first section, I discussed my relationality to the land, where I come from, and how I connect with the land. I acknowledge that I am a colour settler and that I am a guest on Indigenous land. For my learning, I took classes that talked about specific relations between the Canadian government, the Crown, and Indigenous peoples. For me, reconciliation involves educating myself on what treaties are, who was involved, and why they were signed.

If we look at treaty signings through an anticolonial lens, we can decipher what was consensual and what was not. Something that needs to be discussed within Canadian history is the language barrier that was present during contact (Bear Robe, personal communication, May 2021). When treaties were signed, a large language barrier made it impossible for Indigenous communities to truly understand what was being taken from them (Bear Robe, personal communication, May 2021). If we look at treaty signings from a Western standpoint, we will assume that the treaties were righteous documents signed by two contributing members (Bear Robe, personal communication, May 2021). This is the difference between an anticolonial lens and a Western one; one encourages us to look at the reality of inequality, whilst the other looks only at documentation. As we expand our learning, we are able to understand the reality of treaties, where we live, and which treaty territory we live on. Thus, it is essential we understand that treaty signings were the first step in alienating Indigenous communities.

Acknowledgement and Personal Bias

As a person of colour, I am considered inferior to my white counterparts in Western social hierarchy. As a result, I do not hold the same privileges as them. However, I am ranked superior to my Indigenous counterparts, meaning I hold more privileges than them. Although I am a minority, the Western system places Black and Indigenous folks below all others because of their precise history with settler colonialists (Nielson, 2020). The goal is to create safe learning spaces for everyone regardless of who they are and what they look like. To do that, acknowledgement goes a long way. My decolonial learning opportunities provide inherent knowledge if we look deep enough; they tell us where we come from, whose land we are on, and who is surrounding those areas, including living and non-living things (Datta, 2022). Once we get decolonial education, we can overcome personal biases. But because we live in a society that frowns upon encouraging unity, we often have no other choice but to partake in separating ourselves from the other (Nielson, 2020).

Adichie (2009) plays a key role in discussing the troubles of misrepresentation of racialized peoples in Western nations. For example, growing up as an East Indian woman of colour, my image was distorted because people were uneducated and used stereotypes to describe who I was. Similarly, Canadian history and history all around the world surrounding Indigenous communities is written in a single font. For the longest time, the stories I would listen to and the texts I would read were written by white men. Due to this, Indigenous communities around the world were seen only in a single lens—being evil or savage. As a woman of colour, Adichie (2009) speaks on the misrepresentation of so many as she discusses the danger of a single story. For example, using the example of flipping the narrative, she states that if we "start the story with the arrows of the Native Americans, and not with the arrivals of the British, you have an entirely different story" (10:30–10:37). Adichie (2009) helped me acknowledge that when I use a single story to describe a whole community, I am participating in the process of colonization. I am using one stereotype to describe the lived realities of a community. Adichie's speech remains pertinent in the context of international relations and issues because Western narratives are frequently dismissed due to their failure to encapsulate the full diversity of stories and perspectives. I can apply this idea to my life because it has taught me that assumptions are destructive and take away from the lived realities of minority groups. In fact, being able to use this to reconcile is an asset because it encourages us to look at the connections between groups, peoples, and stories.

In addition, scholar Datta (2015) discusses the importance of integrating Indigenous communities and practices in the research process. From what I have learned, introducing and involving the group that is being studied is crucial. When involving Indigenous knowledge in research, information tends to be more accurate and useful in strengthening cultural relationships (Datta, 2015). In other words, a symbiotic relationship navigates the interconnection between science and Indigenous knowledge—both important in decolonization (Datta, 2015). The term "symbiotic" is significant as it states an equally balanced relationship between both parties. However, many of us know that researchers' relationship with Indigenous communities is often one-sided. Therefore, the reading argues the importance and significance of a symbiotic relationship because we can gather more knowledge without excluding the researched group (Datta, 2015). Personally, I use this in my life as it teaches me about respect, integrity, and inclusivity.

Acceptance and Respect

To understand Indigenous ways of knowing, we must be willing to respect where the knowledge comes from. Due to colonial settings, we no longer participate in other cultural activities because we look at it through a single lens—much like Adichie (2009) argues. The concept of respect is often disfigured when discussing racial, cultural, and traditional segregation. We seem to think that because we are living in a modern state that we must also participate in what is "modern." But, considering the land we are on and the reconciliation process, respect must be given to understand the extent of colonization fully.

Gillian Creese (2019), in her works, explores the question "where are you from?" and highlights how those who are not European are automatically listed as foreigners. Creese (2019) explores how the question "'where are you from?' is central to processes of racialization in Canada, and how these encounters mediate identities and belonging" (p. 1476). This is important to note because the question is not asking where you are from; it is asking where are you *really* from (Creese, 2019). It has the connotation that people of colour are foreigners and thus do not belong. I am constantly reminded of this, as I feel I do not belong in Western society, and my identity is distorted by this racist ideology. Moreover, this reading has helped me understand those feelings of discomfort and loneliness in this multicultural state (Creese, 2019). This is something I apply in my life as a reminder not to ask people insensitive and racialized questions. By keeping such statements at bay, it helps prevent negative connotations and racial remarks.

Indigenous scholar Linda Tuhiwai Smith (2012) discusses the importance of oral stories and traditional writings to further discuss ways of respecting traditional knowledge. In Western society, we are taught through strict guidelines that we must use proper English, grammar, and syntax for our work to be considered academic (McWilliam & Nielsen, 2020). In fact, we are taught that writing is the purest form of expression. However, if we look at texts about Indigenous communities today, they hold Eurocentric notions and use Western language. I mean, that is the goal—to eliminate any Indigenous ideologies and make them look bad, whilst making Europeans look good. Tuhiwai Smith (2012) explains that imperialism has done nothing good. She states that "the talk about the colonial past is embedded in our political discourse, our honor, poetry, music, storytelling, and other common-sense ways of passing on both narrative of history and an attitude about history" (p. 1). This statement explores the issue of Western discourse and how it is heavily embedded in everything we see, hear, or touch. To bring this into perspective, we are taught that Western language must be used in written works, and there is little credibility when these written documents discuss Indigenous lives and history. However, when using oral stories and listening to Elders, the story is filled with raw emotion, history, and relevant voices. I have and will continue to use this in the future to tell my story.

Writing is a colonial tool we are forced to use and when we do not abide by those rules, we are penalized and subjected to lower grades (McWilliam & Nielsen, 2020). This ties back into the discussion above because we are taught to be Western beings in a Western world. Additionally, I situate myself a little differently after learning this because I want to avoid participating in the cycle of colonization. I want to speak my truth with my own language and traditional teachings. Another point Tuhiwai Smith (2012) articulated was the differentiation between writing stories and using writing as a theory base. We often need clarification and interconnect stories with theory and because of this, we lose touch with the narrative we are trying to describe (Smith, 2012). For example, in a professional context, the goal is to listen to the stories and make note of the key points. It becomes a problem when everything gets written down and is used to educate others. That oversteps the boundary between what is a story and what is a theory.

CONCLUSION

Learning is everlasting; if we think otherwise, we are not really learning (Datta, 2022). When we think of Canada, we think of multiculturalism, but we mistake multiculturalism for equality. We tend to turn a blind eye when we are not the community being affected. However, it is important to recognize that our privileges can be used to help those below us on the social hierarchy. This paper highlighted the importance of decolonization and reconciliation because they are key components that will help unite us into creating a new system. Moreover, this paper articulated the importance of learning, unlearning, and re-learning as we challenge the Western norm of following one worldview.

For me, this process has been a gift of learning, as I constantly seek to learn new things. The ability to add onto our knowledge and get a deeper understanding through others' perspectives is significant because it allows us to get creative with learning. Learning is never linear, rather, it is abstract and unique. For one it may look like reading a book, but for another it may be going into the community, learning through the environment, and learning as a group—everyone will have a different way of learning and will be at a different stage of learning. That said, our ability to learn and pass on our teachings will further the process of decolonization because we are uniting ourselves and fighting this battle collectively.

I hope my knowledge benefits the community as it expresses my learning process and encourages others to step out of their comfort zones. Additionally, it challenges the hegemonic narrative that we are equal members in society. In fact, it pushes us to look within ourselves and to see how we benefit off the system when some communities do not. Thus, it is essential to deconstruct meanings of decolonization and reconciliation as these terms help reconstruct what it means to be a part of a community.

REFLECTION QUESTIONS

1. What are some ways we can/are actively participating in decolonizing and reconciliation?
2. What do the words reconciliation, decolonization, and land-based learning mean to you?
3. Do you think there is space for us as a community to move past differences to reconcile and respect the land we are on?

SUGGESTED READINGS

- Griffin, J. H. (2010). *Black like me.* Berkley.
- Lorde, A. (1984). *Sister outsider: Essays and speeches.* Crossing Press.
- Wagamese, R. (1994). *Keeper'n Me.* Anchor Canada.

REFERENCES

Adichie, C. N. (2009). *The danger of a single story.* TEDGlobal.

Barnes, E. C., Jamie, I. M., Vemulpad, S. R., Yaegl Community Elders, Breckenridge, D., Froud, A. E., ... & Jamie, J. F. (2021). National Indigenous Science Education Program (NISEP): Outreach Strategies That Facilitate Inclusion. *Journal of Chemical Education, 99*(1), 245–251. https://doi.org/10.1021/acs.jchemed.1c00393

Campbell, A. (1964). *Age of the buffalo.* National Film Board of Canada. https://www.nfb.ca/film/age-of-the-buffalo/

Cook, A. (2018). Recognizing settler ignorance in the Canadian Truth and Reconciliation Commission. *Feminist Philosophy Quarterly, 4*(4), 1–26. https://doi.org/10.5206/fpq/2018.4.6229

Creese, G. (2019). "Where are you from?" Racialization, belonging and identity among second-generation African-Canadians. *Ethnic and Racial Studies, 42*(9), 1476–1494. https://doi.org/10.1080/01419870.2018.1484503

Datta, R. (2015). A relational theoretical framework and meanings of land, nature, and sustainability for research with Indigenous communities. *Local Environment: The International Journal of Justice and Sustainability, 20*(1), 102–113. https://doi.org/10.1080/13549839.2013.818957

Datta, R. (2022). Land-based environmental sustainability: A learning journey from an Indigenist researcher. *Polar Geography*, 1–15. https://doi.org/10.1080/1088937X.2022.2141905

Galeano, E. (2001). *Upside down: A primer for the looking-glass world* (M. Fried, Trans.). Picador.

Haig-Brown, C. (1988). *Resistance and renewal: Surviving the Indian residential school*. Arsenal Pulp Press.

Hart, M. A. (2010). Indigenous worldviews, knowledge, and research: The development of an Indigenous research paradigm. *Journal of Indigenous Voices in Social Work, 1*(1A), 1–16.

Hele, K. S. (2021, January 14). *Indigenous Elders in Canada*. The Canadian Encyclopedia. Retrieved May 17, 2022, from https://www.thecanadianencyclopedia.ca/en/article/indigenous-elders-in-canada

Indigenous Foundations. (n.d.). *Terminology*. First Nations & Indigenous Studies: UBC.

Mahi, D. (2013). The children of Kalihi. *Reclaiming Children and Youth, 22*(1), 50–54.

McWilliam, S. E., & Nielsen, B. B. (2020). Global value chains and development: Redefining the contours of 21st century capitalism. *Journal of International Business Studies, 51*, 1347–1350. https://doi.org/10.1057/s41267-020-00303-3

National Centre for Collaboration in Indigenous Education. (2020, August 21). *Reciprocity: Dene relationship with fish* [Video]. YouTube. https://www.youtube.com/watch?v=h5Nk1Vujli0

Nielson, K. (2020). Type one diabetes mellitus in immigrant and minority pediatric populations. Brigham Young University. https://scholarsarchive.byu.edu/studentpub/270

Regan, P. (2010). *Unsettling the settler within: Indian residential schools, truth telling, and reconciliation in Canada*. UBC Press.

Smith, L. (1999). *Decolonizing methodologies: Research and indigenous peoples*. Bloomsbury Publishing.

Smith, L. T. (2012). Imperialism, history, writing and theory. In *Decolonizing methodologies: Research and Indigenous peoples* (2nd ed., pp. 19–41). Zed Books.

Wagamese, R. (1994). *Keeper'n me*. Anchor Canada.

Wildcat, M., McDonald, M., Irlbacher-Fox, S., & Coulthard, G. (2014). Learning from the land: Indigenous land based pedagogy and decolonization. *Decolonization: Indigeneity, Education & Society, 3*(3), i–xv.

CHAPTER 9

Decolonizing Digital Citizen Science: Driving Self-Governance via Data Sovereignty of Historically Colonized Populations

Jasmin Bhawra

Community-based participatory research (CBPR) methods, which have been used in a variety of disciplines, are now increasingly embracing digital innovation as part of data collection and study design. However, data ownership continues to lie in a grey area as citizens and communities rarely own their data and are often reliant on researchers to share study results. Advances in digital technology and its application in research provide unparalleled opportunities to reimagine how community-based research can be conducted. In particular, CBPR, when implemented with citizen science approaches, can play an important role in driving self-governance by promoting data sovereignty among populations that have been historically colonized. This chapter unpacks the potential of digital citizen science for conducting collaborative CBPR. Using the Bridge Framework, steps for decolonizing traditional citizen science research methods are described alongside activities and resources for readers to explore as part of a decolonizing journey.

This chapter aims to improve readers' understanding of the benefits of digital citizen science for conducting CBPR with a decolonized lens. Through engagement with this text, this chapter also aims to provide steps for decolonizing research using the Bridge Framework and to help readers unpack the relationship between decolonizing research, data sovereignty, and self-governance.

POSITIONALITY STATEMENT

I am a settler scholar and second-generation immigrant with Indian ancestry. As India was formerly colonized by the British, I have witnessed the intergenerational impacts of colonialism on the diaspora. Ranging from health, social, psychological, and economic impacts, I have learned that formerly colonized communities experience common systemic barriers, which has driven my interest in health and social equity. Over the past decade, I have partnered with First Nations and Métis communities in Canada on projects focused on land-based active living, food security, food sovereignty, and mental wellness. Through conversations with Knowledge Keepers and Elders in these communities, as well as through unpacking the complex relationship my family and ancestors have with colonial systems and ways of thinking, my work as a settler scholar aims to reimagine our approach to health research and community engagement.

THE SCOOP ON CITIZEN SCIENCE

Community-based participatory research (CBPR) has been a fundamental practice in a variety of disciplines including social sciences, health, and education. This approach to research plays an important role in elucidating community perspectives and solutions on a range of issues (Holkup et al., 2009; Jull et al., 2017; Smith, 2017). CBPR involves collaboration with community stakeholders as partners in the research process (Baum, 2006; Israel et al., 1998). This practice has evolved in recent decades to take on numerous forms and names, including community-based research, action research, or participatory action research, to name a few (Holkup et al., 2009). Some scholars place these titles on a spectrum, ranging from community-based work that consults and involves communities at specific research phases on one end of the continuum (i.e., data collection, analysis, knowledge dissemination), full collaboration in all research phases including designing project goals and implementation, to action research on the other end of the continuum where there is community leadership and transformation (Holkup et al., 2009; Wallerstein & Duran, 2010). Irrespective of the place on the spectrum or specific research taxonomy, CBPR prioritizes community involvement and outcomes (Holkup et al., 2009; Reason, 2017).

CPBR is a common approach especially when working with vulnerable or marginalized populations, as it focuses on understanding the lived experience of groups of people as they relate to various social and health outcomes of interest

(Baum, 2006; Cyril et al., 2015; Holkup et al., 2009; Israel et al., 1998; Israel et al., 2001). As described by Holkup et al. (2004), characteristics of CBPR include

> a) recognizing the community as a unit of identity, b) building on the strengths and resources of the community, c) promoting co-learning among research partners, d) achieving a balance between research and action that mutually benefits both science and the community, e) emphasizing the relevance of community-defined problems, f) employing a cyclical and iterative process to develop and maintain community/research partnerships, g) disseminating knowledge gained from the CBPR project to and by all involved partners, and h) requiring long-term commitment on the part of all partners. (Holkup et al., 2004)

When CBPR has an action-oriented focus, it can also work to reshape power dynamics between researchers and communities (Baum, 2006).

In practice, there are a variety of methods employed under the umbrella of CBPR. One such approach that has gained in popularity, particularly in ecological and environmental research, is citizen science. Citizen science refers to public participation in data collection and knowledge dissemination for research (Dickinson et al., 2010; Katapally, 2019; Lepczyk et al., 2009; Silvertown, 2009). Some citizen science research is conducted voluntarily (i.e., unpaid) or, similar to CBPR, it may involve scientists leading projects with input from citizens. This approach enables citizens to contribute to or collaborate on all aspects of the research process and promotes open participation, which enables citizens to be active collaborators on research projects (de Sherbinin et al., 2021; Katapally, 2019; Katapally et al., 2018). The benefits of a citizen science approach include, in many cases, a lack of dependence on researchers to carry out projects, as well as the potential to collaborate with researchers on citizen- or community-led projects. In addition, the language of "citizen scientist" can be empowering when applied to CBPR depending on the context or population.

As part of a research design, citizen science has implications for data collection and knowledge translation in particular. With respect to sampling, citizen science projects can collect data using a variety of methods including crowdsourcing, which creates a wider net for data collection depending on the research goal and recruitment method (i.e., social media). There are potential limitations of open-ended data collection methods including lack of representativeness; however, this can be countered by *community-based* citizen recruitment where all citizens in a given organization, school, or whole community are invited to a study (de Sherbinin et al., 2021; Katapally, 2019; Katapally et al., 2018; Silvertown,

2009). Learning from CBPR, community-driven recruitment of citizens has the greatest likelihood of success.

As discussed later in this chapter, a key advantage of citizen science lies in the promise of digital tools for real-time engagement and knowledge dissemination (Jull et al., 2017; Katapally, 2019). Citizen science projects have the potential to employ a diversity of knowledge dissemination strategies outside of the traditional academic scope. For example, citizens may take the lead in sharing ongoing study findings via social media, study-specific digital platforms or apps, or community events. In order to maximize the benefits of this approach, power dynamics between citizens and researchers must be re-evaluated.

> **Citizen Science Projects**
>
> The Government of Canada has a Citizen Science Portal where citizens can identify and join ongoing projects of interest (Government of Canada, 2022). Many projects have an environmental focus and seek citizens' input to help track patterns in nature including wildlife movement, changes in plants or agriculture, or air quality. Citizens' perspectives are critical to understanding the impacts of changes in environment in local jurisdictions on other systems.

HOW PARTICIPATORY METHODS HAVE PERPETUATED A TOP-DOWN RESEARCH APPROACH

While CBPR makes a concerted effort to eliminate power dynamics between participant groups and researchers, hierarchies inevitably emerge based on existing models of research (Holkup et al., 2009; Israel et al., 1998; Wallerstein & Duran, 2010). For example, funding sources (i.e., government or university grants, private or corporate sponsorship, community funds) play a role in the project scope, objectives, target population(s), and included jurisdictions, as well as eligible expenses. If a community has limited financial or personnel capacity to carry out a project, power dynamics may shift to prioritize researchers' and/or funders' interests. As a result, many CBPR projects lead with a priori research questions, academic research agendas, and funding parameters which potentially limit flexibility in community-based work.

In an ideal scenario for community-based participatory *action* research, a grounded theory approach—which involves constructing or deriving theory from systematically obtained data (Chun Tie et al., 2019; Corbin & Strauss, 1990)—can be used to identify research questions in collaboration with communities. However, this approach requires establishing relationships with communities prior to applying for funding and beginning a research project, which contributes to many CBPR projects placing researchers in a lead role. Given the current academic environment, one may argue the inevitability of a top-down approach, as many communities, particularly those already experiencing economic or social disadvantage, are not able to commit to research projects until or unless funding support is offered. The rigid parameters of most research funding may not enable extensive community engagement prior to the start of a research project, especially if travel, honoraria, and incentives are required as part of initial engagement. Overall, this traditional research structure perpetuates a top-down research approach where researcher agendas are prioritized and researchers take the lead even in community-based projects. This scenario is certainly not the case for all CBPR, and there are numerous examples of community-driven grant funding and projects where researchers either act as collaborators in projects or lead initiatives while prioritizing community needs (Israel et al., 1998).

However, this arrangement may also prioritize certain types of knowledge generation. Research conducted in or with academic institutions may have inherent biases in prioritizing Western knowledge and science over local or Traditional Knowledge of communities (Datta, 2018; Wadams & Park, 2018). Local knowledge refers to "skills and understandings developed by groups of individuals in a specific local geographic setting, often informing decision-making in day-to-day life. In contrast with Indigenous knowledge, local knowledge does not presuppose a broader, shared worldview, although it often is associated with a shared local understanding of context" (Eicken et al., 2021). Traditional Indigenous Knowledge refers to perspectives, worldviews, and skills that communities develop over time based on their experiences and interactions (Eicken et al., 2021; Hill et al., 2020). This knowledge is often reflected in cultural practices and language (Eicken et al., 2021; Hill et al., 2020). Eiken et al. (2021) note that "Indigenous and local knowledge systems are empirically tested, applied, contested, and validated through different means in different contexts" (Eicken et al., 2021). In this text, the term Traditional Knowledge is capitalized out of respect for the cumulative body of knowledge, practices, and beliefs that Indigenous Peoples have developed and maintained over time (Magga, 2005; Tengö et al., 2021).

Taking the example of climate change research, there is immense global effort mobilizing against rapid climate change; however, the communities that are most negatively impacted are often not well represented in critical conversations

(Allan & Smylie, 2015; Pörtner et al., 2022; Thomas, 2022). In many regions across Canada and worldwide, Indigenous communities are one of the most adversely affected by climate change because their strong connection to the land means that even subtle changes in the environment can have a disproportionately greater impact on their food systems, economy, and livelihoods (Allan & Smylie, 2015; Barber et al., 2015; Furgal & Seguin, 2006; Lemke & Delormier, 2018; Nash, 2017). The Intergovernmental Panel on Climate Change and United Nations Climate Change Conference (COP26 Goals, 2021; Pörtner et al., 2022) have set targets to reduce climate change impacts, although these goals can only be achieved with consistent and equitable engagement of Indigenous communities. Indigenous Peoples have a wealth of Traditional Knowledge about the environment and healthy ecosystems which is critical to the conversation about climate change preparation and adaptation (Allan & Smylie, 2015; Johnson et al., 2016; Kadykalo et al., 2021; Kipp et al., 2019; Mazzocchi, 2006; Ogar et al., 2020; Pollock & Whitelaw, 2005; Smith, 2021). There is commonly a lack of representation of Traditional Knowledge of Indigenous or racialized groups in research, particularly if the research is not led by recognized institutions (Smith, 2021; Thomas, 2022).

In exploring opportunities for climate change preparedness and adaptation, in particular, integrating Traditional Knowledge with Western research methods such as citizen science could provide unique and timely solutions to mitigate climate and related health issues (Bhawra et al., 2021; Katapally, 2020a; Magga, 2005; Tengö et al., 2021). These methods also lend well to research in the social sciences and medical sciences, as local and historical context has been proven to improve programming and policy interventions when conducted in collaboration with communities (Eden, 1996; Israel et al., 1998; Jameson et al., 2018; Johnson et al., 2016; Katapally et al., 2017; Kipp et al., 2019; Lam et al., 2019; MacKinnon, 2018; Pollock & Whitelaw, 2005). In addition, the use of digital tools in research increases opportunities for equitable and timely engagement and collaboration. Digital citizen science, in particular, offers solutions for these research gaps.

THE ROLE OF DIGITAL CITIZEN SCIENCE IN ETHICAL COMMUNITY-BASED RESEARCH

Digital devices, particularly smartphones, offer a new opportunity to ethically and equitably engage citizens (Katapally, 2020a; O'Dea, 2020; O'Donnell et al., 2016). Smartphones have become ubiquitous, with more than 6 billion smartphone subscription plans globally and 32 million smartphone users in Canada

(O'Dea, 2020). Smartphones provide access to digital tools and platforms, which range from apps to electronic platforms that provide services, support, and communication in real-time. The role of digital technology in providing access to essential goods and services, including groceries and healthcare, has increased significantly since the onset of the Coronavirus (COVID-19) pandemic (Katapally, 2020b; Whitelaw et al., 2020). The COVID-19 pandemic catalyzed the use of digital devices in delivering essential services, information, and programs, especially in rural, remote, or northern communities which previously experienced access issues (Whitelaw et al., 2020).

According to Statistics Canada, 88.1 percent of Canadians aged 15 years and over had a smartphone in 2018 (S. C. Government of Canada, 2021), and this number is expected to be much higher in 2021 based on global reports of how smartphone usage has increased (Turner, n.d.). In 2021, 88.54 percent of Canadians reported using mobile internet, with 70 percent of Canadians spending up to 20 hours per week using mobile internet (Ceci, 2022). Globally, there are an estimated 6.37 billion smartphones users worldwide, with this number projected to increase up to 7.33 billion in 2025 (Turner, n.d.). Approximately 84 percent of people globally have smartphones, making this one of the most commonly used and accessible digital devices (Katapally, 2019; Turner, n.d.). Each device generates an enormous amount of big data—which is data that is high in volume, velocity, variety, and veracity (Anshari & Alas, 2015).

Digital citizen science can play a significant role in leveraging big data, which if used ethically and effectively, can be used to not only inform rapid responses to health and social crises (Johnson et al., 2016; Katapally, 2020a) but also bring together decision-makers and civil society to co-create solutions (Katapally, 2019; Tauginienė et al., 2020; Wald et al., 2016). Digital citizen science is an emerging area whereby digital tools, such as smartphones, are used to capture data and engage with citizens in real-time (Katapally, 2019; Vohland et al., 2021). Digital tools have immense potential to advance citizen science research, as rapid-response interventions and knowledge sharing can be administered in near real-time (Johnson et al., 2016; Katapally, 2020a; Katapally et al., 2018). Combined with artificial intelligence, there is increasing sophistication that can be built into digital platforms to enable time-, user-, event- or location-triggered prompts for citizens' feedback (Johnson et al., 2016; Katapally, 2020a; Katapally et al., 2018; Vohland et al., 2021). The potential for longitudinal big data collection enables the development of machine learning and artificial intelligence algorithms that can simulate or predict health or social crises and help to identify effective nodes of intervention (Gray et al., 2020; Katapally, 2019). Digital technology has an even greater role to play in time sensitive crises such as climate change or pandemic preparedness. For example, advanced artificial intelligence algorithms can be used to anticipate community needs prior to urgent crises and help inform strategies to manage environmental disasters, communicable disease spread, or food supply crises (Gray et al., 2020; Meechang et al., 2020; Smith, 2019; Zhou et al., 2019).

In many rural and remote communities, smartphone ownership is not the limiting factor to participation in digital citizen science projects; rather, the issue is internet inequity—differential internet access based on wealth, location (urban, rural, or remote), gender, age, or ethnicity (Katapally, 2020a). While smartphone ownership is ubiquitous, internet access widely varies even within jurisdictions, with rural and remote communities experiencing greater issues with connectivity and lower bandwidth than their urban counterparts (Hilbert, 2016; Katapally, 2020a). The United Nations has declared internet access as a human right (La Rue, 2011), hence this gap in internet access is not only problematic as an issue of equity but also because lack of internet limits advancements in virtual or remote healthcare, social and other essential services, and timely access to information (Bhawra et al., 2021; Meechang et al., 2020; Smith, 2019; Zhou et al., 2019). In Canada and elsewhere, communities and policymakers are making dedicated efforts towards improving internet access (I. Government of Canada, 2022), which will ultimately improve the utility and potential of smartphone-based big data.

In addition, given the rapidly growing area of digital tools and its potential for community-based research, a key question is: how can we change the top-down approach with digital citizen science? As noted by Katapally (2019), "the technology that powers [digital] devices offer extraordinary research opportunities [...] to overcome traditional constraints in terms of participant recruitment and retention, data collection and analysis, interventions, and knowledge translation." Using smartphones, researchers can more easily collaborate with citizens to collect both quantitative and qualitative data including audio, video, and photo-based data and objective sensor-based data from built-in smartphone sensors (i.e., global positioning system [GPS], accelerometers; Katapally, 2019; Katapally et al., 2018). However, more importantly, using digital citizen science can offer avenues for remote collaboration, consultation, data sharing, and real-time knowledge translation, which has not been possible with other CBPR methods to date. Digital citizen science platforms may be citizen-, community-, or researcher-led and require rethinking how data sharing agreements, consent processes, data collection, and engagement are conducted throughout the course of a study. The potential is described in greater detail below in the Bridge Framework; however, it is critical to first consider how to decolonize digital citizen science if we are to reshape power dynamics in research projects.

SHIFTING THE FOCUS: DECOLONIZING DIGITAL CITIZEN SCIENCE RESEARCH

Decolonizing research decentres the focus from the aims of non-Indigenous researchers to the priorities of Indigenous Peoples (Smith, 2021). It is a process that requires unlearning Western-centric research practices, from data collection and analysis to participant engagement and knowledge sharing, in order to dissociate research from its colonial roots (Datta, 2018; Evans et al., 2020; Smith, 2021). While CPBR is commonly applied for community-focused research (MacKinnon, 2018), not all projects that are community-driven take a "decolonizing" lens. Decolonizing research requires an active stance—it is an iterative process whereby each aspect of research and engagement is unpacked to understand the potential colonial underpinnings, and reassessed with a decolonized lens. Dr. Linda Tuhiwai Smith and other scholars have championed decolonizing research methods and describe this as a necessary challenge for researchers to "simultaneously work with colonial and Indigenous concepts of knowledge, decentring one while centring the other" (Smith, 2021). Decolonizing research requires centring an Indigenous Research Agenda (Smith, 2021). Tuhiwai Smith describes the agenda as a set of approaches which include mobilization, healing, decolonization, and transformation, which can be incorporated into research methods or practices to facilitate self-determination. Tuhiwai Smith's leadership in this space has led to dialogue and reframing CBPR across disciplines over the past two decades, with new frameworks such as the process framework for decolonizing research (Bartlett et al., 2007; Smith, 2021), challenging non-Indigenous and settler scholars to reassess their roles in allyship and reconciliation (Datta, 2018, 2019).

Citizen science has great potential to contribute to decolonizing CBPR methods, as citizens exercise greater control in the research process and can report on health or social issues such as climate change events in real-time with the help of digital tools. A current deficit of this approach, however, is the lack of representation of Indigenous, racialized, and low-income groups in citizen science research studies (de Sherbinin et al., 2021; Jameson et al., 2018; Pandya, 2012). Traditional citizen science approaches stem from Western ideology, with many projects placing the focus on individual participation and data collection rather than the community as a whole (Hecker et al., 2018; Tauginienė et al., 2020). This individualistic approach limits the application of citizen science for community-driven initiatives if not adapted using a decolonized approach, whereby citizens are viewed as members of a larger community for project participation.

Digital citizen science, in particular, has great potential to aid meaningful community engagement and collaboration, if decolonized and viewed as a collective community effort working towards common goals (Johnson et al., 2016; Tengö et al., 2021). With the expansion of smartphone ownership, information is increasingly being shared through digital and social media (Ceci, 2021; S. C. Government of Canada, 2021). The ubiquitous availability and use of smartphones also enables participation in digital citizen science projects for geographically disparate communities, which may otherwise face challenges in research participation (Government of Canada, 2022; Katapally, 2020b; Lam et al., 2019; Pollock & Whitelaw, 2005). Importantly, we do not want to risk further widening gaps in research and information access, thus digital citizen science has a critical role to play in democratizing both technology access and project participation (Katapally, 2020b).

Researchers, scientists, and thought leaders in this space have paved the way for decolonizing research methods (Bartlett et al., 2007; Datta, 2018, 2019; Evans et al., 2020; Smith, 2021), and it is important that we apply these principles to digital citizen science if we are to engage in research projects equitably. Decolonizing research methods involves unlearning the hierarchy attributed to Western research methods and respecting Traditional Indigenous Knowledges as valid science in identifying solutions for health and social crises. A framework for decolonizing digital citizen science called the Bridge Framework is introduced in the next section.

THE BRIDGE FRAMEWORK

Informed by the expertise and wisdom of Indigenous and settler scholars who have paved the way for decolonizing research methods, the Bridge Framework for decolonizing citizen science was developed (Figure 9.1). Stepping out of the status quo in CBPR starts with a self-decolonizing journey, community engagement and capacity building, integrated knowledge translation, and co-creating solutions with communities (Bhawra, 2022). Together, these key pillars can facilitate healing, self-determination, and self-governance (Smith, 2021).

Step 1: Self-Decolonization

Decolonizing digital citizen science starts with a self-decolonizing journey whereby researchers reflect on how colonial processes and institutions have influenced our

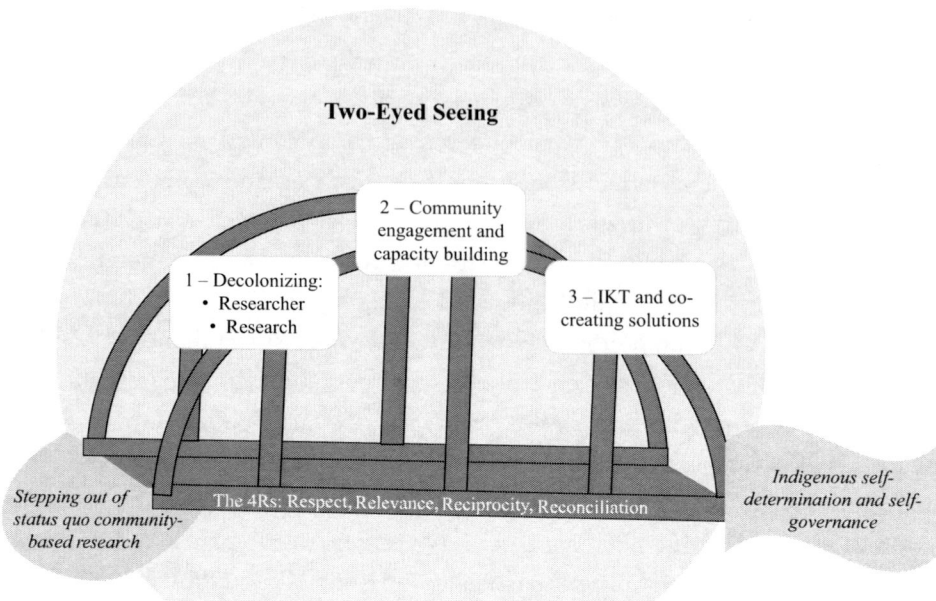

Figure 9.1: The Bridge Framework for Decolonizing Digital Citizen Science. Image adapted from: Bhawra J. (2022). Decolonizing digital citizen science: Applying the bridge framework for climate change preparedness and adaptation. *Societies, 12*(2), 71.

ways of thinking. My personal journey is influenced by my roles as a settler scholar and daughter of Indian immigrants. India was formerly colonized by the British, and witnessing the intergenerational impacts of colonization stemmed my interest in understanding the long-term impacts of these systems on health. Over the past 10 years, I have partnered with First Nations and Métis communities in Ontario and Saskatchewan, Canada, on a range of projects focused on food security and mental health, and I have had the great privilege of learning from Knowledge Keepers and Elders in these communities. These experiences emphasized the importance of acknowledging the extent to which our systems—and therefore our ways of thinking and doing—are colonized, so that we may begin to imagine how our approach to health research and community engagement could shift if we took a decolonized approach.

These partnerships highlight the importance of building relationships based on respect, collaboration, and common goals (Parter & Wilson, 2021; Schelhas,

2020). Decolonizing involves non-Indigenous researchers listening and learning from the colonial history and experiences of Indigenous Peoples. This practice requires identifying and deconstructing Western-centric research training, which may be initiated through self-awareness, reflection, engaging with critical discourse in the area (see Suggested Readings), and formal training workshops.

Step 2: Community Engagement and Capacity Building

Community engagement is a key component of CBPR, where community involvement can range from leadership to collaboration in research projects (Jull et al., 2017; Wallerstein & Duran, 2010). Many racialized and Indigenous communities have a complicated relationship with research as a result of colonialism, and the trauma of exploitation has continued to limit participation in academic partnerships (Sylvestre et al., 2018). For Indigenous Peoples in Canada, health and social inequities can be traced back to the long-term impacts of colonization and residential schools (Cauchie, n.d.; Gracey & King, 2009; King et al., 2009; Waldram et al., 1995). In order to work towards truth and reconciliation (Truth and Reconciliation Commission of Canada, 2015), community-academia relationship building is essential before beginning a research project. Research has well established the need for authentic community-research partnerships that empower citizens to ensure the relevance and sustainability of research projects long term (Datta, 2018; Smith, 2021; Wallerstein & Duran, 2010). Community collaboration in research should not only amplify citizens' voices to increase representation in decision-making but also ensure that projects are developed in alignment with a community's priorities and vision (Wehipeihana et al., 2010).

Community members are the experts of their specific geographies, histories, and cultures, thus they are also the most knowledgeable about potential research priority areas and approaches (Katapally, 2020a; Thomas, 2022; Wadams & Park, 2018). Consistent and meaningful community engagement and capacity building is an important step for not only decolonizing research but also for self-determination to take place, as described in Tuhiwai Smith's Indigenous Research Agenda (Smith, 2021). Self-determination is described not only as a goal but also a process which requires transformation, decolonization, healing, and mobilization of Indigenous Peoples (Smith, 2021).

As part of this process, researchers must appreciate how each community is unique and has different histories, experiences, and understandings of the world. Community engagement is an important part of this learning and helps to identify where and how capacity can be built to ensure long-term project sustainability and longevity (Cairncross, 2002; Carr-Hill & Street, n.d.; Mason et al., 2008; Narayan, 2002; Popay et al., 2007; Pratchett et al., 2009). Ultimately, self-determination and governance rely on community capacity.

Step 3: Integrated Knowledge Translation and Co-Creating Solutions

Given the focus of digital citizen science projects on improving community outcomes, communities should play a leading role in both integrated knowledge translation (IKT) and guiding the generation of solutions. IKT refers to co-production of knowledge as knowledge users work with researchers throughout the research process (Jull et al., 2017). An IKT approach ensures that the knowledge generated and shared throughout a research project is continually disseminated to all relevant stakeholders (Jull et al., 2017). Throughout a project, co-creating solutions to identified problems is an essential component of designing policies, programs, and strategies that will succeed. Co-creation is also a deliberate process to ensure that solutions do not come from the "top" down (MacKinnon, 2018; Martin, 2012; Pandya, 2012).

When applied to digital citizen science projects, there is potential for IKT to take place in near real-time, as research findings can be shared to citizens' smartphones via digital app platforms or social media (Katapally, 2019; Katapally et al., 2017, 2018). While traditional CBPR may disseminate knowledge only at the end of a study timeline, the process of IKT can take place before, during, and after co-creating solutions. This flexibility encourages timely idea sharing, dissemination, and implementation of solutions. Activities may include organizing community events, use of social media, or sharing knowledge via IKT symposia (Katapally et al., 2017).

The 4Rs

Decolonizing digital citizen science cannot take place without respect between researchers and communities, and for Indigenous Knowledges and cultures (Datta, 2018; Pandya, 2012; Smith, 2021). The foundation for the bridge to decolonizing citizen science therefore must be the 4Rs—Respect, Reciprocity, Reconciliation, and Relevance (Darder, 2019; First Nations Information Governance Centre [FNIGC], n.d.). The 4Rs refer to respect for Indigenous cultures and peoples; reciprocity in relationships between non-Indigenous settlers and Indigenous Peoples; a reconciliatory approach to building partnerships, capacity, understanding, and healing; and ensuring relevance of research approaches to engagement, IKT, and co-creating solutions.

The First Nations OCAP principles (FNIGC, n.d.) are also critical to acknowledge and apply in digital citizen science projects. OCAP refers to ownership of knowledge and data, control over all aspects of research, access to information about one's own community, and possession or control of data (McEwan, 2021). These principles ensure First Nations and other Indigenous Peoples the right to their own information and respects the fact that they are stewards of their information. They also reflect commitments to use and share information in a way that maximizes the benefit to a community, while minimizing harm.

As described in Darder's (2019) principles of decolonizing Indigenous education framework, in addition to the 4Rs and OCAP principles, decolonization requires centring Indigenous voices and naming coloniality (Darder, 2019). Removal of hierarchical structures is also a key component, as Western research norms can limit the application of decolonized citizen science and a Two-Eyed Seeing approach. Collaboration at every stage of research, from project conceptualization to knowledge dissemination, is necessary for self-determination and self-governance.

The Bridge

Two-Eyed Seeing forms the backdrop of the Bridge Framework, as the harmonious application of both Western and Indigenous Ways of Knowing is critical to facilitating the change from status quo in CBPR to Indigenous self-governance (Bhawra, 2022). From a digital citizen science perspective, self-governance is not feasible without data sovereignty, as big data generated by citizens plays a central role in informed decision-making (Katapally, 2019).

> **Food Equity and Environmental Data Sovereignty Project**
>
> Decolonization is an especially critical consideration for research related to climate change impacts on health and food systems, as issues of land and food sovereignty, as well as holistic wellness (i.e., the connectedness between environmental and human health, which includes social, physical, mental, spiritual, and emotional well-being; McEwan, 2021). As global conversations are taking place on climate change preparedness, colonial power dynamics are clearly on display. Decolonizing digital citizen science is an essential step in achieving the goals of the Intergovernmental Panel on Climate Change and 2021 United Nations Climate Change Conference (*COP26 Goals*, 2021, p. 26; Pörtner et al., 2022, p. 6). The lack of attention to decolonization may hinder our collective efforts to curb climate change

while we can. The Food Equity and Environmental Data Sovereignty (FEEDS) project is a digital citizen science project that applies the Bridge Framework (Bhawra, 2022; Bhawra et al., 2021). FEEDS aims to capture environmental and health-related data (e.g., weather, permafrost degradation, fire hazards, human movement, etc.) using a custom-built app (Bhawra et al., 2021). Big data is relayed in real-time to a digital dashboard, where citizens and decision-makers have access to valuable information that can be used to mitigate health-related risks of climate change.

CO-Away Digital Epidemiological Platform

CO-Away is a digital epidemiological platform serving remote Indigenous communities for COVID-19 prevention and management (Rodrigues, 2020). Using a front-end smartphone application, citizens provide real-time data that informs a backend digital dashboard for Indigenous decision-makers. The app provides three key precision medicine services: 1) continuous risk assessment of COVID-19 infection; 2) evidence-based public health communication; and 3) citizen reporting of food availability, access to public services, and COVID-19 symptoms and test results. These culturally responsive features have been co-created with Indigenous decision-makers based on imminent community needs and priorities. CO-Away enables real-time data collection through continuous citizen engagement to inform municipal jurisdictional policies, thus enabling self-governance and data sovereignty.

DATA SOVEREIGNTY IS CRITICAL TO DECOLONIZING RESEARCH

Data ownership is an important component of digital citizen science projects as it relates to citizen and community data sovereignty. Data sovereignty refers to meaningful control or ownership of one's data (Hummel et al., 2021). Digital citizen science projects, which collect data using digital devices including smartphones, have the potential to generate big data from both objective (i.e., sensor-based) and subjective (i.e., survey-based) sources (Bhawra et al., 2021; Katapally, 2019; Katapally et al., 2018; Vohland et al., 2021; Whitelaw et al., 2020). However, for many research projects, there are often unclear parameters around data ownership (Resnik et al., 2015; Vohland et al., 2021).

A decolonized approach to digital citizen science requires dedicated conversations between researchers and citizens about data, including development of digital platforms that incorporate nuanced access to citizen and community data (Bhawra et al., 2021; Katapally, 2019, 2020; Katapally et al., 2018). For example, a digital platform may provide differential access to citizens, researchers, and community decision-makers, whereby citizens have access to personal and aggregate-level data, researchers have anonymized access to specific data agreed upon with the community, and community decision-makers have autonomy to access all data to make informed, timely decisions. This process is important for all CBPR to ensure that communities can effectively use collected data, especially when IKT is not the norm and research findings may only be published after study completion (Evans et al., 2020; Jull et al., 2017; Smith, 2021; Smith, 2017). Time-sensitive crises such as the COVID-19 pandemic also require data to be relayed in near real-time, thereby increasing the ethical implications of who has access and ownership of data (Katapally, 2020b; Smith, 2021; Whitelaw et al., 2020).

In addition to data-related concerns, academic ownership of data can further perpetuate a top-down relationship with communities, and for population groups that have historically experienced discrimination and disadvantage, dynamics of data ownership may discourage some communities from research participation (Holkup et al., 2004; Israel et al., 1998; Wallerstein & Duran, 2010). Research has identified lower participation of marginalized and lower socioeconomic status groups in citizen science projects (Pandya, 2012; Tauginienė et al., 2020). Lower participation may be a result of deficits in study recruitment, a history of exploitation which discourages specific groups from engaging in research, and mistrust of research, among other reasons. (Allan & Smylie, 2015; Pandya, 2012; Smith, 2021). Given that these groups are also most likely to be adversely affected by health and social issues, their participation is critical in digital citizen science projects. Data sovereignty plays an important role in promoting equity, inclusivity, and collaboration in research, thus decolonizing research approaches can facilitate ethical community partnerships.

DECOLONIZING DIGITAL CITIZEN SCIENCE RESEARCH FOR SELF-GOVERNANCE

Data sovereignty and self-governance are interconnected. Digital citizen science projects have the potential to collect vast amounts of big data, and if owned and applied by communities, these initiatives can play an important role in self-governance. Self-governance refers to the ability of a group to determine their own practices, priorities, and method of governance based on their own values, beliefs, and culture (Bowie, 2013; Pierre, 2019). Indigenous peoples who were colonized in countries including Canada and the United States were forced to replace existing governance structures with colonial systems (Pierre, 2019; Smith, 2021). Colonial governance systems continue to impede on Indigenous self-governance.

As described by Nikolakis (2019), "sovereignty and self-governance have different yet interdependent meanings in theory and practice. Sovereignty is a social, legal and political construct—the term conveys absolute power over people, land, water, and natural resources. Self-governance is an arrangement where a collective governs its own affairs, as a unit or subunit of sovereign power." Consequently, sovereignty is shaped by self-governance (Pierre, 2019). More on this topic can be explored in the book *Reclaiming Indigenous Governance: Reflections and Insights from Australia, Canada, New Zealand, and the United States* (Pierre, 2019).

In CBPR, self-governance is a relevant and long-standing issue because traditional research methods have commonly posed barriers to data access and ownership (Smith, 2021). Data generated through research and other activities can play a critical role in decision-making, thus lack of data sovereignty can severely limit the potential of communities to engage in the process of self-governance (Bowie, 2013; Pandya, 2012; Smith, 2021). Traditional data collection and knowledge dissemination practices used in research do not promote self-governance due to limited data sharing, lack of access, and delayed results sharing. The lack of transparency and data access can potentially be addressed through co-creation of projects using digital tools in CBPR and citizen science.

Community-based digital citizen science can give communities ownership of their own data so that they have power to act on digitally collected information in the best interests of their community members. Communities are the experts in local issues, and taking an empowerment approach and decolonizing digital citizen science methods can promote self-governance and allow communities timely access to information and data. For example, climate change action to date has largely been led by organizations and institutions rather than communities (Kipp et al., 2019; Lam et al., 2019; Thomas, 2022). Indigenous Peoples have been stewards of the land since time immemorial (Johnson et al., 2016; Kipp et al., 2019; Lam et al., 2019; Pollock & Whitelaw, 2005), thus it is not only problematic that the colonial systems, corporate structures, and nations responsible for expedited climate change have taken the reigns in addressing the problem they created, but it is also inappropriate for these groups to lead in generating climate change solutions when many are disconnected from the health, social, economic, and environmental impacts on the ground (Allan & Smylie, 2015; Pörtner et al., 2022). Digital citizen science can bring together citizens and communities to lead in solutions to crises, such as climate change, and work to amplify the Traditional Knowledge of communities.

In Canada and abroad, colonization has impeded on the sovereignty and ability to self-govern for Indigenous peoples. Colonization is a mindset, and in addition to the multitude of tangible impacts it has on peoples' livelihoods, many racialized communities in formerly colonized countries also feel the repercussions for generations. Thus, in a global context, decolonizing digital citizen science can empower Indigenous and other historically colonized groups to promote local and Indigenous Knowledges, self-determination, and sovereignty.

CONCLUDING REMARKS

Decolonizing digital citizen science is a powerful method for conducting CBPR in partnership with Indigenous communities in the digital age, and it can also facilitate equity among other marginalized populations and developing countries who have historically been impacted by colonization. The Bridge Framework provides a practical guide to engaging in the decolonization of digital citizen science to conduct ethical research with Indigenous and marginalized communities. Decolonizing citizen science requires meaningful engagement between researchers and citizens and emphasizes the participation of communities. Community-oriented data collection, analysis, and knowledge sharing will promote the application of research findings and facilitate the generation of relevant, creative, and engaged solutions to societal health and social issues.

REFLECTION QUESTIONS

1. How would you define data sovereignty? What are the key aspects that comprise data sovereignty? Consider what knowledge, resources, infrastructure, or conditions would need to be in place to enable data sovereignty.
2. How does data sovereignty relate to data privacy and security?
3. Think about a project you are currently working on or interested in. How could you apply digital citizen science? Reflect on how digital citizen science methods can be applied at various stages of the project, including data collection, analysis, and knowledge dissemination.

4. Decolonization is a process that begins with self-reflection and understanding of one's positionality. Consider the following questions as part of your reflection:
   a. What is your relationship with colonialism?
   b. In what ways have you potentially benefited from or been disadvantaged by colonial systems?
   c. What are some actionable steps you can take towards truth and reconciliation (see Leah Thomas's work in the suggested readings below)?
5. The Bridge Framework provides steps for decolonizing digital citizen science projects. How could you apply the Bridge Framework to your work? Reflect on:
   a. What steps would you take to apply the Bridge Framework?
   b. What are potential barriers you expect to face in decolonizing research projects?
   c. How would you work to overcome these barriers?

SUGGESTED READINGS

- Bhawra, J. (2022). Decolonizing digital citizen science: Applying the bridge framework for climate change preparedness and adaptation. *Societies, 12*(2), 71. https://doi.org/10.3390/soc12020071
- Datta, R. (2019). *Reconciliation in practice: A cross-cultural perspective*. Fernwood Publishing.
- Katapally, T. R. (2019). The SMART framework: Integration of citizen science, community-based participatory research, and systems science for population health science in the digital age. *JMIR MHealth and UHealth, 7*(8), e14056. https://doi.org/10.2196/14056
- Lam, S., Dodd, W., Skinner, K., Papadopoulos, A., Zivot, C., Ford, J., Garcia, P. J., IHACC Research Team, & Harper, S. L. (2019). Community-based monitoring of Indigenous food security in a changing climate: Global trends and future directions. *Environmental Research Letters, 14*(7), 073002. https://doi.org/10.1088/1748-9326/ab13e4
- Smith, L. T. (2021). *Decolonizing methodologies: Research and Indigenous peoples* (3rd ed.). Zed Books.
- Tengö, M., Austin, B. J., Danielsen, F., & Fernández-Llamazares, Á. (2021). Creating synergies between citizen science and Indigenous and local knowledge. *BioScience, 71*(5), 503–518. https://doi.org/10.1093/biosci/biab023
- Thomas, L. (2022). *The intersectional environmentalist: How to dismantle systems of oppression to protect people + planet*. Voracious.
- Truth and Reconciliation Commission of Canada. (2015). *Honouring the truth, reconciling for the future: Summary of the final report of the Truth and Reconciliation Commission of Canada.*

REFERENCES

Allan, B., & Smylie, J. (2015). *First peoples, second class treatment*. Wellesley Institute. https://www.wellesleyinstitute.com/publications/first-peoples-second-class-treatment/

Anshari, M., & Alas, Y. (2015). Smartphones habits, necessities, and big data challenges. *The Journal of High Technology Management Research, 26*(2), 177–185. https://doi.org/10.1016/j.hitech.2015.09.005

Barber, M., Jackson, S., Dambacher, J., & Finn, M. (2015). The persistence of subsistence: Qualitative social-ecological modeling of Indigenous aquatic hunting and gathering in tropical Australia. *Ecology and Society, 20*(1), 60. https://doi.org/10.5751/ES-07244-200160

Bartlett, J. G., Iwasaki, Y., Gottlieb, B., Hall, D., & Mannell, R. (2007). Framework for Aboriginal-guided decolonizing research involving Métis and First Nations persons with diabetes. *Social Science & Medicine, 65*(11), 2371–2382. https://doi.org/10.1016/j.socscimed.2007.06.011

Baum, F., MacDougall, C., & Smith, D. (2006). Participatory action research. *Journal of Epidemiology & Community Health, 60*(10), 854–857. https://doi.org/10.1136/jech.2004.028662

Bhawra, J. (2022). Decolonizing digital citizen science: Applying the bridge framework for climate change preparedness and adaptation. *Societies, 12*(2), 71. https://doi.org/10.3390/soc12020071

Bhawra, J., Buchan, M. C., Skinner, K., Favel, D., & Katapally, T. R. (2021). A guiding framework for needs assessment evaluations to embed digital tools with Indigenous communities. *Preprints.org*. https://doi.org/10.20944/preprints202112.0375.v1

Bowie, R. (2013). Indigenous self-governance and the deployment of knowledge in collaborative environmental management in Canada. *Journal of Canadian Studies, 47*(1), 91–121. https://doi.org/10.3138/jcs.47.1.91

Cairncross, L. (2002). *Tenants managing: An evaluation of tenant management organisations in England*. Office of the Deputy Prime Minister.

Carr-Hill, R., & Street, A. (2008). *Economic analysis of cost-effectiveness of community engagement to improve health*. Centre of Health Economics, University of York.

Cauchie, L. (n.d.). *National Collaborating Centre for Indigenous Health*. Retrieved April 26, 2022, from http://www.nccah-ccnsa.ca/en/

Ceci, L. (2022, October 18). *Mobile internet usage in Canada—Statistics and facts*. Statista. https://www.statista.com/topics/3529/mobile-usage-in-canada/

Chun Tie, Y., Birks, M., & Francis, K. (2019). Grounded theory research: A design framework for novice researchers. *SAGE Open Medicine, 7*. https://doi.org/10.1177/2050312118822927

COP26 Goals. (2021). *COP26 explained*. UN Climate Change Conference UK 2021. https://webarchive.nationalarchives.gov.uk/ukgwa/20230311034236/https://ukcop26.org/cop26-goals/

Corbin, J. M., & Strauss, A. (1990). Grounded theory research: Procedures, canons, and evaluative criteria. *Qualitative Sociology, 13*, 3–21. https://doi.org/10.1007/BF00988593

Cyril, S., Smith, B. J., Possamai-Inesedy, A., & Renzaho, A. M. N. (2015). Exploring the role of community engagement in improving the health of disadvantaged populations: A systematic review. *Global Health Action, 8*(1). https://doi.org/10.3402/gha.v8.29842

Darder, A. (Ed.). (2019). *Decolonizing interpretive research: A subaltern methodology for social change*. Routledge. https://doi.org/10.4324/9781351045070

Datta, R. (2018). Decolonizing both researcher and research and its effectiveness in Indigenous research. *Research Ethics, 14*(2), 1–24. https://doi.org/10.1177/1747016117733296

Datta, R. (Ed.). (2019). *Reconciliation in practice: A cross-cultural perspective*. Fernwood Publishing.

de Sherbinin, A., Bowser, A., Chuang, T.-R., Cooper, C., Danielsen, F., Edmunds, R., Elias, P., Faustman, E., Hultquist, C., Mondardini, R., Popescu, I., Shonowo, A., & Sivakumar, K. (2021). The critical importance of citizen science data. *Frontiers in Climate, 3*. https://doi.org/10.3389/fclim.2021.650760

Dickinson, J. L., Zuckerberg, B., & Bonter, D. N. (2010). Citizen science as an ecological research tool: Challenges and benefits. *Annual Review of Ecology, Evolution, and Systematics, 41*(1), 149–172. https://doi.org/10.1146/annurev-ecolsys-102209-144636

Eden, S. (1996). Public participation in environmental policy: Considering scientific, counter-scientific and non-scientific contributions. *Public Understanding of Science, 5*(3), 183–204. https://doi.org/10.1088/0963-6625/5/3/001

Eicken, H., Danielsen, F., Sam, J.-M., Fidel, M., Johnson, N., Poulsen, M. K., Lee, O. A., Spellman, K. V., Iversen, L., Pulsifer, P., & Enghoff, M. (2021). Connecting top-down and bottom-up approaches in environmental observing. *BioScience, 71*(5), 467–483. https://doi.org/10.1093/biosci/biab018

Evans, M., Miller, A., Hutchinson, P. J., & Dingwall, C. (2020). Decolonizing research practice: Indigenous methodologies, Aboriginal methods, and knowledge/knowing. In P. Leavey, *The Oxford handbook of qualitative research* (2nd ed., pp. 263–281). Oxford University Press. https://doi.org/10.1093/oxfordhb/9780190847388.013.18

First Nations Information Governance Centre (FNIGC). (n.d.). The First Nations Principles of OCAP. Retrieved April 24, 2022, from https://fnigc.ca/ocap-training/

Furgal, C., & Seguin, J. (2006). Climate change, health, and vulnerability in Canadian northern Aboriginal communities. *Environmental Health Perspectives, 114*(12), 1964–1970. https://doi.org/10.1289/ehp.8433

Government of Canada. (2022). *Citizen science portal*. https://www.ic.gc.ca/eic/site/063.nsf/eng/h_97169.html

Government of Canada. (2022, April 22). High-speed internet for all of Canada. https://ised-isde.canada.ca/site/high-speed-internet-canada/en/high-speed-internet-all-canada

Gracey, M., & King, M. (2009). Indigenous health part 1: Determinants and disease patterns. *The Lancet, 374*(9683), 65–75. https://doi.org/10.1016/S0140-6736(09)60914-4

Gray, D. M., Joseph, J. J., & Olayiwola, J. N. (2020). Strategies for digital care of vulnerable patients in a COVID-19 world—Keeping in touch. *JAMA Health Forum, 1*, e200734. https://doi.org/10.1001/jamahealthforum.2020.0734

Hecker, S., Haklay, M. E., Bowser, A., Makuch, Z., Vogel, J., & Bonn, A. (Eds.). (2018). *Citizen science: Innovation in open science, society and policy*. UCL Press. https://doi.org/10.2307/j.ctv550cf2

Hilbert, M. (2016). The bad news is that the digital access divide is here to stay: Domestically installed bandwidths among 172 countries for 1986–2014. *Telecommunications Policy, 40*(6), 567–581. https://doi.org/10.1016/j.telpol.2016.01.006

Hill, R., Adem, Ç., Alangui, W. V., Molnár, Z., Aumeeruddy-Thomas, Y., Bridgewater, P., Tengö, M., Thaman, R., Adou Yao, C. Y., Berkes, F., Carino, J., Carneiro da Cunha, M., Diaw, M. C., Díaz, S., Figueroa, V. E., Fisher, J., Hardison, P., Ichikawa, K., Kariuki, P., … Xue, D. (2020). Working with Indigenous, local and scientific knowledge in assessments of nature and nature's linkages with people. *Current Opinion in Environmental Sustainability, 43*, 8–20. https://doi.org/10.1016/j.cosust.2019.12.006

Holkup, P. A., Tripp-Reimer, T., Salois, E. M., & Weinert, C. (2004). Community-based participatory research: An approach to intervention research with a Native American community. *Advances in Nursing Science, 27*(3), 162–175.

Hummel, P., Braun, M., Tretter, M., & Dabrock, P. (2021). Data sovereignty: A review. *Big Data & Society, 8*(1). https://doi.org/10.1177/2053951720982012

Israel, B. A., Schulz, A. J., Parker, E. A., & Becker, A. B. (1998). Review of community-based research: Assessing partnership approaches to improve public health. *Annual Review of Public Health, 19*(1), 173–202. https://doi.org/10.1146/annurev.publhealth.19.1.173

Israel, B. A., Schulz, A. J., Parker, E. A., & Becker, A. B. (2001). Community-based participatory research: Policy recommendations for promoting a partnership approach in health research. *Education for Health: Change in Learning & Practice, 14*(2), 182–197. https://doi.org/10.1080/13576280110051055

Jameson, S., Lämmerhirt, D., & Prasetyo, E. (2018). Acting locally, monitoring globally? How to link citizen-generated data to SDG monitoring. *SSRN*. https://doi.org/10.2139/ssrn.3229753

Johnson, N., Behe, C., Danielsen, F., Krümmel, E.-M., Nickels, S., & Pulsifer, P. L. (2016). *Community-based monitoring and Indigenous knowledge in a changing Arctic: A review for the Sustaining Arctic Observing Networks*. Inuit Circumpolar Council.

Jull, J., Giles, A., & Graham, I. D. (2017). Community-based participatory research and integrated knowledge translation: Advancing co-creation of knowledge. *Implementation Science, 12*(1), 150. https://doi.org/10.1186/s13012-017-0696-3

Kadykalo, A. N., Cooke, S. J., & Young, N. (2021). The role of western-based scientific, Indigenous and local knowledge in wildlife management and conservation. *People and Nature, 3*(3), 610–626. https://doi.org/10.1002/pan3.10194

Katapally, T. R. (2019). The SMART framework: Integration of citizen science, community-based participatory research, and systems science for population health science in the digital age. *JMIR mHealth and uHealth, 7*(8), e14056. https://doi.org/10.2196/14056

Katapally, T. R. (2020a). A global digital citizen science policy to tackle pandemics like COVID-19. *Journal of Medical Internet Research, 22*(5), e19357. https://doi.org/10.2196/19357

Katapally, T. R. (2020b, December 10). *Are democratic nations ready to democratize technology?: Tarun Katapally for* Inside Policy. Macdonald-Laurier Institute. https://macdonaldlaurier.ca/democratic-nations-democratize-technology/

Katapally, T. R., Abonyi, S., Episkenew, J.-A., Ramsden, V., Karunanayake, C., Kirychuk, S., Rennie, D., Dosman, J. A., & Pahwa, P. (2017). Catalyzing action on First Nations respiratory health using community-based participatory research: Integrated knowledge translation through strategic symposia. *Engaged Scholar Journal: Community-Engaged Research, Teaching, and Learning, 2*(1), 57–70. https://doi.org/10.15402/esj.v2i1.198

Katapally, T. R., Bhawra, J., Leatherdale, S. T., Ferguson, L., Longo, J., Rainham, D., Larouche, R., & Osgood, N. (2018). The SMART study, a mobile health and citizen science methodological platform for active living surveillance, integrated knowledge translation, and policy interventions: Longitudinal study. *JMIR Public Health and Surveillance, 4*(1), e31. https://doi.org/10.2196/publichealth.8953

King, M., Smith, A., & Gracey, M. (2009). Indigenous health part 2: The underlying causes of the health gap. *The Lancet, 374*(9683), 76–85. https://doi.org/10.1016/S0140-6736(09)60827-8

Kipp, A., Cunsolo, A., Gillis, D., Sawatzky, A., & Harper, S. L. (2019). The need for community-led, integrated and innovative monitoring programmes when responding to the health impacts of climate change. *International Journal of Circumpolar Health, 78*(2). https://doi.org/10.1080/22423982.2018.1517581

La Rue, F. (2011). *Report of the Special Rapporteur on the promotion and protection of the right to freedom of opinion and expression, Frank La Rue: Addendum.* United Nations. http://digitallibrary.un.org/record/706200/files/A_HRC_17_27_Add-1-EN.pdf

Lam, S., Dodd, W., Skinner, K., Papadopoulos, A., Zivot, C., Ford, J., Garcia, P. J., IHACC Research Team, & Harper, S. L. (2019). Community-based monitoring of Indigenous food security in a changing climate: Global trends and future directions. *Environmental Research Letters, 14*(7), 073002. https://doi.org/10.1088/1748-9326/ab13e4

Lemke, S., & Delormier, T. (2018). Indigenous Peoples' food systems, nutrition, and gender: Conceptual and methodological considerations. *Maternal & Child Nutrition, 13*, e12499. https://doi.org/10.1111/mcn.12499

Lepczyk, C. A., Boyle, O. D., Vargo, T. L., Gould, P., Jordan, R. C., Liebenberg, L., Masi, S., Mueller, W., Prysby, M. D., & Vaughan, H. (2009). Citizen science in ecology: The intersection of research and education. *Bulletin of the Ecological Society of America, 90*(3), 308–317.

MacKinnon, S. (Ed.). (2018). *Practising community-based participatory research: Stories of engagement, empowerment, and mobilization*. Purich Books.

Magga, O. H. (2005, August 12). *Indigenous knowledge systems—The true roots of humanism*. World Library and Information Congress: 71th IFLA General Conference and Council, Oslo, Norway.

Martin, D. H. (2012). Two-eyed seeing: A framework for understanding Indigenous and non-Indigenous approaches to Indigenous health research. *Canadian Journal of Nursing Research, 44*(2), 20–42.

Mason, A. R., Carr Hill, R., Myers, L. A., & Street, A. D. (2008). Establishing the economics of engaging communities in health promotion: What is desirable, what is feasible? *Critical Public Health, 18*(3), 285–297. https://doi.org/10.1080/09581590802277366

Mazzocchi, F. (2006). Western science and traditional knowledge: Despite their variations, different forms of knowledge can learn from each other. *EMBO Reports, 7*(5), 463–466. https://doi.org/10.1038/sj.embor.7400693

McEwan, C. (2021). Decolonizing the Anthropocene. In D. Chandler, F. Müller, & D. Rothe (Eds.), *International relations in the Anthropocene: New agendas, new agencies and new approaches* (pp. 77–94). Palgrave Macmillan. https://doi.org/10.1007/978-3-030-53014-3_5

Meechang, K., Leelawat, N., Tang, J., Kodaka, A., & Chintanapakdee, C. (2020). The acceptance of using information technology for disaster risk management: A systematic review. *Engineering Journal, 24*(4), 111–132. https://doi.org/10.4186/ej.2020.24.4.111

Narayan, D. (2002). *Empowerment and poverty reduction: A sourcebook*. Open Knowledge Repository. https://openknowledge.worldbank.org/handle/10986/15239

Nash, J. C. (2017). Foreword: Extractive industries in global economies. In K. Jalbert, A. Willow, D. Casagrande, & S. Paladino (Eds.), *ExtrACTION: Impacts, engagements, and alternative futures* (pp. xix–xxiii). Routledge.

Nikolakis, W., Cornell, S., & Nelson, H. (2019). *Reclaiming Indigenous Governance: Reflections and Insights from Australia, Canada, New Zealand, and the United States*. University of Arizona Press. http://www.jstor.org/stable/j.ctvqc6jwv

O'Dea, S. (2020). *Smartphone users in Canada 2018–2024*. Statista. https://www.statista.com/statistics/467190/forecast-of-smartphone-users-in-canada/

O'Donnell, S., Beaton, B., McMahon, R., Hudson, H.E., Williams, D., & Whiteduck, T. (2016). *Digital technology adoption in remote and northern Indigenous communities in Canada*. Canadian Sociological Association 2016: Annual Conference. University of Calgary, Calgary, Alberta.

Ogar, E., Pecl, G., & Mustonen, T. (2020). Science must embrace traditional and Indigenous knowledge to solve our biodiversity crisis. *One Earth, 3*(2), 162–165. https://doi.org/10.1016/j.oneear.2020.07.006

Pandya, R. E. (2012). A framework for engaging diverse communities in citizen science in the US. *Frontiers in Ecology and the Environment, 10*(6), 314–317. https://doi.org/10.1890/120007

Parter, C., & Wilson, S. (2021). My research is my story: A methodological framework of inquiry told through storytelling by a doctor of philosophy student. *Qualitative Inquiry, 27*(8–9), 1084–1094. https://doi.org/10.1177/1077800420978759

Pollock, R. M., & Whitelaw, G. S. (2005). Community-based monitoring in support of local sustainability. *Local Environment, 10*(3), 211–228. https://doi.org/10.1080/13549839.2005.9684248

Popay, J., Attree, P., Hornby, D., Milton, B., Whitehead, M., French, B., Kowarzik, U., Simpson, N., & Povall, S. L. (2007). *Community engagement in initiatives addressing the wider social determinants of health: A rapid review of evidence on impact, experience and process.* University of Lancaster.

Pörtner, H. O., Tignor, E. S., Poloczanka, K., & Roberts, D. C. (2022). *Climate change 2022: Impacts, adaptation and vulnerability.* IPCC. https://www.ipcc.ch/report/sixth-assessment-report-working-group-ii/

Pratchett, L., Durose, C., Lowndes, V., Smith, G., Stoker, G., & Wales, C. (2009). *Empowering communities to influence local decision-making: Evidence-based lessons for policy makers and practitioners.* University of Southampton, Department for Communities and Local Government.

Reason, P. (2017). Three approaches to participative inquiry. In N. K. Denzin & Y. S. Lincoln (Eds.), *Handbook of qualitative research* (pp. 324–339). SAGE.

Resnik, D. B., Elliott, K. C., & Miller, A. K. (2015). A framework for addressing ethical issues in citizen science. *Environmental Science & Policy, 54*, 475–481. https://doi.org/10.1016/j.envsci.2015.05.008

Rodrigues, M. (2020, July 10). *Co-Away: A digital tool to help northern communities address COVID-19.* Graduate School of Public Policy. https://www.schoolofpublicpolicy.sk.ca/news-events/news-articles/2020/co-away-a-digital-tool-to-help-northern-communities-address-covid-19.php

Schelhas, J. (2020). Research and reconciliation: Unsettling ways of knowing through Indigenous relationships. *Society & Natural Resources, 33*(10), 1328–1329. https://doi.org/10.1080/08941920.2020.1789795

Silvertown, J. (2009). A new dawn for citizen science. *Trends in Ecology & Evolution, 24*(9), 467–471. https://doi.org/10.1016/j.tree.2009.03.017

Smith, B. C. (2019). *The promise of artificial intelligence: Reckoning and judgment.* The MIT Press. https://doi.org/10.7551/mitpress/12385.001.0001

Smith, L. T. (2021). *Decolonizing methodologies: Research and Indigenous peoples* (3rd ed.). Zed Books.

Smith, L. U. (2017). Community engagement framework for community assessment and improvement planning. *Journal of Public Health Management and Practice, 23*, S22–S28. https://doi.org/10.1097/PHH.0000000000000600

Statistics Canada. (2021, June 21). *Table 22-10-0115-01: Smartphone use and smartphone habits by gender and age group, inactive*. https://www150.statcan.gc.ca/t1/tbl1/en/tv.action?pid=2210011501

Sylvestre, P., Castleden, H., Martin, D., & McNally, M. (2018). "Thank you very much... you can leave our community now.": Geographies of responsibility, relational ethics, acts of refusal, and the conflicting requirements of academic localities in Indigenous research. *ACME, 17*(3), 750–779.

Tauginienė, L., Butkevičienė, E., Vohland, K., Heinisch, B., Daskolia, M., Suškevičs, M., Portela, M., Balázs, B., & Prūse, B. (2020). Citizen science in the social sciences and humanities: The power of interdisciplinarity. *Palgrave Communications, 6*(1), 89. https://doi.org/10.1057/s41599-020-0471-y

Tengö, M., Austin, B. J., Danielsen, F., & Fernández-Llamazares, Á. (2021). Creating synergies between citizen science and Indigenous and local knowledge. *BioScience, 71*(5), 503–518. https://doi.org/10.1093/biosci/biab023

Thomas, L. (2022). *The intersectional environmentalist: How to dismantle systems of oppression to protect people + planet*. Voracious.

Truth and Reconciliation Commission of Canada. (2015). *Honouring the truth, reconciling for the future: Summary of the final report of the Truth and Reconciliation Commission of Canada*.

Turner, A. (n.d.). *How many people have smartphones worldwide (Apr 2022)*. BankMyCell. https://www.bankmycell.com/blog/how-many-phones-are-in-the-world

Vohland, K., Land-Zandstra, A., Ceccaroni, L., Lemmens, R., Perelló, J., Ponti, M., Samson, R., & Wagenknecht, K. (Eds.). (2021). *The science of citizen science*. Springer Cham. https://doi.org/10.1007/978-3-030-58278-4

Wadams, M., & Park, T. (2018). Qualitative research in correctional settings: Researcher bias, Western ideological influences, and social justice. *Journal of Forensic Nursing, 14*(2), 72–79. https://doi.org/10.1097/JFN.0000000000000199

Wald, D. M., Longo, J., & Dobell, A. R. (2016). Design principles for engaging and retaining virtual citizen scientists: Design principles for virtual citizen science. *Conservation Biology, 30*(3), 562–570. https://doi.org/10.1111/cobi.12627

Waldram, J. B., Herring, D. A., & Young, T. K. (1995). *Aboriginal health in Canada: Historical, cultural, and epidemiological perspectives*. University of Toronto Press.

Wallerstein, N., & Duran, B. (2010). Community-based participatory research contributions to intervention research: The intersection of science and practice to improve health equity. *American Journal of Public Health, 100*(S1), S40–S46. https://doi.org/10.2105/AJPH.2009.184036

Wehipeihana, N., Davidson, E. J., McKegg, K., & Shanker, V. (2010). What does it take to do evaluation in communities and cultural contexts other than our own? *Journal of MultiDisciplinary Evaluation, 6*(13), 182–192. https://doi.org/10.56645/jmde.v6i13.265

Whitelaw, S., Mamas, M. A., Topol, E., & Van Spall, H. G. C. (2020). Applications of digital technology in COVID-19 pandemic planning and response. *The Lancet Digital Health, 2*(8), e435–e440. https://doi.org/10.1016/S2589-7500(20)30142-4

Zhou, L., Zhang, C., Liu, F., Qiu, Z., & He, Y. (2019). Application of deep learning in food: A review. *Comprehensive Reviews in Food Science and Food Safety, 18*(6), 1793–1811. https://ift.onlinelibrary.wiley.com/doi/abs/10.1111/1541-4337.12492

CHAPTER 10

Land-Based Learning as Cross-Cultural Youth Community Building: A Cross-Cultural Children's Learning Journey

Prarthona Datta and Prokriti Datta

In this chapter, we (two sisters) share our learning experiences, focusing on how land-based learning from an Indigenist perspective can help us to understand who we are as second-generation settlers of colour in this Indigenous land and our responsibilities to the land and people. In an Indigenist worldview, our land-based activities have helped us to understand the meanings of decolonization from and within land-based learning. For the last eight years, we have been actively involved in land-based children's activities, including learning the meanings of land from Indigenous Elders and educators, music, artwork, growing foods, and building relationships with plants and insects. Following land-based learning activities, we share our learning stories in three parts: first, who we are in this Indigenous land and our responsibilities to the land and people; second, how to build relationships with soil, insects, plants, gardener friends, and parents; and third, how our Indigenous land-based learning stories help to build resilience. We hope our land-based learning stories may inspire other children and youth to create a deeper understanding of decolonization in their everyday practice.

INTRODUCTION

One of the main challenges in Western education is that there is only classroom-based education; learning is unrelated to every practice (Folkestad, 2006). In Western education, everything is only human-based learning, so students must learn from the land, animals, insects, soil, etc. The Western approach to education can hinder students from learning valuable knowledge passed down from parents, their cultural heritage, Indigenous Elders, and their connection to the land. This can have harmful consequences, as these teachings risk being disconnected from everyday, land-based practices (Bowra et al., 2021).

Land-based learning and land-based stories from Indigenous Elders and Knowledge Keepers can help teach youth in a community garden about relationships with the land and the importance of connecting with the land (Datta et al., 2022; Wilson, 2008). Land-based learning can challenge Western perspectives and help strengthen children's belongingness with the land and understanding of the importance of Indigenous rights, traditional culture, and practice (Datta, 2022a). Indigenous land-based stories can also help to teach children about their identity and their responsibility as part of decolonization (Hansen, 2018).

This paper aims to fill gaps in land-based education as cross-cultural youth community building. Many studies touch on this subject but do not explain the responsibilities of youth. There needs to be more information on how land-based activities can help cross-cultural children take responsibility for creating a connection with the land. In this chapter, we aim to explore how land-based education can decolonize. To achieve this goal, we have organized this chapter into five parts: first, we situate ourselves regarding who we are and why we are writing this chapter; second, we explain the challenges in Western education; third, we present a case study; fourth, we discuss our theoretical framework and methods; and fifth, we discuss our decolonial learning through relational stories.

SITUATING OURSELVES

Situating us as learners is an integral part of this chapter. It is a significant aspect of who we are today and who we will become (Datta et al., 2015; Wilson, 2008) in this Indigenous land as second-generation colour settler learners.

We are two sisters who are 14 and 15 years old. As colour settler children, we situate ourselves from an intersectional perspective, including as community gardeners, dancers, artists, and musicians. Our intersectional identities have multiple implications for building cross-cultural children's communities through our community garden activities.

We see ourselves as cross-cultural dancers. For instance, we have done a lot of cross-cultural dancing (i.e., ballet, lyrical, Bangla folk, classical Indian Kathak and Bharatanatyam, Indigenous powwow, Russian, and German folk dance) in the community garden. We have had the opportunity to learn a variety of cultural dances. We have learned the importance of various cultural dances in our everyday practice as cross-cultural dancers, particularly Indigenous dance.

We also consider ourselves cross-cultural musicians, performing Bengali and English music. Cross-cultural music has deep meaning, as it respects all cultures and inspires us to learn. Cross-cultural singing in the community garden has exposed us to many types of global music and helped us appreciate the diversity of people in our garden.

Playing cross-cultural instruments in the community garden has taught us about the diversity of cultures and instruments. An Indian classical harmonium was the first instrument we learned to play. We always sing and play the harmonium together in our community garden.

Therefore, our intersectional identities have significantly influenced the land-based learning and activities we have been doing for the last eight years. Our intersectional identities have played a significant role in bridging our formal and informal learning.

CHALLENGES IN WESTERN EDUCATION

Learning that is unrelated to everyday practices and classroom-only and human-centric education are some of the many issues that Western education presents (Datta, 2018). Here we discuss some of the many challenges of Western education and decolonization as they are related to our learning.

Challenges in Classroom-Based Education

There are many challenges with using only classroom-based learning. First, many studies show that classroom-based education has limited interaction with the land, insects, plants, animals, and more. Without interaction with other living things, there is no relationship or connection with the land, which will result in learning that is not meaningful (Cajete, 2004). Learning solely in a classroom setting does not provide relevant education, promote opportunities for knowledge and stories, and create safe spaces for healing and learning. Relationships with the land are vital aspects of life that encourage us to take responsibility for the land. Building connections will help the land because we will protect the things we have meaningful relationships with.

Challenges in Unrelated Learning

Western education only sometimes teaches skills that will help students in their lives (Merriam & Kim, 2011). It is essential to relate learning with everyday practices because learning from the land creates relationships between the land and people. Meaningful learning with the land can take place by incorporating related knowledge from Indigenous teachings and forming connections with animals, plants, insects, soil, and so on. These teachings help us to learn traditional knowledge from Elders and Knowledge Keepers. Connecting learning with everyday land-based practices is of paramount importance. This integration of land-based education into daily routines fosters a stronger connection to the land and empowers individuals with greater self-determination.

Challenges in Human-Based Learning

In Western education, there is only human-based learning; there is no connection with the land or relationships with animals, insects, plants, and more. The relationships created with other living things also teach us to be compassionate because they force us to look beyond our needs and imagine those of others. Building relationships with non-humans allows us to understand the circle of life and how everything is connected. While watching an animal, we can see how one thing leads to another; without one animal, the entire cycle would collapse. For example, foxes eat rabbits, and rabbits eat grass. If the rabbit were to be gone, so would the foxes; everything is connected, so we need to engage in learning aside from just human-based learning.

All of these challenges in Western education (such as learning that is human-based, classroom-based, and unrelated to everyday practices) create many difficulties; this is why students must also learn from the land and stories. Classroom-based learning can impede students' connection with the land, cutting off the opportunity to build relationships with animals, plants, insects, soil, and more. Learning that is unrelated to everyday practices prevents students from learning the necessary skills they need in life with a connection to the land (Spillman, 2017). Human-centric learning does not allow students to take responsibility for and learn with non-humans.

THEORETICAL PERSPECTIVES AND METHODS

To understand the storytelling and learning in the community garden, we used an Indigenist theoretical framework to understand our relationships with non-humans, relationships with children, stories from Indigenous Elders and parents, and climate change and our responsibilities (Datta, 2022a; Barlo et al., 2021). This Indigenist theoretical framework helps us learn about our relationships in the community garden. Following an Indigenist theoretical framework, we used six methods to achieve our decolonial learning: listening to traditional storytelling, creating artwork, growing food, playing, dancing, and playing music.

Land-Based Learning

The understanding that we have a connection to and a relationship with the land we live on is the main idea of Indigenous land-based learning (Datta, 2022b). Our goal is to employ land-based education based on Indigenous knowledge and teachings to create our belongingness with the land and people. Indigenous land-based learning is significant for us because it teaches us how to connect with the land and understand that the land is part of us and that we should treat it with respect and kindness as we do to ourselves. In the community garden outside our apartment, we learned how to connect our school learning with land-based learning and connect with the land and insects from this community garden. In our school, our teachers taught us about the soil and the insects; however, we never actually got to learn about them with real examples from the land. We would sit in the classroom instead of going outside to learn about insects and soil. We learned about the soil and insects in the community garden while practising it. The community garden gave us unlimited opportunities to learn with the land and non-humans.

Traditional Storytelling

Land-based storytelling is an important technique for sharing knowledge in a community garden, according to anti-racist and decolonial academic Ranjan Datta (2018). Traditional storytelling aids in the sharing of important knowledge among generations, which assists in understanding culture, heritage, and land (Chan, 2021). Storytelling has enhanced our understanding of Canada's past. We heard many stories about the land from Indigenous Elders, Knowledge Keepers, Indigenous and non-Indigenous artists, our parents, and immigrant children through various community garden activities.

Growing Food, Children's Artwork, Music, and Dancing

Growing food, creating art, music, and dancing in a community garden are important for children's education (McVittie et al., 2019). This method helps children to connect their learning to practice. Growing food, creating art, music, and dancing have helped me learn and understand my responsibilities to help the earth by reducing the impact of climate change. These methods have helped us better understand the land, animals, insects, and more. We have also used this method to showcase how growing food in a community garden can assist with environmental education.

We have used these three methods to understand the storytelling and learning in the community garden. These methods have helped us to understand our relationships with children and non-humans; they have also helped us to understand stories from Indigenous Elders and parents, and to understand climate change and our responsibilities. This Indigenist theoretical framework helped us learn about our relationships in the community garden.

CASE STUDY: CROSS-CULTURAL CHILDREN'S JOURNEY IN A COMMUNITY GARDEN

For eight years, we have been engaged with the community garden right beside our apartment building on Treaty 6 Territory. Our community garden was a learning space for everyone and a place to build relationships with the land. Our community garden helped us develop a relationship with the land through playing with the soil, insects, and plants. Our parents inspired us to help in the garden by showing us and sharing their land-based stories. There were many cross-cultural children our age playing and working in the garden and encouraging us to build relationships with the land. Further, many Indigenous Elders came and shared their knowledge with all the cross-cultural children; they told stories about the land animals, insects, soil, and so on. These stories helped us build resilience and grow our love for the community garden.

Our Decolonial Learning through Relational Stories

Building relationships with non-humans has helped us decolonize our learning processes. For example, in our community garden, we built many relationships with non-humans. Through relationships with non-humans, we understood that we must care for all living things because they are part of the circle of life; if one is harmed, so is every other living thing, including us. Non-humans have taught us many things about the land.

Insects
In our community garden, we always played with ladybugs, butterflies, and worms. We were always excited to build new relationships. While growing up, insects and plants became our friends and kept us company. We always treated them with

care, because we always thought of them as a part of our bodies. We don't want to hurt a part of us so we would never hurt an insect. They taught us that every living thing is important because everything is connected. Harming one insect could harm many others. Watching and playing with all the insects helped us create a connection with them and the land.

Plants

Helping our family and friends in the garden helped us understand that building relationships with the plants we are growing is important. We must care for the plants because they help us and other living things stay alive; everything is interconnected and has a purpose. Learning this helped us understand that we need more diversity in the garden to help other animals and insects, which is why we always kept a plot with different weeds. This was done because it would provide a home to different insects and animals; this is important because we wouldn't just be feeding ourselves. Therefore, we were helping other living things like insects, soil, and animals. This is crucial to the well-being of the land because there would not just be one kind of plant, but diversity in the plants. We helped our parents in the garden and found it so much fun to see the little seeds slowly become full-grown plants that we could harvest and eat. We went out to the garden every day and took care of the seeds we planted. Growing foods in the community garden has always been a way for us to connect with the land.

We learned through our decolonial relational stories that we must care for all living things as part of the circle of life, and that if one is hurt, so are all other living things, including ourselves. Helping our family and friends in the garden taught us the importance of cultivating relationships with the plants we nurture. We assisted our parents in the garden and had a chance to watch the little seeds grow into full-grown plants that our family could harvest and enjoy together.

Decolonization with Land-Based Stories

The land-based stories of Elders, Knowledge Keepers, and our parents in our community garden have helped us to decolonize our mindsets. These important stories have helped cross-cultural children in the community learn about the importance and history of the land, and also learn about our past, heritage, and culture from the land.

Learning from Indigenous Elders' and Knowledge Keepers' Stories

Through Elders and Knowledge Keepers, we have learned the importance and history of the land. For numerous activities, we planned to learn directly from the land, Indigenous Elders, and Knowledge Keepers. For example, many workshops and storytelling activities, such as blanket exercises, were organized to help youth learn about the land we live on. Their stories helped us understand the importance of native plants and the importance of connecting with the land, insects, soil, animals, and other beings. Learning about the history of the land from Indigenous Elders and Knowledge Keepers helps us understand the wrongdoings of the past and understand who we are on this Indigenous land. It has helped us unlearn, relearn, and understand what we must do to move forward.

Learning Parents' Stories

Through land-based stories, we learned about our past, heritage, and culture with the land. Together as a family, we learned the importance land has in all cultures and how it affects us because of our ancestry. Our parents would tell us many of their stories and stories from our grandparents regarding who we are and where we came from in the community garden, because it was a space for learning. While spending time with the land, our parents shared many stories about our culture through gardening and playing with insects and animals. We looked forward to these stories because it was interesting to learn more about ourselves from our parents and the land.

Learning from Art, Music, and Dance Activities

Creating art with the land was beneficial to us because it gave us inspiration for our art, and we also used different materials from the land. It allowed us to broaden our creativity while learning from the land. In the community garden, there are lots of art workshops so our art skills have developed because of our surroundings and the environment. When we were younger, we usually drew the land—flowers, butterflies, ladybugs, simple landscapes, and trees inspired by the community garden. The garden sparked our interest in creating art about the things around us. Now, because of the community garden, we like to go outside and watch insects and birds for inspiration when we draw. Making art and music and dancing with the land has helped us feel more connected and rooted to the land, which is why learning from the land is important to us.

We have learned about the value and history of the land by listening to Elders and Knowledge Keepers. Learning about the land's history from Indigenous Elders and Knowledge Keepers helps us understand previous misdoings. We have learned about our past, traditions, and culture with the land through land-based stories. It has helped us discover who we are in this Indigenous country and establish our connection to it. Stories from our parents helped us understand who we are, and art with the land allowed us to create a deeper connection with the land.

DISCUSSION AND CONCLUSION

Our land-based learning in a cross-cultural community garden helped us to learn many things and take responsibility for building a decolonial youth community. In the previous section, we discussed the two most important areas that helped us to reshape our responsibility as youth in building a youth-led decolonial community and practising decolonization through land-based learning.

Decolonization is a task we all share, no matter where we are. Learning through Indigenous teachings will help undo and relearn colonialism (Wildcat et al., 2014). As we mention in the case study findings, the stories from Indigenous Elders and Knowledge Keepers have helped us learn more about the land and the history of Canada and its Indigenous people. By learning from these stories, we understand what needs to be done so history does not repeat itself. It is important to learn and relearn past mistakes so that things will change moving forward (Fitznor, 2005). Learning from and on the land allowed us to understand decolonization from stories told in our community garden.

Children need to take responsibility for decolonization because we are the next generation and it is up to us to make a change. Children need to learn about the history of Canada and acknowledge the things done to Indigenous people, so as not to allow the wrongdoings of the past to be repeated. In our community garden, children are taught about decolonization and building relationships with Indigenous people through stories from parents, Elders, and Knowledge Keepers, as well as through music, art, and dance activities.

REFLECTION QUESTIONS

1. Why and how can children learn more about land-based learning?
2. What responsibilities should youth have for land-based learning?
3. How can children practice land-based learning?
4. How can land-based learning help to decolonize our learning and practice?

SUGGESTED READINGS

- Bishop, R., Berryman, M., Cavanagh, T., & Teddy, L. (2009). Te Kotahitanga: Addressing educational disparities facing Māori students in New Zealand. *Teacher and Teacher Education, 25*(5), 734–742.

- Mahi, D. (2013). The children of Kalihi. *Reclaiming Children and Youth, 22*(1), 50–54.
- Manuel, G., & Posluns, M. (2019). *The fourth world: An Indian reality*. University of Minnesota Press.
- Maracle, L. (1991). *Bobbi Lee Indian Rebel*. Women's Press.
- Maracle, L. (2003). *I am woman: A native perspective on sociology and feminism*. Press Gang Publishing.

REFERENCES

Barlo, S., Boyd, W. E., Hughes, M., Wilson, S., & Pelizzon, A. (2021). Yarning as protected space: Relational accountability in research. *AlterNative: An International Journal of Indigenous Peoples, 17*(1), 40-48.

Bowra, A., Mashford-Pringle, A., & Poland, B. (2021). Indigenous learning on Turtle Island: A review of the literature on land-based learning. *The Canadian Geographer/Le Géographe canadien, 65*(2), 132–140. https://doi.org/10.1111/cag.12659

Cajete, G. (2004). A philosophy of Native science. In A. Waters (Ed.), *American Indian thought* (pp. 45–57). Wiley-Blackwell.

Chan, A. S. (2021). Storytelling, culture, and Indigenous methodology. In A. Bainbridge, L. Formenti, & L. West (Eds.), *Discourses, dialogue and diversity in biographical research: An ecology of life and learning* (Vol. 10, pp. 170–185). Brill.

Datta, R. K. (2018). Rethinking environmental science education from Indigenous knowledge perspectives: An experience with a Dene First Nation community. *Environmental Education Research, 24*(1), 50–66.

Datta, R. (2022a). Cross-cultural community gardening as an Indigenist methodology: A learning ceremonial journey from a colour settler perspective. In P. Liamputtong (Ed.), *Handbook of qualitative cross-cultural research methods: A social science perspective* (pp. 324–334). Edward Elgar Publishing.

Datta, R. (2022b). Land-based environmental sustainability: A learning journey from an Indigenist researcher. *Polar Geography*, 1–15. https://doi.org/10.1080/1088937X.2022.2141905

Datta, R., Kayira, J., & Datta, P. (2022). Land-based environmental education as a climate change resilience: A learning experience from a cross-cultural community garden. In E. M. Walsh (Ed.), *Justice and Equity in Climate Change Education: Exploring social and ethical dimensions of environmental education* (pp. 214–233). Routledge.

Datta, R., Khyang, N. U., Prue Khyang, H. K., Prue Kheyang, H. A., Ching Khyang, M., & Chapola, J. (2015). Participatory action research and researcher's responsibilities: An experience with an Indigenous community. *International Journal of Social Research Methodology, 18(6)*, 581-599.

Fitznor, L. (2005). *Aboriginal educational teaching experiences: Foregrounding Aboriginal/Indigenous knowledges and processes*. University of Manitoba.

Folkestad, G. (2006). Formal and informal learning situations or practices vs formal and informal ways of learning. *British Journal of Music Education, 23*(2), 135–145.

Hansen, J. (2018). Cree elders' perspectives on land-based education: A case study. *Brock Education: A Journal of Educational Research and Practice, 28*(1), 74–91.

McVittie, J., Datta, R., Kayira, J., & Anderson, V. (2019). Relationality and decolonisation in children and youth garden spaces. *Australian Journal of Environmental Education, 35*(2), 93–109.

Merriam, S. B., & Kim, Y. S. (2011). Non-western perspectives on learning and knowing. In S. B. Merriam & A. P. Grace (Eds.), *The Jossey-Bass reader on contemporary issues in adult education* (pp. 378–389). Jossey-Bass.

Spillman, D. (2017). A share in the future… only for those who become like 'us'!: Challenging the 'standardisation' reform approach to Indigenous education in the northern territory. *The Australian Journal of Indigenous Education, 46*(2), 137–147.

Wildcat, M., McDonald, M., Irlbacher-Fox, S., & Coulthard, G. (2014). Learning from the land: Indigenous land based pedagogy and decolonization. *Decolonization: Indigeneity, Education & Society, 3*(3), i–xv.

Wilson, S. (2008). *Research is ceremony: Indigenous research methods*. Fernwood Publishing.

PART III

COLOUR SETTLER REFUGEE AND DISABLED WOMEN COMMUNITY REFLECTIONS ON DECOLONIZATION IN PRACTICE

Indigenous scholars Eve Tuck and K. Wayne Yang have argued that decolonization is not a metaphor (Tuck & Yang, 2012). Decolonization requires action throughout all facets of society, deconstructing the prevailing power structures from academia to all forms of everyday practices. The chapters in this section critically discuss why and how refugee and disabled lives matter and how decolonial practice can help achieve their visions.

1. **Najla Mohammadi,** as a colour settler refugee woman, shares her decolonial learning stories focusing on how we as a collective community can build a decolonial community to create positive change in our everyday practices.
2. **Tasnim Jaisee,** as a colour settler disabled woman, shares her decolonial lived experiences navigating race and disability in Bangladesh and Canada.

CHAPTER 11

Learning the Importance of Building a Decolonial Community: From and within a Colour Settler Former Refugee Woman's Reflections

Najla Mohammadi

As a colour settler refugee woman from Afghanistan who is currently living on the Indigenous land known as Canada, in this chapter I share my decolonial learning stories focusing on how we as a collective community can build a decolonial community to create positive change in our everyday practices. From my personal learning journey, I learned that we all need to ask ourselves: *How should we take responsibility for understanding and implementing Indigenous meanings of decolonization in our everyday lives?* Our decolonial learning journey may create many positive possibilities in our lives, including the significance of sitting in a circle and providing a safe space free of judgment for every person in the family to share their thoughts and opinions. Learning the importance of building a decolonial community and Indigenous meanings of reconciliation from Indigenous perspectives has become a celebration for me.

In my decolonial learning journey, I have learned that reconciliation is everyone's responsibility; it involves learning, unlearning, and relearning to tackle barriers, stereotypes, prejudices, and inequalities experienced by Indigenous peoples. In this chapter, I use my decolonial stories to explain how our responsibilities for learning, acknowledging, and honouring Indigenous perspectives and implementing them in our everyday practices help to unfold who we are on this Indigenous land and create our belongingness with Indigenous land and people.

The process of decolonial learning is a significant step in building decolonial communities and recognizing Indigenous history and trauma. When we become an active part of this decolonial journey, we allow ourselves to have a better understanding of Indigenous perspectives, backgrounds, history, and sovereignty. Once we have accurate and adequate education on this matter, we can then share our knowledge with our family members, friends, and community.

When I came to Canada, I had very little knowledge of Indigenous history and survival stories. I did not know Canada had a history of discrimination and cultural genocide against the Indigenous population. I did not know about the impacts of colonization on Indigenous communities, its severity, or that it continues to affect Indigenous peoples today. The ideal picture of Canada that I had in mind was shattered when I was first introduced to the Indigenous history of this land in school. I could not believe that a country as peaceful and prosperous as Canada could commit such horrible crimes against some of its people. I learned that Canada is not perfect after all. From believing Canada to be a predominantly white, safe, equal, inclusive, and racism-free country to unlearning and relearning decolonial teachings, I strongly believe it should be our top priority to put decolonial learning at the centre of our focus for rebuilding a Canada that includes, values, and respects all races, backgrounds, and religions. We can build a better and more tolerant Canada together when we as Canadians are ready to accept the past, hear the truth, and be willing to change our attitudes and actions. Therefore, it is important that educational institutions focus on decolonial learning at an early age because there are hundreds of newcomers arriving every year who call Canada home but are still unaware of its history. I sincerely hope my decolonial journey will encourage every newcomer in this country to pause for a minute and think about what it means to live on Indigenous lands, what it means to challenge colonized thoughts and teachings, and finally, what it means to be home.

SITUATING MYSELF

I started my decolonial stories focusing on who I am, where I am coming from, and why I am writing this chapter. I am a colour settler feminist woman currently residing in Treaty 7 Territory, Alberta, Canada. Originally, I am from the Shia Hazara community in Afghanistan and was born and raised in a Hazara Shia Imami Ismaili family in Kabul. Hazaras, who primarily follow the Shia branch of Islam, are the most discriminated-against ethnic and religious minority group in Afghanistan, subjected to persecution for centuries. Due to our distinct facial features and our faith, Shia Hazaras have been the victims of continuous genocide, persecution, assimilation, expulsion, and enslavement by every Afghan ruler since the 1800s. Like thousands of Shia Hazara families, my family was forced to flee the country and become refugees in a different country. By sharing my story with the world, I hope to shift the narrative of Hazaras, Shias, and refugees from victims to survivors and warriors. By telling my decolonial stories, I hope to create my belongingness with this Indigenous land and Indigenous peoples in Canada. At the same time, my stories also help to achieve my dreams of dismantling the patriarchy. My goal is to challenge Western perspectives, such as the colonization of Canada and other countries in the world.

My birth country became the victim of a Western war when the barbaric Taliban once again took control of Kabul in August 2021. Today more than ever, Shia Hazaras face the grave threat of being persecuted by the Taliban once again. The fact that we are being killed because of our physical features and our faith, besides political and financial gains, is entirely heartbreaking and enraging. Continued targeted attacks on Shia Hazara mosques, schools, and neighbourhoods have become the new reality for thousands of Shias and Hazaras still living in Afghanistan. As a Shia Hazara myself, I feel uncertain, hesitant, and fearful to announce my birth country because my birth country never felt like home; I never felt the belongingness, the safety, the warmth, and the content feeling that a home should offer. In other words, Afghanistan has never been my country, nor was I ever fully accepted as a citizen of Afghanistan. It has never been a safe place for Shia Hazaras to reside and make progress. We, as Shia Hazaras, were never accepted nor treated equally to other Afghans by numerous Afghan leaders and Afghan people. As a result of the ongoing genocide and ethnic cleansing against Shia Hazaras, it is difficult not to feel alienated and hateful towards the Afghan government and its people.

At the age of 14, preceding the Taliban's continuous threat, my family was forced to leave Afghanistan. With hearts full of pain and sorrow, we became refugees in India for three years. It was painful to leave the place where our ancestors lived and made a livelihood and memories. It was scary to embark on a new journey full of challenges and uncertainties. Our refugee life in India was full of challenges, disappointments, dejection, and rejections every day. The challenges I faced as a refugee in India have taught me to become a stronger, more responsible, more humble, sensible, kinder, and more compassionate person towards our beautiful mother earth and all living organisms. I feel a significant amount of gratitude towards the people of India for their generosity in letting my family stay in their country for three years.

Like every Shia Hazara family, my family's and my own experiences of racism began in Afghanistan when I was just a little kid trying to achieve excellent grades in school. I was particularly concerned about getting higher grades than anyone else in the classroom to validate my intelligence, hard work, and determination as a Shia Hazara. Colonized thoughts and ways of life have taught us that good grades determine a person's worth, while in reality, it is the good heart of a person that indicates how kind and successful a person can be.

The education system in Afghanistan is one of the biggest failures in a nation that still persecutes its native people through cultural assimilation, cultural cleansing, and deliberate attacks. In other words, the Afghan education curriculum is exclusive and based on a "one size fits all" approach. It has undermined and continues to undermine the significance of teaching all faiths in classrooms. When I was a student in Kabul, my faith was deemed wrong. Students like me were forced to learn, pray, and think according to mainstream Islam, which is Sunnism. Any student who did not follow the rules was punished physically—beaten up—and sometimes given an F on the exam paper. This is a particular example of assimilation through academics in Afghanistan against Shia Muslims.

As refugees in India, my family was not financially independent nor did we have the privileges, opportunities, or resources to thrive and prosper. Living as refugees with limited to no opportunities made it inconvenient for my family to send me to school to get the best education possible. However, my family saw a significant amount of potential, faith, and drive in my future. My oldest sister, who was doing her master's in Canada at the time, worked day and night to earn more money to be able to pay for my tuition. She sacrificed a lot of her time, energy, and money to help me get an education. I am forever grateful for the sacrifices each family member made to give me a better life. I feel incredibly privileged and fortunate to have been able to continue my education despite encountering several setbacks as a refugee in India. I am thankful for my family, who made it possible for me to be here today—to write my stories, stories that reflect my strength, ambition, resilience, and determination in my journey of decolonization. I can feel that my stories challenge the patriarchal system through my thoughts on decolonization. My stories and lived experiences of racism give me the strength to fight for justice for the most vulnerable groups in our communities, particularly the Shia Hazara in Afghanistan, and to create solidarity with Indigenous peoples in Canada.

One of the benefits of living in three different countries is learning new languages. Since I was born in Kabul and lived in India for three years, I can speak Farsi/Dari and English, and I understand Hindi very well. I started learning

English at the age of seven, thanks to my parents and Hazar Imam (the current spiritual leader of Shia Ismailis), who always emphasizes how important it is to speak the global language of today. It is also significant to mention that while it is essential to learn English, it is also necessary to know our native language because our native language plays an important role in establishing our identity. Remembering and speaking our native language is a reminder of the struggles and discrimination we continue to face to fit better in our societies. It is also a personal approach to fighting colonization and patriarchy by rejecting what is considered the norm. Thus, learning and speaking English does not mean one should be distant from their roots, culture, or identity.

My family and I are very grateful to the Indigenous peoples here in Canada for sharing their land with us. I come from a place where cultures and traditions are practised to enhance the reputations of men while suppressing the roles of women and the values they add to life. Ask an Afghan woman living in Afghanistan today how it feels to be stripped of her basic human rights and dignity. Ask her how it feels to be ordered by a group of terrorists to fully submit to the men of her house. The Taliban are taking away the very core being of women in Afghanistan. Afghan women and girls no longer have the liberty to be women but rather are objects, controlled by men. Women everywhere in the world, but especially in male-dominated societies such as Afghanistan, are no stranger to being treated as second-class citizens. I hope and I fight for the day when women everywhere no longer have to fight or risk being murdered for their right to bodily autonomy, education, and the right to say no.

As mentioned earlier, Afghanistan has a history of genocide, persecution, and expulsion against Shia Hazaras. While it is imperative that one should not generalize or compare experiences of racism or levels of trauma and oppression between and among groups, I believe there needs to be a clearer connection between the experiences of racism and oppression we Shia Hazaras continue to face and those of Indigenous peoples. Both Shia Hazaras and Indigenous peoples are minority native groups that continue to face racism on a daily basis. Both have experienced loss of life, culture, traditions, and languages through decades of continued genocide and colonization. There is a little comfort that the world is somewhat aware of the crimes and atrocities committed against Indigenous peoples in Canada. On the other hand, unfortunately, Shias and Hazaras still continue to tell the world of the crimes being committed against them in Afghanistan without getting much attention. Canadians and those in power have begun to accept, listen, and learn from past events to ensure that Indigenous peoples' rights and freedoms are not sacrificed again while moving forward. However, the continued oppression and cultural cleansing of Shia Hazaras continues to impact thousands of lives in Afghanistan. To be willing to change our actions, behaviours, and colonized thoughts means giving land acknowledgements to those who were assimilated and sent away from their homes. A land acknowledgement is a way of giving honour and thanks to those forced to flee home and those forced to change their identity. In Canada, we listen to land acknowledgements in the beginning of every speech. This shows our appreciation and gratitude towards Indigenous lands that we live on. My hope for the thousands of Shias and Hazaras who continue to suffer is to receive a land acknowledgement, a sincere and heartfelt apology from those in power as well as people who benefit from their oppression, meaningful compensation, and a strong commitment to make life better and safer for the Shia Hazara groups in Afghanistan. In addition, a land acknowledgement does not achieve any significant outcome if we do not change our actions and behaviours towards Indigenous perspectives, ways of life, and trauma. A land acknowledgement is not just to show appreciation but, more importantly, to learn, unlearn, and relearn one of Canada's most hurtful times in history.

I may be living on the colonized territories of Indigenous people, but I shall remain determined and purposeful in my journey to challenge and dismantle the patriarchy. Through meaningful self-reflection and Indigenous land-based studies, I hope to bring a positive change to society and to myself, and in the ways I see myself and those around me. By writing my decolonial stories, I hope to discover how I can effectively use my past and my identity as a Hazara Shia Imami Ismaili colour settler feminist woman to find meaning in life.

RESPONSIBILITIES FOR DECOLONIZATION

As a colour settler refugee woman, I learned from my Indigenous studies that every Canadian's responsibility is to learn, unlearn, relearn, communicate, and engage in Indigenous matters (Corntassel, 2012; Datta, 2018). I also learned from Indigenous and decolonial readings how we need to act collectively to bring positive change and take responsibility for understanding and implementing Indigenous meanings of decolonization and reconciliation in our everyday lives.

Through my Indigenous decolonial studies, I came to understand the significance of Indigenous research and researchers in the process of decolonization and reconciliation. The vital role Indigenous researchers play in the process of anti-colonial struggle helps us better understand and respect Indigenous history and sovereignty (Wilson et al., 2021). As non-Indigenous colour settler people, we must put Indigenous researchers at the centre of our research and studies so we can be a part of a meaningful dialogue that supports Indigenous peoples' efforts to fully regain their sovereignty and the right to self-governance. By conducting anticolonial research and studies with Indigenous researchers, we are amplifying Indigenous voices and resistance and prioritizing their liberation from oppression and racism. Indigenous researchers' works help to strengthen social and cultural institutions, protect and restore environments, revitalize languages and cultures, and rebuild leadership and governance structures (Smith, 2021).

As a colour settler woman who experienced racism and discrimination at a young age and learned the colonial histories towards Indigenous peoples in Canada, I can understand how significant it is to challenge colonial thoughts and perspectives. I feel I need to take responsibility for learning about colonial history and the challenges that come along with it. Without decolonial education, we may not be able to undo the colonial events of the past. I learned from Indigenous Elders and Indigenous readings that land-based Indigenous teachings as decolonial education would enable us to raise awareness and educate new generations to prevent similar genocide against Indigenous people and people of colour.

When I first came to Canada, I had minimal to no knowledge of Canada's history with Indigenous peoples. In my journey of learning about decolonization and reconciliation responsibilities, I learned that decolonization is an ongoing process of anticolonial struggle that gives Indigenous people the voice to speak up about the challenges they face daily (Wilson et al., 2021). It is about learning, unlearning, acknowledging, respecting, and honouring those who bore the burden of hardships before us (Datta, 2018). Decolonization is neither a concept nor an event but a lifelong process of welcoming, including, and healing (Datta, 2018; Wilson, 2008). It is about learning history and trying not to make the same errors again, learning instead from Indigenous people (Battiste, 2013). I am unsure if it is possible to heal generations of people who have gone through so much pain and loss; however, I would like to take responsibility to do my part to work together towards Indigenous peoples' sovereignty and their right to live and make their own decisions.

One of the effects of colonization I (as a native person of Afghanistan) face is the loss of fluency in my native language. In schools and public spaces in Afghanistan, we Hazaras were constantly made ashamed of our language, Hazaragi. The people of Afghanistan have zero respect for the minor languages spoken across the country. My mother tongue was always seen as invalid and less worthy. We could not speak our language freely in public because it would bring us and those around us embarrassment. It makes me sad and angry that I fully cannot comprehend

Hazaragi today due to the linguistic cleansing I experienced in Afghanistan. It was a clear example of assimilating an ethnic group into mainstream society. While we Hazaras were made uncomfortable speaking our language outside, we felt at peace when we were among our own people because we had the freedom to speak our language. We felt most connected to our culture and roots when there was nobody to mock or punish for speaking our language.

While learning about history in an academic setting is important, it is even more important to learn Indigenous histories from Indigenous Elders, knowledge keepers, and leaders. This learning process needs to be respectful. In most cases, academic readings may not be able to inform the truth. Often, Western academic books written by settler scholars misrepresent histories. Therefore, people should not entirely rely on these books; they should ask Elders and community leaders for accurate information and guidance. As a Hazara student in Kabul, I was never taught the history of the Hazara genocide and persecution in school. Our history books were full of heroic stories of Pashtun leaders who would go to battlefields and conquer other peoples' lands and homes. I did not find those stories heroic or inspiring, nor did I think of those leaders as "heroes"; rather, I think of them as murderers for destroying and killing innocent people, both inside and outside Afghanistan. Since my academic books did not discuss the Hazara genocide, I would always turn to my parents and siblings for true, reliable, and lived experiences and knowledge. I believe the absence of accurate information and reports on Hazara persecution is the reason the world is so silent towards a genocide that has cost the Hazara community far too many lives for far too many years. Similarly, the history of Indigenous peoples in Canada and the colonial ways of life forced on Indigenous peoples are not discussed as early as they could be in schools. Therefore, we must try to put our Elders and knowledge keepers at the centre of our decolonization journey to avoid further disappointments from academic institutions.

Learning about the process of decolonization is as equally important as implanting what we learn in our daily lives. What we learn in academic settings should be the first step in our journey of decolonization. The next and most important step is how we actually utilize our knowledge and put it into action in our daily lives. It is crucial to ask ourselves, do we discuss what we learn in school with our family members? Standing up to racism against Indigenous peoples in all places should be encouraged as there is no real benefit to studying Indigenous studies if we do not break the vicious cycle of colonization.

A historic policy in the history of Canada's mistreatment of Indigenous peoples is the formation of the *Indian Act* (Joseph, 2018). Created in 1876 by European colonizers, the *Indian Act* attempted to assimilate, eliminate, destroy, and control every aspect of Indigenous cultures and identities (Joseph, 2018). Its primary goal was to create colonial laws and legislation that would coerce Indigenous peoples to assimilate into the new Euro-Canadian society where white power prevailed (Leslie, 2002). Through the implementation of this act, countless Indigenous peoples witnessed the undermining of their cultures, identities, languages, traditions, and practices.

I have learned that the *Indian Act* gave the federal government unwavering power to control and manipulate Indigenous rights, freedoms, and sovereignty for decades. I have also learned that one of the powers given to the federal policymakers was the establishment of residential schools across Canada. Residential schools in Canada were government-funded religious schools that were established to "educate" and "civilize" Indigenous children. I have learned that the residential school system was an extensive boarding school system set up and run by the government of Canada and administered by churches from the 1880s to 1996. The colonial objective was to educate Indigenous children as a way to assimilate them into mainstream white Canadian society. It was intended to indoctrinate young Indigenous generations into Euro-Canadian and Christian ways of life. The residential school system was perpetrated to decimate the Indigenous population and remove their cultures and traditions from Canada (Gray, 2011). The annihilation of the Indigenous population and cultures could only be substantially carried out by implementing the residential school system because it was convenient to assimilate and "civilize" Indigenous children at a young age.

From my Indigenous readings, I have learned that the Sixties Scoop was another distressing historical attempt to assimilate and eliminate Indigenous identity and cultures (Stevenson, 2020). The Sixties Scoop refers to the thousands of Indigenous children who were forcefully taken from their homes and families and put in foster care only to be adopted by white families. This act was particularly effective at assimilation because young Indigenous children were made to live with white families so they would be more immersed in settler culture and leave their Indigenous cultures behind.

Another major learning tool in decolonization and reconciliation is the Truth and Reconciliation Commission Calls to Action (2015). This document highlights the importance of honouring the treaties and respecting the sovereignty of Indigenous peoples. Learning the 94 Calls to Action is an effective way of learning, relearning, and unlearning colonized teachings. Decolonization should, for example, place Indigenous communities at the centre when conducting research on their lives. I have learned that Indigenous communities should be consulted and included in every decision that is going to affect them, for who can better understand their needs than Indigenous people themselves.

As a student, community member, colour settler woman, and family member, it is my responsibility to educate myself on Indigenous matters. I am responsible for challenging the patriarchy by learning, unlearning, and relearning Indigenous history and colonial policies and laws. When I am educated enough and brave enough to question Canada's treatment of Indigenous peoples, I will be able to set an example for other newcomers who come to Canada unaware of its painful history.

RESPONSIBILITIES FOR RECONCILIATION

Through my learning from Indigenous readings, I understand that Canada and those in power have failed Indigenous peoples on multiple occasions throughout history, but now is the time to reverse this (Eyford, 2016). Indigenous history is unique, and there is so much we can learn and apply in all aspects of our lives. Every person and every culture represents Canada as a diverse and multicultural nation; therefore, their protection should be a collective responsibility of all Canadians.

Reconciliation is neither an event nor a trend but a lifelong collective goal that requires a collaborative approach in the battle to fight colonization and achieve Indigenous sovereignty (Wilson et al., 2021). It will be accomplished if we all work together as a collective society. In my learning journey to decolonization and reconciliation, I learned that Indigenous people do not need to reconcile with the government; it is the government that needs to do their part in making changes and corrections to how they approach Indigenous peoples' right to live, be on the land, and exercise sovereignty (Wilson, 2008). I learned from my Indigenous readings and Elders that the government is responsible for building trust between various government platforms and Indigenous peoples. It must make sure that every Indigenous person's voice is heard and their needs met. By emphasizing the importance of reconciliation, we can correct and stop the misunderstandings, stereotypes, lack of trust and respect, and negligence among Canadians regarding Indigenous people, their past trauma, and their future.

The TRC is an example of a reconciliation method that addresses the ongoing social, economic, psychological, and physical impacts of residential schools on survivors, victims, and families. I have learned that the main goal of the TRC is to provide a path for the government and all citizens of this country to create a joint vision of reconciliation. Our responsibility to learn from the TRC can bring all people together despite their differences in one circle to address the issues and challenges faced by Indigenous peoples for decades and find meaningful yet effective solutions. Reconciliation must concern people of all cultures, history, and backgrounds. One of the first steps towards reconciliation that I learned from Indigenous Elders is the dedicated discussion of what reconciliation means and why it should matter to every person in this society. The re-education and cultural regeneration processes are critical to building trust between Indigenous peoples and the government (Datta, 2019). I have also learned that when trust is built, treaties are respected and honoured, and stories and truth are heard across the country, we are one step closer to achieving the goal of decolonization and reconciliation (Datta, 2019). When I learn about this process, I feel like I am beginning to build my belongingness with the land and Indigenous people.

Indigenous representation in all aspects of life, such as economic, social, and political, must be encouraged and respected. While there is a Western perspective to problems, there is also an Indigenous perspective. When approaching a task or a challenge, it is necessary to understand that there can be more than one way to approach problems. Similarly, in Indigenous cultures, there is not only one truth but many. One of the serious contemporary challenges we are facing today is climate change. Indigenous knowledge keepers and Elders have the knowledge and experience that we need to fight climate change. Climate change has become a real challenge for many Indigenous families, affecting their lives and livelihoods. It is affecting Indigenous lands, waters, and territories the most. Protecting these elements of life should be our collective goal since they are sacred and a symbol of a spiritual connection with nature. Hence, it is extremely important that Indigenous leaders take the lead on this issue because Indigenous communities are more vulnerable to climate change given their lifestyles and geography. When climate change is affecting Indigenous communities the most in Canada, the United States, and around the world, those in power need to include Indigenous leaders in all matters.

I have come to understand that if one wants to explore topics such as nature, land, and sustainability, one must work with local Indigenous communities. Through local perspectives, we will be able to correct the misunderstandings and misrepresentations that exist in our communities. If we want to build a connection with the land, we must first understand our spiritual connection with the land and what the land means to us. Traditional experiences and knowledge, customs, and cultures of Indigenous communities can be a useful tool in combatting issues such as sustainability and environmental issues. After all, climate change is a real threat to our planet; we must welcome every perspective and all the help we can get on this issue.

I feel privileged to have the opportunity to learn about Indigenous history and struggle for sovereignty and freedom. Unfortunately, hundreds of newcomers come to Canada every year who never get the chance to reflect upon Canada's history. Providing new Canadian citizens with accurate information to learn about Indigenous history will go a long way to supporting efforts towards decolonization. I see it as my responsibility to encourage the federal and provincial governments to provide funding to social and educational programs that will boost newcomers' knowledge of Canada and its history with Indigenous peoples.

CONCLUSION

Indigenous communities have profound and unique histories. It takes all of us as a collective community to work hard to ensure that Indigenous people have access to necessities. Providing safe neighbourhoods and genuine opportunities that will lead to progress of Indigenous inclusion must be a joint vision for all Canadians. The process of decolonization may seem a long and heart-wrenching one, but if we truly believe that we are all in this together, if in different roles, and want to bring change, we can achieve our goal, individually and collectively, by taking small but bold and concrete steps. From standing up to racism and discrimination to holding our government and leaders responsible, we can make Canada a better place for every Canadian, a Canada that is peaceful, inclusive, and tolerant of all races and backgrounds.

After writing my decolonial stories and my own experiences of racism and discrimination, I feel I am beginning to establish my belongingness with these Indigenous lands. Crafting this chapter has helped me to look deeper into my own hidden, unconscious biases against Indigenous people and people of colour, as well as prejudices I direct at myself. I am finally beginning to feel joy and pride in telling my story. I am beginning to feel more comfortable in my skin, being more appreciative of my origin and all the elements that contribute to defining my unique identity.

My decolonial stories are important to me because, first, they keep me in check with who I am and where I come from, and second, they provide me with the insight and encouragement to fight for justice and equality and to constantly try to dismantle patriarchy by challenging colonial thoughts and ways of life in everything I do. My stories inspire me to stay humble and conscious of my privileges and always remember whose land I am living on and how I should be an active part of the decolonization and reconciliation process in Canada.

While my stories help me become a better person for myself and the land I am living on, I hope others will benefit as well. My story is a tale of a young Shia Hazara Ismaili Muslim woman of colour who, despite challenges and conflicts, is still trying to explore her identity as a new Canadian on these colonized lands. I hope other young newcomers benefit from reading my stories and experiences as a refugee and a new Canadian citizen and know that they are not alone in discovering Canada's history of colonization.

To my fellow new Canadians who come to Canada in search of hope, safety, and prosperity, know that you are safer here. I understand our new life in Canada can be hectic, difficult at first, and hard to manage, but we should make some time for reading and engaging with Indigenous matters. We should make time to understand Canada's history with Indigenous peoples and what role we play in the process of decolonization and reconciliation.

REFLECTION QUESTIONS

I would like to leave my readers with a few questions in the hopes of encouraging them to be responsible towards Indigenous history and trauma.

1. What action are you taking to challenge and change your colonized thoughts and mindsets?
2. Are you spreading the information you gain about Indigenous history with your family, friends, and community?
3. It is understandable that the process of decolonization and reconciliation is correlated to dismantling the patriarchy; how can you, as an individual, see it as your responsibility to ensure we are moving forward in the right direction?

SUGGESTED READINGS

- Carleton, S. (2020). *21 things you may not know about the Indian Act: Helping Canadians make reconciliation with Indigenous Peoples a reality* by Bob Joseph, and: *Talking back to the Indian Act: Critical readings in settler colonial histories* ed. by Mary-Ellen Kelm and Keith D. Smith. *The Canadian Historical Review, 101*(4), 648–649.
- Leslie, J., Maguire, R., Moore, R. G., & Department of Indian Affairs and Northern Development. (1978). *The historical development of the Indian Act*. Government of Canada.

- Palmater, P. D. (2011). *Beyond blood: Rethinking Indigenous identity.* Purich Publishing.
- Wagamese, R. (2011). *Keeper'n me.* Anchor Canada.

REFERENCES

Battiste, M. (2013). *Decolonizing education: Nourishing the learning spirit.* UBC Press.

Corntassel, J. (2012). Re-envisioning resurgence: Indigenous pathways to decolonization and sustainable self-determination. *Decolonization: Indigeneity, Education & Society, 1*(1), 86–101.

Datta, R. (2018). Decolonizing both researcher and research and its effectiveness in Indigenous research. *Research Ethics, 14*(2), 1–24. https://doi.org/10.1177/1747016117733296

Datta, R. (Ed.). (2019). *Reconciliation in practice: A cross-cultural perspective.* Fernwood Publishing.

Eyford, R. (2016). *White settler reserve: New Iceland and the colonization of the Canadian West.* UBC Press.

Gray, R. R. R. (2011). Visualizing pedagogy and power with urban Native youth: Exposing the legacy of the Indian residential school system. *Canadian Journal of Native Education, 34*(1), 9–27. https://doi.org/10.14288/cjne.v34i1.196528

Joseph, B. (2018). *21 things you may not know about the Indian Act: Helping Canadians make reconciliation with Indigenous Peoples a reality.* Indigenous Relations Press.

Leslie, J. (2002). *The Indian Act: An historical perspective.* Canadian Parliamentary Review.

Smith, L. T. (2021). *Decolonizing methodologies: Research and Indigenous Peoples.* Bloomsbury Publishing.

Stevenson, A. (2020). *Intimate integration: A history of the Sixties Scoop and the colonization of Indigenous kinship* (Vol. 51). University of Toronto Press.

Truth and Reconciliation Commission. (2015). *Truth and Reconciliation Commission: Calls to action.*

Tuck, E., & Yang, K. W. (2012). Decolonization is not a metaphor. *Tabula Rasa,* (38), 61–111. https://doi.org/10.25058/20112742.n38.04

Wilson, S. (2008). *Research is ceremony: Indigenous research methods.* Fernwood Publishing.

Wilson, S., Breen, A. V., & DuPré, L. (2021). Mining for culture or researching for justice? Unsettling psychology through Indigenist conversation. In K. C. McLean (Ed.), *Cultural methods in psychology: Describing and transforming cultures* (pp. 410–426). Oxford University Press.

CHAPTER 12

Decolonial Lived Experiences in Bangladesh and Canada: Navigating Race and Disabilities

Tasnim Jaisee

Racism and ableism can be viewed as two sides of the same coin when it comes to recognizing oppression and hierarchies. While there have been studies done to show how race and disabilities can influence one's lived experiences, often there is a lack of understanding of the duality they bring to this discussion if one's identity involves both of these identity markers. In this chapter, I share my personal decolonial lived experiences as a woman of colour with disabilities living in Bangladesh and Canada. I speak on my lived experiences navigating my decolonial identities simultaneously while recognizing barriers of racism and ableism. In the first section, I discuss an overview of my unique experiences with my race and disabilities, having to be resilient against extreme forms of systemic oppression in action in Bangladesh, due to having a lack of accessibility to education and other aspects of my life. Moving to Canada, I began to notice that racism has transformed my racial identity as a factor that has shaped my experiences co-existing with my disabilities. Living on Treaty 6 Territories as I grew up, in my postsecondary education I began to learn more and educated myself to acknowledge the colonial harms that existed on this land and back home in Bangladesh, which was a key factor in enabling ongoing suppression. My decolonial and anti-racist stories are about my strength, self-determination, and resilience. In the second section of this chapter, I discuss the importance of decolonizing education and representational tools, specifically to address racism and ableism. Using a cross-discipline understanding of disability and critical race theory, DisCrit (Annamma et al., 2018), I discuss the necessity to decolonize our learning about race and disabilities. I also discuss the influence of the media's effects on how people misrecognize and misrepresent these issues of racism and ableism. I conclude by sharing my visions for decolonizing the need for community support and amplifying marginalized perspectives of people of colour with disabilities.

DECOLONIAL REFLECTIVE STORIES FROM BANGLADESH AND CANADA LIVED EXPERIENCES

For a long time in my life, I often found myself confused about my intersectional identities. The feeling of belonging in this world was difficult. I was either "too disabled" or "too brown" or both. In Bangladesh, I grew up acknowledging how my disabilities set me apart from children my age. While racism was an added layer of oppression that found its way to me when I moved to Canada, I also experienced ableism in the Bangladeshi community in Canada. Navigating these intersections was challenging. In an effort to revitalize my identity, I made the active choice to be resilient and feel proud to be a woman of colour with disabilities. In this section, I explain how my decolonial stories help me understand how racism and ableism are alive in our everyday practice, culture, and institutional policy in Bangladesh and Canada.

Situating Discussion

I struggled to write this chapter. I struggled because my goal is not to complain but to be critical of the lived experiences I had due to my racial and disability identity. I felt second-hand embarrassment in re-writing the stories of how people in the communities closest to me treated me. It felt as though if I spoke about these experiences, it would allow the marginalized communities around me to be negatively misunderstood. The sharing of my experiences is not to take away from the marginalization of people of colour and people with disabilities and intersecting identities. I realized that if I did not write from my heart and share my true experiences, these issues will continue to cycle systems of oppression. Writing this chapter further re-emphasized for me the need to have space for discussions on the complexities between marginalized communities and identities, along with their struggles with the larger hegemonic systems.

Navigating resilience. For me, the concept of self-resilience as a woman of colour with disabilities is not one that shifts away the critique and discourse of colonial systemic barriers. It is rather that I make an active choice in not allowing myself to internalize ableism and racism perpetuated in society against my identity. Simultaneously, I can admit this work is tiring when the whole system is full of purposeful oppression. It is a lot more than trying to find silver linings in the current state of the colonial institutions around us. The systems around us were not designed to allow marginalized folks to thrive and find success. In the midst of this tension, I find strength in recognizing the resilience of my decolonial identity. I know that I will continue to fight back against institutional harm and systems that seek to erase my experience. This does not mean spreading myself thin to prove that my existence is worth acknowledging to the world. Validation from the system does not drive me to do better. The resilience I seek for myself is one of radical self-acceptance. I know that my experiences are worth sharing. My decolonial perspectives of resilience are each moment that I am able to live authentically as a woman of colour with disabilities.

Childhood in Bangladesh

Taking a look back into my childhood, I began to see the many ways in which a lack of understanding of the intersections of disabilities creates barriers. When disabilities are not widely understood from either a medical or social perspective, it can result in further societal rejection. As my parents' first child, my birth was full of excitement and joy. I was born on a Friday, which has significant meaning in my parents' Muslim faith—Fridays are sacred and full of good fortune. This happiness and excitement soon halted with the sudden acknowledgement that something was wrong from the moment I was born. I was a baby; babies are supposed to cry the minute they are born, but my mother knew at that moment that my cries were not normal but rather cries of agony. Upon going in for multiple tests, it was found out that both my femurs, the strongest bones in the body, were immediately broken at birth. In the late '90s in Bangladesh, there were no smartphones, no easy access to the internet and information to tell my parents what was wrong with me. In a post-war country after British- and American-fuelled colonization that negatively affected the growth of every aspect of resources for the Bangladeshi people, including healthcare, my parents knew that they could only receive limited resources and answers about my condition. While my parents stayed at the hospital with me, confused and stressed about my health, there was only one doctor in the whole hospital who knew about my condition. My parents were advised by doctors that I had Osteogenesis Imperfecta (OI). OI is a rare bone disorder that causes its carriers to have very soft bones compared to the average human, meaning my bones can break very easily everywhere in my body. The slightest physical pressure would be enough to cause a fracture in any part of my body at an exponentially higher rate than the average able-bodied person. There is no cure for this condition. Doctors told my parents that I would not be able to walk or live independently and would potentially pass away in six months. While I made it past the six-month period, living in this world remains challenging.

Systemic Challenges in Bangladesh

Decolonizing disability is a direct challenge to hegemonic systems. In a racialized land such as Bangladesh where being able-bodied is normalized, being disabled goes against the status quo of society. In the environments I grew up in, it was ingrained in me that if I do not speak about my experiences and just continue to focus on life's successes, that everything would fall into place. This is not the reality. While I was too young to know the word "ableism," I knew it existed around me in every moment of my life. Ableism is defined by Merriam-Webster (n.d.) as "discrimination or prejudice against individuals with disabilities." Runcan (2022) describes ableism towards people with disabilities as the oppression that spreads over "attitudinal, economic, environmental, and institutional barriers" through "dependency, exclusion, isolation, and segregation" (p. 58). Ableism can seep into every type of social relationship and interaction. As soon as I was able to start making sense of the world, I recognized how people looked at me from a very young age. Even children my age understood the discrepancies of how different I was compared to able-bodied children. I was far from "normal." I heard it all, including that it would be better if I hadn't been born. It is comments like this that have unfortunately stuck with me into my adulthood. It was unsafe for me to be around other people who did not understand my condition. The outside world in Bangladesh was often not accessible; I didn't even have access to go to school. I felt isolated and dysphoric from a very young age. In a country with a massive lack of resources and education, disabled children in Bangladesh are frowned upon as an added burden to society—a hindrance. Emotional pain came attached to the physical pain. I knew I was different; I could not walk, and I was much shorter than average children my age. I was seen as so far from the aesthetics of "normalcy." The stares and comments were based on disgust and repulsion. Sheer looks of horror that said I was an awful sight to see. I did not have control over the ways my disabilities impacted my body. They gave me the opportunity to observe not only how my community was misguided on this issue, but also how the actions of the community can negatively impact people with disabilities.

Bangladeshi Able-Bodied Parenting of a Child with Disabilities

While I have able-bodied parents, they did their best to try and understand me and help me feel supported. They could not physically experience the pain I felt but they tried to do their best to be there for me emotionally, whenever I needed them. My parents spent the early years of my life searching for answers. My femurs breaking at birth was not the end of the side effects of my health condition. Because of these health situations, I would break bones from the slightest motions or movements. I would break ribs from sneezing, break a femur from kicking a blanket off my legs, break an arm from turning to my side, and more. These fractures were unpredictable, and they were tremendously physically painful. My parents wanted to know why this happened to me and how I could get better so that I could live a life that was "normal." Normal meant not having to live in pain. My parents searched and tried to communicate with doctors all over Bangladesh and all over the world using the limited access to the internet and phones that they had at that time. It was not the norm for the average person in Bangladesh to have access to those resources in their homes at that time. Since they did not have computers or phones in our house, they would often take turns after work: one of them would come home to me, while the other would continue their research using the internet at work. My parents spent every living moment outside of work trying to take care of me and figure out a plan for me to live. I often felt this was a place of privilege for me. I know that it can be more difficult having disabled parents as a disabled child navigating this world. My able-bodied parents were able to shield me, even if minutely, from some aspects of the vicious attitudes I experienced in my childhood.

However, my parents too were unable to fully escape the grips of ableism despite being able-bodied. Often they experienced ableism through me. People told them that my disability was the equivalent of a lifelong curse. They assumed that my parents must have sinned in their past lives. These comments were a complete rejection of my identity. Selway and Ashman (1998) and Zhang and Bennett (2001), as cited by Stienstra (2002), suggest that "different religions (as well as different people within each religion) have inconsistent approaches to disability, ranging from acceptance of people with disabilities as a gift from god(s) and therefore special, to rejection of those with disabilities as a punishment from god(s)" (p. 6). These approaches overlook the experiences of people with disabilities and characterize them in a black-and-white way, through a religious lens. Colonial religious practices with ties to patriarchal religious values create internal colonization within the self. Disabilities as negative consequences for parents, family, and the community. Many times, my parents were told by family members and strangers to give me away. These comments came from a disregard for my life as a child with disabilities; both medically and socially, I was not recognized as someone worthy of life.

Disability and Education

While disability is a significant challenge/stigma in both Canada and Bangladesh, my parents had big dreams for me; they wanted me to grow and be a changemaker. My parents tried to create a cultural connection between me and this world at an early age. They wanted me to expand my mind and understand the life that surrounded me. I was taught by my mother to read in Bangla and English. When my extended family wanted to buy me a present, my parents would tell them to give me books. I would stay in my own world with my books, trying to keep my mind busy and stay occupied as a shield against the ableism I faced in this challenging world. As a child, I was fully struck down by the weights of oppression, but I was eager and curious to learn about the world outside. There were times when I used to feel powerless, and my voice was taken away by a society that was not willing to understand me. I blamed my disabilities for a lot of my shortcomings at that time, that if only I hadn't been born with these conditions, maybe life would be better and I would not feel so much pain in every aspect of my life. The moments I felt punished for having to live in this world with such conditions, books would help to alleviate those thoughts. My parents believed that education would lead to the freedom that I did not have. They hoped that I could use education to free my mind.

Complex New Beginning in Canada

At the age of seven, after years of trying to reach medical care across the world, my parents connected with Shriners Hospital in Montreal, Canada. They were the first hospital in the country that had treatment plans for children with OI. Off we went, navigating the complex immigration system and seeking a new life in Canada while I was being treated for OI. We knew the treatment would not be a cure but rather one that would make my bones stronger and slow down the worsening of my condition. It was an adventure of new beginnings and new hope. My access to education remained of high priority to my parents; they wanted me to continue with schooling, a resource that I did not have back in Bangladesh due to inaccessibility. In Canada, I was able to access education in public schooling, a concept that neither I nor my parents were able to imagine before. I was now using a wheelchair to go to school; I was learning and doing my best to "fit in." I would do my best to study for good grades, raise my hand actively in class, travel around the school freely, go on field trips, and do the everyday things children my age would do. I loved creative projects and I loved learning about history, social movements, and justice. While it felt good to be in an environment where I was not constantly belittled for who I was, this new dream life brought in new challenges. I was one of the only children of colour in the school, and one of the only children with visible disabilities. I stood out without even being able to stand up. This was a barrier my parents and I did not expect because we initially believed that coming to Canada would remove all past barriers I had in Bangladesh. While coming to Canada alleviated some issues such as access to education and healthcare, the new societal issues I was facing of ableism and racism were ones that I had to learn to navigate in my childhood.

Interactions with Non-Racialized Children with Disabilities

My parents started noticing that I was not interested in engaging with able-bodied children. They thought that going to school and participating in classes would stop the isolation I had felt back home. That was far from reality. They saw how upset I was at being rejected, not invited to birthday parties or asked on play dates. At that age, I could not understand what was happening; I felt like I was quite a social person and I felt like I had a lot of friends but I was almost never included in activities. To bring me comfort, my parents tried to send me to youth groups and hangouts full of children with disabilities. This did not bring me the comfort that they hoped for. While I did have positive interactions getting to know other children with disabilities, getting to discuss our shared experiences, often my interactions in those spaces left me feeling confused. A lot of these children in these disability-group spaces were wheelchair users like me. But I still felt excluded and uncomfortable. Initially, my parents were concerned that I was too often around able-bodied people to be able to be comfortable around people with disabilities. I still was not able to explain to them how I was truly feeling.

It took me until my adulthood to recognize why I have turned away from those youth-disability spaces. While we had shared identity markers, my race was a part of my identity that I could not simply hide. Often as the only child of colour in the youth disability spaces, I faced unfortunate backhanded compliments and microaggressions. Comments about my skin, my hair, and misconceptions about my culture and background made me feel excluded and hurt, mostly because I could not understand where it was coming from. I thought this space would make me feel safe—after all, we all faced the same adversities, did we not? We all had disabilities, so what made our experiences so different?

Interactions with Bangladeshi Communities in Canada

At times I felt similarly excluded when I would try to connect with Bangladeshi community groups; our shared racial identities brought us closer but my disabilities created distance between me and able-bodied people of colour. The Bangladeshi communities around me were often very kind in their interactions with my able-bodied parents until it came to factors that involved me. For example, community gathering through sharing food is a big part of Bangladeshi culture. My family expected to be uninvited from large dinners, with the hosts claiming that my wheelchair would take up too much space in the house or venue. For the dinner invites that we did receive, often children would be asked to hang out upstairs, without considering accessibility. This would leave me quietly isolated from children my age and instead sitting with my parents for the whole gathering. These exclusionary tactics, whether implicit or explicit, made me feel excluded from my community, the community that I longed to be a part of as a person of colour.

Adulthood as a Racialized Woman with Disabilities in Canada

During my childhood and growing into adulthood, I often envisioned that if I did all the "right things" in life, such as getting educated and starting a career, everything would fall into place, and I would no longer face ableism or racism. This was not the case. Ableism and racism did not just stop; they continued in every corner of my life. My first professional job interview was a unique experience. I was all ready and excited to speak to the hiring managers but when I arrived at the location, I was met with a flight of stairs as the only entrance into the building. I was told by the hiring managers that we would simply head to a nearby cafe across the street to do the interview. Little did they know that it was my first time crossing a street by myself as up until then I had always had a caregiver support me when I was mobilizing outside. I remember my heart beating and feeling extremely uncomfortable because, at the same time, I felt that I could not ask for a push on my chair to cross the street as that would make me look dependent and unable to do things for myself. I have too many memories of barriers such as this. It is not just isolated incidents of discriminatory intent from people, but also physical barriers that have sought to hold me back.

Another very recent memory I have of facing racism and ableist discrimination occurred when I accidentally dropped my cell phone on the ground right in front of my workplace. I asked a passerby to kindly pick it up for me, as I am usually unable to pick things up from the ground. I was told no and questioned whether I was the owner of the cell phone in the first place. I was being targeted for my identity. Interactions like these are hurtful but often too representative of how people of colour with disabilities are viewed in society. Too often we are used to seeing people with identities like mine represented negatively as having sinister or malicious intentions or as untrustworthy, simply because they are "different." We do not fit in the status quo of "successful" adults who are simply trying to get by and live their lives. These types of barriers are discouraging towards people of colour with disabilities, and it takes an active choice and desire for us to continue to fight against a society that perpetuates these oppressive stereotypes.

I have spent a lot of time in my adulthood trying to understand the many ways in which my identities connect and conflict with one another. It has helped me to make sense of the frustration I feel living in world that benefits whiteness and able bodies. It has been an ongoing journey of unlearning and learning. In Bangladesh, as a woman belonging to the dominant racial group while having disabilities, I did not experience racism but I did experience ableism. In Canada, I faced the dual identity markers of being part of a marginalized racial group and a disabled person, while still experiencing ableism in Bangladeshi communities in Canada. In order to navigate these identities, I continued to challenge myself to become a decolonized learner and actively seek to challenge the systems around me.

DECOLONIZED AND INTERSECTIONAL COMMUNITIES' IMPACTS ON MY LIVED EXPERIENCES

A large part of my life was spent without a community that recognized my experiences as a disabled woman of colour. I was often isolated, confused, and conflicted about my experiences. I felt safer living in my shell, away from interactions. Being unable to fit into communities made me lonely and my dissatisfaction with myself grew. I was internalizing the ableism and racism I received as a consequence of the rejection I felt. The isolation I felt from being rejected from various communities and groups was only healed when I found communities that were accepting of my intersectional identity. In this section I explain the need for intersectional community empowerment, which supported me in challenging ongoing systemic racism and ableism. Without this support, I would be isolated and I would not have the courage to share my perspectives with the world. I emphasize the importance of intersectional community support to uplift each other's voices towards a more inclusive future.

My desire to seek out community support grew stronger, and it wasn't until I took classes in my postsecondary educational journey in intersectional feminist studies that I discovered the language to articulate my frustrations. I began to understand the colonial mindsets that surrounded us in these institutions and related them to my lifelong experiences in both Canada and Bangladesh. I finally had the language to speak my feelings. I was starting to become more aware of a representational gap in content published by and about people of colour with disabilities. It was not until well into my adulthood that I found community spaces that accepted me for who I was. Community strength holds the power to navigate layers of oppression; chosen families led me to find my voice again. I wanted to be a part of the communities that shared my lived experiences. I met some of the best people by exploring my intersectional identities and speaking to people who wanted to see me succeed as much as I wanted them to succeed as well. I later recognized my identities as a part of me that make me who I am. It took a long time for me to understand that my race and disabilities are powerful identities, and that no one could ever take that away from me.

As an adult, I wanted to live in an inclusive world, full of communities that valued decolonized mindsets and intersectional understandings of the world. I wanted to live in a world where everyone can feel safe being themselves, embracing their identities and living unconditionally as themselves. I knew that if I did not speak up, no one would. I chose to enrol in a postsecondary education stream that gave me the opportunity to write about these topics within political and gender studies. I was later elected as president of the student union at my campus, and I was the first woman of colour and the first person with visible disabilities to take the seat in the university's history. From there, I sought to continue working in the equity, diversity, and inclusion sectors and continue to challenge system structures in my path ahead.

For a more equitable future, we must create a sense of community built on supporting and providing safe spaces for people with disabilities and people of colour. I share my stories as part of this discussion to uplift decolonial perspectives through intersections of race and disabilities in my childhood and adulthood. Each day was an active choice for me to keep on living and pushing against the current system. My identity is of strength and power, no matter how much the system wants to hold me back. We as people of colour with disabilities have existed since the beginning of time and will continue to exist. It is up to us to make others recognize our perspectives and values. Allies must create space to amplify our perspectives. We cannot be equitable without inclusionary practices for all people of colour with disabilities.

WHY DO WE NEED DECOLONIAL EDUCATION AND REPRESENTATION?

From my lived experiences in my twenties, I have learned that decolonial education and representation are useful ways to challenge systemic racism and ableism. Being brought up in an environment that did not embrace those values made it really difficult to understand systemic barriers in my way. Through my decolonial learning, I have learned that to create inclusive practices for people with disabilities and diverse racial identities, society must understand these identities on an individual basis, but also address the ways in which systemic barriers overlap and oppress these identities. Using recent studies, I am going to explain why we need decolonial and anti-racist perspectives in order to understand systemic racism and disability in our everyday practice. We need to see the concept of disability from decolonial and anti-racist perspectives.

Intersectional scholar Crenshaw (1991) discusses the history of social movements often leaving out intersectional identities. She expresses the tensions between marginalized communities and their identities when they seek to dominate each other in competition. She noted that studying identities together should "be the source of empowerment and reconstruction" (p. 1250). When identities are pitted against each other based on imbalanced prioritization, this causes space for harm. Rather than competing against each other, being aware of our shared struggles allows for a more comprehensive approach to dismantling barriers through implementable action.

Disability Critical Race Theory (DisCrit) is a framework to understand how the interconnected struggles of racism and ableism act parallel to one another, which can allow the development of a new understanding of how we recognize the works of intersectional identities (Annamma et al., 2018). Annamma et al. (2018) emphasize that the DisCrit framework must work concurrently with other critical theories. This framework identifies the ways in which racism and ableism interact with each other to disenfranchise and disempower. Annamma et al. (2018) also highlight the importance of affirming the knowledge generated from these communities. Similarly to Crenshaw, Annamma et al. (2018) mention that DisCrit recognizes that some identities hold more power than others, and identify the system's eagerness to place different identities at odds with one another to ensure continued marginalization. I know that if we can create a comprehensive tool for education surrounding disabilities and race, we can begin to seek the proper tools to dismantle these barriers. Far too often, society will only uplift one set of voices from marginalized communities when in reality, different people have many different intersectionalities and lived experiences.

There are many ways colonial practices mark disabilities and racialized minorities as inferior identities. Colonialism often seeks to only give power and value to individuals based on their output of productivity. Simultaneously, colonial values are inherently built on disenfranchising racial and disability groups. This means that people with disabilities are held back from receiving equitable opportunities while being labelled as unfit to provide to the capitalist system. Imada (2017) broadly speaks of the history of how colonial regimes' "perceived unproductivity as laborers; embodied racial-sexual differences; 'unchaste' proclivities of their women; susceptibility to moral contagion and infectious diseases; or inability to learn" (para. 2). Imada's research explores how colonizers deemed people with marginalized identities as inferior and unfit to survive. Being deemed worthy of value by the colonial system is dependent on how much labour one can contribute to the hegemonic system. Those who cannot provide labour are marked as lesser than.

Stereotyping race and disability into simplified and categorized identities plays a big role in determining how people of colour with disabilities are viewed. I have experienced that when people of colour with disabilities are not able to share their dual lived experiences with accurate portrayals, negative stereotyping can occur. There is no one way to be disabled and no one way to embrace your race. For instance, Mercado (2019) discusses the importance of teaching students in the classroom that the media has a certain agenda in mind about who they want to present as successful (i.e., white, able-bodied, etc.). When students are able to recognize these patterns, they have the tools to challenge these narratives from the beginning and identify more intersectional examples. I often felt that if the children around me were more receptive and understanding of my racial and disabled identity, I would have felt more comfortable in my educational experiences. Children are not inherently ableist or racist; these are concepts that they are taught.

Attention to race and disability intersections can allow us to be a more cognizant society that is aware of our issues first-hand. For example, findings from Horner-Johnson et al. (2021) show the need for growing care when it comes to women of colour with disabilities and their health needs, especially for reproductive healthcare. Some healthcare providers may prioritize providing reproductive care to white women based on personal biases. These assumptions about health can be detrimental to one's autonomy. Another ongoing example can be found in workplaces that failed to provide disability and race-based care during the COVID-19 pandemic. Bowleg (2020) expresses that the pandemic disproportionately affected racial minority groups such as Black Americans. People with disabilities also tended to be vulnerable to the effects of the pandemic health-wise. Two identity markers caused greater harm to people of colour with disabilities, yet there is limited information about the impact of the pandemic on people with disabilities. Once again, issues have been minimized through the erasure of intersectional voices.

Annamma et al. (2013), as cited by Beneke (2021), distinguish features of how DisCrit explains the conceptualization of race and disability in children's development. First, being non-white and able-bodied is generally desirable. Next, there is a lack of educational opportunities to learn the intersections of race and disabilities. Challenges related to race and disability have been ingrained in society, with historical precedents particularly impacting children. Furthermore, dominant racial identities and able-bodied traits serve as property with advantage. Lastly, the experiences of children of colour with disabilities must be acknowledged. These facets encompass the need for DisCrit as an active subject of discussion with an ongoing impact on the growth of children's understandings of race and disabilities.

Living in a colonial system full of racism and ableism, my life is also directly connected with the above studies. For instance living in Bangladesh, able-bodied children were very aware of my disabilities. I was considered to be a part of the dominant and hegemonic race in Bangladesh, so I did not face active racial discrimination, but I did face ableism. This experience quickly changed in my interactions with able-bodied and white children in Canada, where my identity was being picked apart on two different levels. Further complexities occurred when I experienced forms of racism in disability safe spaces, as most of the children in the space were not used to interacting with children of colour. Simultaneously, interacting with able-bodied children of colour in Canada still led to differential treatment as my disabilities impacted their perspectives of me. While the examples I have used for this discussion related to experiences in my childhood, the same patterns were replicated in some of my adulthood experiences as well. I think about how different my life would be if I had had the tools to learn these concepts at an earlier age, rather than only learning about how my race and disabilities intersect only when I reached postsecondary education. I feel that I would have been much better equipped to handle the barriers I faced throughout my life.

I believe that being brought up with an understanding of my intersecting identities would have made me better equipped to navigate my life. I grew up feeling frustrated with the unfairness, wondering what my life would be like without my racial identity and disabilities. Yet I did not understand why I despised my identities like this. I saw myself as a burden to everyone around me, including myself; I believed there was something inherently wrong with me. I believed that I did not deserve to feel comfortable in my own skin or in my sense of self.

I had all sorts of internalized ableist and racist perceptions towards myself from a very young age. Children are prone to understanding differences when it comes to race and disability. This is not a bad thing. When we choose to actively ignore identities, they in turn become minimized experiences. The issue begins when certain races and/or abilities start to gain power over one another, in this case, whiteness and able-bodiedness. Children are not inherently born racist or ableist. These concepts are created to form hierarchies. They are ingrained into us from a young age to replicate the needs of oppressive structures.

Decolonial education has to be a lifelong journey. We must be ready to constructively critique academic institutions. Bhakta (2020) acknowledges the push for postsecondary academia to move towards inclusion and diversity. However, race and disability as a combined conversation have often received little attention, fuelled by the "absence or invisibility" of racialized scholars. They go on to explain that the barriers that allow the alienation of students of colour with disabilities in academic institutions can help us recognize the various issues at play for what they are. Additionally, it is mentioned that only a limited number of scholars can break through institutional barriers, which allows them to have limited access to the benefits of academia itself. As a woman of colour with disabilities, I also acknowledge the critique of DisCrit itself. Jaulus (2020) mentions the need to include perspectives from the disability rights activism of the Global South in its discussion to further include transnational understandings such as race and class in DisCrit. Real systemic change must be one that values all perspectives. This journey of intersectionality in understanding how to better reflect on disability and race must be ongoing.

Being a decolonial and anti-racist learner, I faced many of these barriers myself as a student of colour. While the team of the disability services office did seek to support me in my education, the barriers often became very frustrating as they piled up with ongoing and continuous structural and institutional issues. The uphill battle often became exhausting from inaccessible classrooms, washrooms, and study spaces, and a lack of resources on racial sensitivity and diverse ways of understanding and knowing. What kept me moving forward was hopes of a better future for myself and all, especially the future generations of our society. These efforts cannot be made alone. There is strength in numbers in building anti-racism and disability activism communities. Thorius and Waitoller (2017) discuss the importance of initiating pedagogies that specifically target exclusion on the basis of intersectional identities. To eliminate systemic barriers from our daily lives, it is essential to grasp the complexities of intersectional challenges, including those related to race, gender, and disabilities.

From my experiences, I learned that amplifying the voices of people of colour with disabilities has to be done in a way where both of the identities are recognized as having unique experiences as well as shared struggles. To liberate people of colour with disabilities is to understand that they cannot pick and choose which identity they want for the day. Both of these identities have to be simultaneously addressed in order to accurately represent the barriers faced by these communities.

MY VISION OF HOW TO MOVE FORWARD

In fostering anti-racist and decolonial disability activist communities, we must seek to acknowledge dual identities as intersecting with one another. To be open to learning and sharing knowledge with one another. For this conversation of intersectionality, race and disability have to coexist. Living in dichotomies and binaries is often what colonial institutions and structures want us to seek out. Simplistic answers to complex questions are not the way these layered issues are resolved. We must be critical of how racism and ableism play an active role in our daily lives.

My journey is far from over—it is a cycle of continued resiliency. My race and disabilities are identities of power. They make me who I am. I write this discussion as an active reminder that we must work together to live in a decolonial world full of communities that are aware of the needs of people of colour with disabilities and that this knowledge can be shared with people of all identities. Education and representation must include accurate portrayals of people of colour with disabilities. It is about not just tolerance but also acceptance, and we must be unapologetic about advocating for race and disability liberation. We need to be open to actively challenging systems and creating progress.

I want to see a future where children of colour with disabilities do not have to experience the pain and hardships I did while I was growing up. Firstly, this can only be done by educating our future generations about racism and ableism and how we all have a shared responsibility to dismantle these systems. Secondly, we need to prioritize the perspectives of people of colour with disabilities in all aspects of our society. No projects to combat racism and ableism should be done without understanding the needs of the demographic. Thirdly, marginalized communities must continue fostering spaces that support decolonized perspectives and intersectional identities. There is power in numbers, and allies must continue creating the space for people of colour with disabilities.

At a point in my life, I believed that if I was able to get a job and live independently, I would finally be able to beat the oppressive forces that sought to hold me back, and the racial and accessibility barriers would naturally alleviate themselves. This was far from the truth. The battle against oppression in our current system is an active force of power. I recognize my experiences as ones that replicate themselves over multiple systems. For me, it is an ongoing journey acknowledging the current oppressive forces around us in society and being active in seeking to address them. This decolonial journey is one of continuous solidarity, uplifting one another and building relationships. Because if we don't do it, then who will?

REFLECTION QUESTIONS

1. How would you begin to introduce the concept of racism and ableism to someone who does not know about intersectionality?
2. Have you encountered any media featuring people of colour with disabilities, and was the portrayal accurate?
3. How do you think the dynamic experiences of people of colour with disabilities would change upon the addition of other identities (e.g., women of colour with disabilities, queer people of colour with disabilities, etc.)?
4. What are some of the accessibility issues you have noticed in the environment around you?

SUGGESTED READINGS

- Annamma, S. A. (2014). Disabling juvenile justice: Engaging the stories of incarcerated young women of color with disabilities. *Remedial and Special Education, 35*(5), 313–324. https://doi.org/10.1177/0741932514526785
- Gillborn, D. (2015). Intersectionality, critical race theory, and the primacy of racism: Race, class, gender, and disability in education. *Qualitative Inquiry, 21*(3), 277–287. https://doi.org/10.1177/1077800414557827
- Harpur, P. (2009). Sexism and racism, why not ableism? Calling for a cultural shift in the approach to disability discrimination. *Alternative Law Journal, 34*(3), 163–167. https://doi.org/10.1177/1037969X0903400304
- Pieper, M., & Mohammadi, J. H. (2014). Ableism and racism: Barriers in the labour market. *Canadian Journal of Disability Studies, 3*(1), 65–92. https://doi.org/10.15353/cjds.v3i1.147

REFERENCES

Annamma, S. A., Ferri, B. A., & Connor, D. J. (2018). Disability critical race theory: Exploring the intersectional lineage, emergence, and potential futures of DisCrit in education. *Review of Research in Education, 42*(1), 46–71. https://doi.org/10.3102/0091732X18759041

Beneke, M. R. (2021). Investigating young children's conceptualizations of disability and race: An intersectional, multiplane critique. *Educational Researcher, 50*(2), 97–104. https://doi.org/10.3102/0013189X21992029

Bhakta, A. (2020). "Which door should I go through?" (In)visible intersections of race and disability in the academy. *Area, 52*(4), 687–694. https://doi.org/10.1111/area.12554

Bowleg, L. (2020). We're not all in this together: On COVID-19, intersectionality, and structural inequality. *American Journal of Public Health, 110*(7), 917.

Crenshaw, K. (1991). Mapping the margins: Intersectionality, identity politics, and violence against women of color. *Stanford Law Review, 43*(6), 1241–1299. https://doi.org/10.2307/1229039

Horner-Johnson, W., Akobirshoev, I., Amutah-Onukagha, N. N., Slaughter-Acey, J. C., & Mitra, M. (2021). Preconception health risks among U.S. women: Disparities at the intersection of disability and race or ethnicity. *Women's Health Issues, 31*(1), 65–74. https://doi.org/10.1016/j.whi.2020.10.001

Imada, A. L. (2017). A decolonial disability studies? *Disability Studies Quarterly, 37*(3). https://doi.org/10.18061/dsq.v37i3.5984

Jaulus, D. (2020). Review of *DisCrit: Disability studies and critical race theory in education* by David J. Connor, Beth A. Ferri & Subini A. Annamma, Eds. (2016). *Canadian Journal of Disability Studies, 9*(5), 554–558. https://doi.org/10.15353/cjds.v9i5.709

Mercado, A. (2019). Mediated images of success: Hegemonic media representations and social justice. *Communication Teacher, 33*(2), 94–98. https://doi.org/10.1080/17404622.2018.1500701

Merriam-Webster. (n.d.). Ableism. In *Merriam-Webster.com dictionary*. Retrieved May 11, 2023, from https://www.merriam-webster.com/dictionary/ableism

Runcan, R. (2022). The ablism: Impairment, disability, handicap. *Revista de Asistență Socială, 21*(1), 55–64.

Stienstra, D. (2002). *The intersection of disability and race/ethnicity/official language/religion.* Canadian Centre on Disability Studies, University of Winnipeg.

Thorius, K. A. K., & Waitoller, F. R. (2017). Strategic coalitions against exclusion at the intersection of race and disability—A rejoinder. *Harvard Educational Review, 87*(2), 251–257.

PART IV

BLACK AND ASIAN IMMIGRANT COMMUNITY REFLECTIONS ON DECOLONIZATION IN PRACTICE

Both Black and Asian immigrants' perspectives on decolonization are critical, particularly in relation to the current Black Lives Matter movement and COVID-19 pandemic. These chapters discuss how decolonial understanding and practices can be beneficial for all. Students, teachers, and all other professionals will have the opportunity to read community reflections, continue critical discussions, and reflect on their own lives.

1. Focusing on sub-Saharan African immigrant communities in western Canada, **John B. Acharibasam** and **Ranjan Datta** explore why researchers need to decolonize the meaning of climate research, who we are as environmental researchers, and how we need to be.
2. Focusing on working-class senior residents and allies in Chinatown, **Jade Ho** explores why aligning anti-racism efforts are important for a decolonial community.

CHAPTER 13

Decolonizing Meanings of Climate Risks: A Learning Experience from and within Sub-Saharan African Immigrant Communities' Perspectives in Western Canada

John B. Acharibasam and Ranjan Datta

As part of an ongoing study, this chapter adopts decolonizing phenomenology to examine how sub-Saharan African immigrants in western Canada, Alberta and Saskatchewan, cope with increasing climate disaster risks. Our research with sub-Saharan African immigrant communities in western Canada helps us understand why we need to decolonize the meaning of climate research, who we are as environmental researchers, and how we need to be. Both researchers took responsibility for learning from the communities and implementing our learning into our practices in significant ways to understand the meanings of decolonization. Following decolonizing phenomenology as our research framework, we used four research methods, such as story sharing, informal conversation, and reflective writing. The findings of this chapter show why we need to relearn and redo the meanings of climate change research from and within community everyday practice to build decolonial communities. This chapter is part of a more extensive study of BIPOC communities in Canada, particularly the western part of Canada (i.e., Alberta and Saskatchewan). This study focused on sub-Saharan African immigrant communities in Saskatchewan and Alberta. Our goals were to learn decolonial community perspectives about some of the extreme climate events that sub-Saharan African immigrants have experienced in their communities; know the decolonial strategies they have adopted to cope and the challenges they face in adapting to extreme climates; and relearn the capacity of the community to adapt to climate change and identify available resources within their communities to help cope with climate risks. The Indigenous researchers who were part of this study investigated the impacts of climate change on First Nations and Métis communities.

Following a decolonial phenomenology theoretical framework, we collected data through story-sharing, informal conversation, and reflective writing. Our chapter goals are interconnected with both the Paris agreement and the United Nations Sustainable Development Goal 13, to which Canada is a signatory, a task for all countries to take urgent action to combat climate change and its impacts (Government of Canada, 2022; Gupta & Vegelin, 2016; Nerini et al., 2019).

WHY DO WE NEED DECOLONIAL PERSPECTIVES?

Black, Indigenous, and people of colour (BIPOC) are Canada's fastest-growing population segments, yet Canada's climate change (CC) solutions fail to meet their needs (Ford et al., 2010; Ford et al., 2006; Simmons, 2020; Waldron, 2021a; Walker, 2021). CC research has primarily focused on technical solutions and physical infrastructure. However, little is known about how social context and relations affect the capacity of BIPOC communities to adapt to CC. CC policies in Canada are also often drafted from a Western colonial perspective. No BIPOC community-led policy in Canada responds to CC, which is a glaring oversight, especially in the era of the Black Lives Matter movement and threats related to pandemics (e.g., COVID-19) and natural disasters. Increasing the resilience of Black populations is instrumental in enhancing their capacity to adapt to the extreme effects of climate change. As Walker (2021) states, Canada must take urgent steps to address the impacts of climate change on vulnerable populations, including children. Recent times have witnessed an unprecedented increase in extreme climatic events, including snowstorms, floods, forest fires, droughts, and heatwaves in western Canada, and these have had devastating impacts on immigrants and other marginalized populations, threatening their ability to cope with climate disaster risks. The Climate Action Network (2020) observes that the regions of western Canada are very vulnerable to climate change-related extreme weather events. The International Institute for Sustainable Development (2022) also concludes that extreme weather events in the Prairie regions of Canada "such as heat waves, droughts, floods, and intense storms are projected to increase in intensity and frequency" (para. 1). Coupled with this, some of the land-use activities that have been identified as contributing more to climate change are predominant within the prairie provinces. As DeMarco (2021, as cited in Zimonjic, 2021) observes, together with Newfoundland and Labrador, Alberta and Saskatchewan "produce 97 percent of Canada's oil and gas" (para. 10). The Intergovernmental Panel on Climate Change (IPCC, 2022) report on impacts, adaptation, and vulnerability has highlighted how climate change is impacting vulnerable populations around the world and the need to enhance their adaptive capacity. Additionally, there are calls "to minimize exposure to disasters and enhance resilience and adaptive capacity" (Gupta & Vegelin, 2016, p. 442). As Waldron (2021b) observes, climate change exacerbates health inequities among Mi'kmaw and African Nova Scotian communities.

In summary, we argue that specific climate solutions tailored to the unique needs of BIPOC populations are needed to enhance their capacity to adapt to increasing climate risk in western Canada.

DECOLONIAL THEORETICAL FRAMEWORK AND METHODOLOGY

For this research, we used a decolonial phenomenology theoretical framework to guide our research. Decolonial phenomenology as our research methodology allowed us to decolonize both researcher and research (Datta, 2018) and explore the phenomenon of climate change from the point of view of those experiencing it (Connelly, 2010). The decolonial research framework makes us responsible to our research community and our relationships with our co-researcher participants (Datta, 2018). As part of our responsibilities as decolonial researchers, we learned from co-researcher participants. We, as Black and colour settler researchers, considered ourselves as learners from the community. Co-researcher participants were considered experts for this research, and we were learners. Specifically, in-depth informal storytelling conversations were held with sub-Saharan immigrants (i.e., co-researchers) living in the provinces of Saskatchewan and Alberta during 2021 and 2022. We used the term "co-researchers" instead of research participants because they played active roles in the research beyond participation (Datta, 2022). We also used decolonial research methods such as story sharing, informal conversation, and reflective writing methods, which were adopted from our long-time relationships with our co-researchers (Datta, 2022; Smith, 2012). Because of the COVID-19 pandemic, we did in-person and Zoom story-sharing with our co-researchers depending on whichever one they were comfortable with and at a location of their choice. We used our ongoing relationship to find knowledgeable co-researchers for our decolonial research. We first approached a few individuals we had networks with, who in turn referred us to other co-researchers who they thought would be interested in the study. We strongly followed institutional research ethics and community research protocols.

DECOLONIAL DATA ANALYSIS

Our decolonial data analysis helped us to follow a collaborative process, involving the research team and the co-researchers in the analysis process. We adopted a thematic analysis approach to analyze the data. Thematic analysis is "a form of pattern recognition within the data, where emerging themes become the categories for analysis" (Fereday & Muir-Cochrane, 2006, p. 82). Braun and Clarke (2006) observe that it "is a method for identifying, analysing, and reporting patterns (themes) within data" (p. 6). In this decolonial data analysis, we adopted a thematic analysis approach because it is flexible and can be modified. Thus, providing "a rich and detailed, yet complex account of data" (Braun & Clarke, 2006, p. 5). The decolonial analysis process began with transcribing interviews, coding, and categorizing codes into themes. The co-researchers reviewed all codes and themes to ensure the themes truly represented their views.

DECOLONIAL FINDINGS

The community guided our decolonial findings. The collaborative analysis process led to the emergence of different themes as they relate to climate change. Community-led identified themes that emerged were extreme climatic events, extreme climatic impacts, adaptation challenges, knowledge of community resources, strengths, and resilience. In the following, we share our decolonial learning findings.

EXTREME CLIMATIC EVENTS

According to the community, we need to decolonize how we understand the meanings of extreme climatic events. For instance, the community discussed that extreme climatic events have become more frequent in Canada. Particularly in the western provinces of Saskatchewan and Alberta, where land use activities have been shown to contribute to climate change, the co-researchers described experiencing different extreme climatic events in their provinces. These extreme events included heatwaves, wildfires, colder winters, snowstorms, and droughts. As one co-researcher described,

> So, there have been many changes recently. For instance, last year's summer, we had a wildfire in the northern part of the city, and that caused lots of problems because there was air pollution in the whole city. For people with respiratory tract issues like myself, it was hard for us because I experienced allergic reactions and bronchitis, and the rest. Also, we had extreme heat, that is, the heatwave; the temperature was so high that even in the news, I heard people had serious I mean fatal issues with the heatwave. And also, the extreme snowfall, we had a snowstorm last year, and I couldn't even go to work for a couple of days. So those three experiences are what I can pinpoint. I know there are more, but these are the three major ones I can remember. (Co-researcher 1, 2022)

Another co-researcher spoke about the extreme heat and droughts experienced in the summer of 2021 in Saskatchewan by stating,

> So predominantly, it is extreme heat like really hot in the past summer, I wasn't expecting it to be that hot; it was above records. I typically drive out of town once every weekend to go to the lake, and you see all the wetlands are dried up. In my entire time here, I have never seen it. I could see huge ponds and wetlands around driving two hours out, and now it is all dry, and I am like something is really happening. (Co-researcher 5, 2022)

DECOLONIZE EXTREME CLIMATIC IMPACTS

The adverse effects of climate change are felt by everybody. However, the co-researchers face a much heavier burden because they do not have other forms of support from family or the community. We observed most of these co-researchers had no other family members within Canada, and therefore had to face these extreme events all by themselves. Based on this, the co-researchers described some of the adverse impacts these extreme climatic events had on them. These included health-related issues, impacts on their livelihoods, feeling of personal safety and security, food security, and other financial issues. For example, it emerged that some of these co-researchers suffered several health issues as a result of climate change. These health issues tend to affect their finances because they cannot work and have no other source of support. Subsequently, this also affected their food security.

A co-researcher described how reduced air quality resulting from the 2021 wildfires in Saskatchewan exacerbated her health issues and impacted her finances and food security:

> Well, I will look at it from my health first. I had bronchitis because of the air pollution from the wildfires. The whole of that week I had to be taken to the emergency because I had bronchitis and my allergies were so terrible. In fact, it even affected my eyes, my nostrils, everything. So yeah, it affected my health and finances. And now food prices have increased. (Co-researcher 1, 2022)

Due to climate change, droughts are also becoming more frequent in the prairie provinces of Saskatchewan and Alberta. This is also impacting food security within these households. Regarding food shortages resulting from the droughts experienced in 2021, a co-researcher stated,

> What touches me most is, because I am coming from the agriculture sector, anything that happens and touches the food production field really affects me, and that is the recent drought. This summer, there was a severe drought. When I drove out of Saskatoon one time into the neighbourhood, one conclusion I already made in my mind was that food production this year is going to be very low. Because if you go out of the city and you have lived in Saskatoon before, you will see what the canola looks like when it is in its regular bloom. You could see wheat growing to a particular height before they start flowering. The canola was just so stunted. (Co-researcher 2, 2022)

As among most marginalized groups, our decolonial learning outcome here is that the adverse impacts of climate change are interconnected. Given that the co-researchers had no other source of support, we found that extreme climatic events had cascading impacts on this population group. For example, health issues resulting from extreme climate impact co-researchers' finances because they could not work and had no other source of support. This affected their food security and other areas of life, including overall health and well-being.

DECOLONIAL ADAPTATION CHALLENGES

We learned that there were many challenges that impeded the co-researchers' efforts in adapting to these changing climatic events. Especially with most of our co-researchers living alone in Canada and doing jobs that paid minimum wage. These challenges affected all aspects of life in adapting to climate change.

Reporting on the financial challenges and increasing bills in coping with extreme climatic events, a co-researcher stated,

> My gas bill, would you call it my utility bill here because when it gets hot, we have to turn the AC on, with the extreme winters, I need to get winter tires because the winter is highly unpredictable. It could be very heavy, or it could be very light, depending on changes in the climate. But those are some of the things that impact me directly. The heatwave was very, very bad because it was extremely hot, nothing could cool it down. You couldn't even go for a run because you will burn out. Yeah, so like, personally, climate change affects almost every facet of my life. (Co-researcher 7, 2022)

Other important challenges were the lack of community-based resources and government policies not factoring in socioeconomic impacts on ordinary people, especially our co-researchers. The co-researchers faced challenges with government policies implemented to tackle climate change. For example, some of the co-researchers complained that there was no community-level consultation before the implementation of the federal carbon tax. As a result of this, the tax did not factor in social impacts. According to one co-researcher,

> The tax is imposed so that people who are into agriculture will know how to go about their agricultural activities such that there is less emission of gases. People into industrialization will also begin to cut down emissions of gases from whatever byproducts affect the climate. From the policy perspective, this was how they were looking at it. But as to whether the social impacts and social ramifications were carefully considered is questionable because every additional dollar deducted from whoever is producing will go to the consumer, so that is how I see it. The policy level is just looking at the bigger picture, but they don't look at the social impacts. (Co-researcher 3, 2022)

A second co-researcher concluded,

> The immigrant's opinions, I think when it comes to policy, I don't know much about Canadian policy, but it is more or less like a debate between intellectuals and politicians. Policy deliberations are more or less, even though there is community engagement, the conversations always end up between what the intellectuals think that is the scientific community like the university professors, those who do research, research organizations and then the politicians. (Co-researcher 2, 2022)

Again, we find that the challenges sub-Saharan African immigrants face in adapting to climate change are like other BIPOC populations. Besides the financial challenges, the co-researchers also reported the lack of community-level resources and marginalization in terms of government climate policies. The lack of inclusion in the climate change decision-making process leads to the implementation of policies that do not meet the specific needs of these populations.

DECOLONIAL STRENGTH AND RESILIENCE

As decolonial researchers, we learned that we need to relearn the meanings of strength and resiliency from the community so that community can guide all CC policymakers to create sustainable and meaningful climate change adaptations. Community-level resources and initiatives, social relations, and families are crucial for enhancing resilience. The co-researchers explained strength and resilience in coping with some of these extreme climatic events. Particularly, these were seen in some of the experiences they brought from their home countries and the strategies they adopted to cope with climate risk. It emerged that some of the co-researchers came to Canada with certain experiences that could be harnessed to help cope with extreme climatic events and enhance resilience. One area where the co-researchers showed strength and resilience was coping with extreme heat. As one co-researcher asked,

> Do you know of a disease called CSM (cerebrospinal meningitis)? It is related to extreme heat, so I know it hits hard every year on communities back home (Ghana). I know that in that season, there are community sensitizations on public address systems, urging people to open windows and doors at night for fresh air, you don't have to be congested in a room. That was what I did here during the extreme heat and survived it. (Co-researcher 4, 2022)

One strong theme we observed in the co-researchers' responses on strength and resilience in adapting to climate change was the need for community-based initiatives. To most co-researchers, community-based initiatives can provide the strength and resources for coping with extreme climatic events. As one co-researcher concluded,

> So, it's more like at the personal level, I'm not really sure what exactly I can do to be very impactful in this climate change agenda. For instance, can I take the bus instead of driving? Yes. But I will spend two hours getting to my job. So, it

doesn't make sense for me to do that. But if there were other community-based projects like, for instance, carpooling. And the time it takes for me to get to my place of work is relatively the same as I will drive, that will be a cheaper option, and I will definitely take up that option. So, on an individual basis, I always feel like I can't really do much. (Co-researcher 7, 2022)

Moving beyond the Western-centred climate solutions, BIPOC communities possess rich experiences, knowledge, and worldviews that can be harnessed to enhance climate resilience in Canada.

DECOLONIAL KNOWLEDGE OF COMMUNITY RESOURCES

Sub-Saharan African immigrants recognize the need for community-led resources to help cope with extreme climate events. However, the co-researchers described limited community resources available to support coping with extreme climatic events within their communities. Additionally, information on the few available resources was limited. Although they admitted that information on climate change, in general, was provided through the internet and media, they described the need for more specific information about available community resources. For example, one co-researcher described how expensive winter clothing and even tires were and the fact that there is no community support to help cope with these extreme climatic events:

> You need to buy some winter jackets, winter boots, and all those things with the extreme cold. If, for example, you were wearing a light jacket because the snow wasn't that cold in the previous years, now it is getting very colder, and we need to get heavy clothing to keep ourselves warm. We all know the cost of winter coats and jackets and boots. Yeah so, talking about the automobile you need to also keep buying winter tires. These are the basic little things that sometimes go unnoticed, we don't know. These are the impacts that affect our livelihoods, we must bear them without support. (Co-researcher 4, 2022)

Even within most organizations, some co-researchers observed there were no resources available to employees to help cope with extreme climatic events. As one co-researcher described,

> I told you I had bronchitis, and since last year because of the air pollution all around, I had to go through a series of sicknesses, and I stayed out of my job for some time. Yeah, it affected me financially. If you stay out of work past your sick leave you are on your own. (Co-researcher 1, 2022)

Empowering communities can play a key role in enhancing the capacity of BIPOC people to adapt to climate change in western Canada.

DECOLONIAL LEARNING

In this section, we discuss our decolonial learning regarding how to decolonize the meanings of CC research from the community. Our decolonial findings from this study show climate change is devastatingly impacting immigrants from sub-Saharan African countries in the prairie provinces of Alberta and Saskatchewan. In other words, our co-researchers are disproportionately impacted by climate change. Yet, there needs to be more community-level resources and initiatives to help them cope. This means as extreme climatic events are projected to increase in these geographical locations, so will the adverse impacts on these marginalized populations. Therefore, decolonizing our learning and enhancing the capacity of these vulnerable groups to cope with extreme climatic events must be given adequate attention. Particularly, resources must be provided and initiatives taken at the community level to help increase adaptive capacity. As technical solutions and physical infrastructure are being provided at the top level, community-based initiatives within the social context are equally important.

Due to already existing inequities, the BIPOC communities, including sub-Saharan African immigrants, are disproportionately impacted by climate change. We learned that some co-researchers did not feel enough was being done to help them cope. They indicated there were insufficient initiatives, resources, and services, especially in coping with extremely cold winters, heatwaves, droughts, and snowstorms. Where certain initiatives exist, access to these services is limited. As a result, most co-researchers are not even aware of the few initiatives their communities and cities are taking, like the extreme snowstorm response plan introduced by the city of Saskatoon in 2021 to help cope with snowstorms (Giles, 2021). Therefore, a significant gap exists in accessing these resources. Furthermore, instituting more programs to support people during winter will enhance resilience to climate risk. For example, introducing community-based approaches to snow removal will go a long way to help ease some of the problems co-researchers face during winter. Unfortunately, most of the neighbourhoods these co-researchers live in either do not get their snow cleared, or get it cleared very late. In Saskatoon, for example, we learned that most co-researchers lived in poor neighbourhoods. Community-based snow-clearing programs can also help improve the co-researchers' mental health and feelings of personal safety.

We discovered that these gaps, including the lack of community-based resources and initiatives, the lack of consideration for social context, and the failure to promote strong community initiatives and relationships, exist because of the approaches Canada has adopted to tackle climate change. According to Ness et al. (2020), Canada's response to climate change has not given adaptation enough consideration. The scholars observe that "over the past five years, just 13 percent of federal government spending on climate change has financed adaptation measures" (para. 1). This partly explains why fewer community-level resources exist within some provinces to support marginalized populations, like our study group, coping with climate change. Even with the fewer community services that existed within Alberta and Saskatchewan, we found access to them was limited and did not reach most of the co-researchers. As a result, this impeded their ability to adapt to some of these climate challenges. Climate resilience is achieved when adaptation is given more attention. More resources and outreach programs targeting these populations are, therefore, needed to enhance the capacity of sub-Saharan immigrants to cope with climate risk. Outreach programs have proven effective in raising climate awareness within vulnerable populations and providing adaptation options (Aakre & Rübbelke, 2010).

Through our decolonial learning journey, we learned that in addition to the non-availability of community resources and financial challenges—including food shortages and rising food prices emerging from extreme heat and droughts—there were also major challenges to the co-researchers in coping with climate risk and adapting to climate change. In 2021, for example, food prices in Canada rose to about 5.73 percent (Zaidi, n.d.). This was without any corresponding increase in wages. According to Zaidi (n.d.), part of the reason for this was the floods, heatwaves, and droughts experienced in the western provinces of Canada. Another financial challenge raised was increased transportation costs resulting from the combined effects of climate change and the subsequent introduction of the carbon tax. Studies have shown that a carbon tax burden can be significantly higher for marginalized populations and lower-income groups (Grainger & Kolstad, 2010). Based on this, most of the co-researchers attributed rising prices of goods and services and increased transportation costs to the carbon tax. Some co-researchers explained every dollar charged to businesses will be passed on to consumers. They therefore argued that although the policy has good intentions, it needs to examine the social impacts on marginalized groups more closely, especially the impacts on people employed in jobs that pay minimum wage.

The carbon tax is a very divisive issue in Canada, especially within the provinces of Alberta and Saskatchewan, with these provinces even challenging the decision all the way to the Supreme Court of Canada (Dryden, 2021). This is reflected in the study, as some co-researchers thought that although the policy could have done more to cushion marginalized populations, they still supported the introduction of the carbon tax for the greater good. Some co-researchers even stated their provinces were among the highest polluters in Canada and it was only fair they did their part to mitigate climate change. Others, however, were against the policy. Overall, the co-researchers described that there was no broader consultation with the BIPOC community before implementing this policy.

LEARNING ABOUT COMMUNITY RESILIENCE AND STRENGTH

Decolonial learning refers to looking beyond deficits. Many immigrants and refugee populations have been found to possess rich experiences and cultures that have the potential to positively benefit host countries (Weng & Lee, 2015). Irrespective of the challenges faced, we realized most of the co-researchers showed strength and resilience in coping with some of these extreme climatic events. This strength and resilience is drawn from experiences they bring with them from their countries of origin. For example, in coping with extreme heat. Temperatures are comparatively higher in the tropics than those in western Canada, making it possible that they may have had similar experiences of heat. As a result, most co-researchers showed extensive experience in coping with extreme heat and some health issues that arise from the heat. As one co-researcher outlined, some of the strategies he used in coping with the 2021 extreme heat in Saskatoon were things he learned coping with heat to avoid cerebrospinal meningitis (CSM) in Ghana. In most parts of sub-Saharan Africa, cerebrospinal meningitis is a major health issue that has received wide attention. Hence, annual vaccinations and public education are major steps that several sub-Saharan African countries have taken to help people cope with heat to prevent this health issue. Based on this, most co-researchers have extensive experience coping with heat in Alberta and Saskatchewan.

As temperatures continue to rise in western Canada, these coping strategies sub-Saharan African immigrants bring into Canada have the potential to help enhance the climate resiliency of their host country when given consideration. Hilder (1994) observed looking past the deficits; immigrants carry some lifestyles, cultures, and experiences that can enhance positive health outcomes of their host countries when considered. Given that temperatures are projected to continue to rise in western Canada, it may be time to draw on immigrants' experiences to engage in public health education and sensitization on certain diseases that thrive in higher temperatures, like cerebrospinal meningitis. As the IPCC (2022) recommends, early response systems are an effective adaptation option for building climate resilience.

COMPARING SUB-SAHARAN AFRICAN AND FIRST NATIONS/MÉTIS CLIMATE EXPERIENCES

Comparing our findings from sub-Saharan African immigrants' climate experiences to previous studies that examined climate vulnerabilities within First Nations and Métis communities in Saskatchewan (See: Akobundu, 2021; Blackburn, 2022), we see similar vulnerabilities to climate change. Particularly, we see the relationship between climate vulnerability and these communities' preexisting socioeconomic inequities. However, the communities face unique climate vulnerabilities, and we advocate climate solutions should be tailored to meet their specific climate needs. For instance, the continuous process of colonialism has caused most of the climate challenges Indigenous communities to face today. As Akobundu (2021) observes, the Indigenous communities in northern Saskatchewan are more exposed to climate risk because of the Canadian government's policies of relocating and forcing Indigenous Peoples into small parcels of lands and reserves. Unique climate solutions that meet the specific needs of BIPOC communities are essential to addressing the climate risk in Canada.

MOVING FORWARD

In our decolonial study, we as a community and BIPOC researchers together explored how extreme climatic events emerging from climate change are having adverse impacts on sub-Saharan immigrant populations in western Canada. Several challenges, including financial, health, and government climate policies (carbon tax) and the non-availability of community programs, initiatives, and resources, were some of the challenges these people faced in trying to cope with extreme climate events and adapt to climate change in general. These, therefore, reduced the capacity of these communities to cope with climate change. To build resilience to climate risk, community-level initiatives and resources are needed and access to these resources must be enhanced. Therefore, respectful engagement of immigrant populations through community-based approaches can enhance their capacity to cope with climate risks. We also found that sub-Saharan immigrants come into Canada with experiences that can be harnessed to help cope with extreme climatic events and have provided them with strength and resilience in coping with extreme climate change in western Canada. As the temperature continues to increase in western Canada, sub-Saharan immigrants' experiences may hold the potential to build more resilience in the face of increasing climate risks.

REFLECTION QUESTIONS

Finally, we conclude with these broader questions for readers.

1. What community-based resources can be provided to help sub-Saharan immigrant communities cope with climate risk in western Canada?
2. How can access to these resources be enhanced in a culturally safer way?
3. How can we harness the experiences of sub-Saharan immigrants to help adapt to increasing climate risk in western Canada?

SUGGESTED READINGS

- Cochran, P. A. L., Marshall C. A., Garcia-Downing, C., Kendall, E., Cook, D., McCubbin, L., & Gover, R. M. S. (2008). Indigenous ways of knowing: Implications for participatory research and community. *American Journal of Public Health, 98*(1), 22–27. https://doi.org/10.2105/AJPH.2006.093641
- Koster, R., Baccar, K., & Lemelin, R. H. (2012). Moving from research ON, to research WITH and FOR Indigenous communities: A critical reflection on community-based participatory research. *The Canadian Geographer / Le Géographe Canadien, 56*(2), 195–210. https://doi.org/10.1111/j.1541-0064.2012.00428.x
- Owusu-Kwarteng, L. (2019). Livin and learnin, tellin stories, challengin narratives: Critical reflections on engaging students from marginalised groups in academic research activities. *Compass: Journal of Learning and Teaching, 12*(1). http://dx.doi.org/10.21100/compass.v12i1.951
- Tobias, J. K., Richmond, C. A. M., & Luginaah, I. (2013). Community-based participatory research (CBPR) with Indigenous communities: Producing respectful and reciprocal research. *Journal of Empirical Research on Human Research Ethics, 8*(2). https://doi.org/10.1525/jer.2013.8.2.129

REFERENCES

Aakre, S., & Rübbelke, D. T. G. (2010). Adaptation to climate change in the European Union: Efficiency versus equity considerations. *Environmental Policy and Governance, 20*(3), 159–179.

Akobundu, A. C. (2021). *A First Nations political ecology of climate change in Saskatchewan* [Master's thesis]. University of Saskatchewan. Retrieved December 19, 2022, from https://harvest.usask.ca/bitstream/handle/10388/13448/AKOBUNDU-THESIS-2021.pdf?sequence=1&isAllowed=y

Blackburn, M. (2022, February 11). Indigenous communities to be hit with "ecological grief, loss of land and traditional knowledge" because of climate crisis. *APTN*. https://www.aptnnews.ca/national-news/indigenous-communities-to-be-hit-with-ecological-grief-loss-of-land-and-traditional-knowledge-because-of-climate-crisis

Braun, V., & Clarke, V. (2006). Using thematic analysis in psychology. *Qualitative Research in Psychology, 3*(2), 77–101.

Climate Action Network (2020, August 7). *Climate Action Network—Réseau action climat Canada (CAN-Rac): Written submission for the pre-budget consultations in advance of the upcoming federal budget 2021.* https://www.ourcommons.ca/Content/Committee/432/FINA/Brief/BR10974084/br-external/ClimateActionNetworkCanada-e.pdf

Connelly, L. M. (2010). What is phenomenology? *Medsurg Nursing; Pitman, 19*(2), 127–128.

Datta, R. (2018). Decolonizing both researcher and research and its effectiveness in Indigenous research. *Research Ethics, 14*(2), 1–24. http://journals.sagepub.com/doi/pdf/10.1177/1747016117733296

Datta, R. (2022). Indigenous trans-systemic research approach. *Qualitative Inquiry, 28*(6), 694–702. https://doi.org/10.1177/10778004211066878

Dryden, J. (2021, March 28). The Supreme Court has ruled in favour of the carbon tax—here's what might happen next. *CBC*. https://www.cbc.ca/news/canada/calgary/kenney-jonathan-wilkinson-west-centre-kathleen-petty-1.5967214

Fereday, J., & Muir-Cochrane, E. (2006). Demonstrating rigor using thematic analysis: A hybrid approach of inductive and deductive coding and theme development. *International Journal of Qualitative Methods, 5*(1), 80–92. https://doi.org/10.1177/160940690600500107

Ford, J. D., Berrang-Ford, L., King, M., & Furgal, C. (2010). Vulnerability of Aboriginal health systems in Canada to climate change. *Global Environmental Change, 20*(4), 668–680.

Ford, J. D., Smit, B., & Wandel, J. (2006). Vulnerability to climate change in the Arctic: A case study from Arctic Bay, Canada. *Global Environmental Change, 16*(2), 145–160.

Giles, D. (2021, September 28). Extreme snowstorm response plan approved by Saskatoon city councillors. *Global News*. https://globalnews.ca/news/8226948/saskatoon-extreme-snowstorm-response-plan-blizzard/

Government of Canada. (2022). *Planting 2 billion trees: A natural climate solution.* Retrieved May 14, 2022, from https://www.canada.ca/en/campaign/2-billion-trees.html

Grainger, C. A., & Kolstad, C. D. (2010). Who pays a price on carbon? *Environmental and Resource Economics, 46*(3), 359–376.

Gupta, J., & Vegelin, C. (2016). Sustainable development goals and inclusive development. *International Environmental Agreements: Politics, Law and Economics, 16*, 433–448. https://doi.org/10.1007/s10784-016-9323-z

Hilder, A. S. (1994). Ethnic differences in the sudden infant death syndrome: What we can learn from immigrants to the UK. *Early Human Development, 38*(3), 143–149. https://doi.org/10.1016/0378-3782(94)90205-4

Intergovernmental Panel on Climate Change (IPCC). (2022). *Climate change 2022: Impacts, adaptation and vulnerability*. Retrieved May 30, 2022, from https://www.ipcc.ch/report/ar6/wg2/

International Institute for Sustainable Development. (2022). *Climate change impacts on the Prairies: Impacts of climate change on the Canadian Prairies*. Retrieved May 20, 2022, from https://www.prairiesrac.com/climate-impacts/

Nerini, F. F., Sovacool, B., Hughes, N., Cozzi, L., Cosgrave, E., Howells, M., Tavoni, M., Tomei, J., Zerriffi, H., & Milligan, B. (2019). Connecting climate action with other Sustainable Development Goals. *Nature Sustainability, 2*, 674–680. https://doi.org/10.1038/s41893-019-0334-y

Ness, R., Sawyer, D., & Street, R. (2020, December 3). *Climate impacts are getting worse. Canada must adapt*. Canadian Climate Institute. https://climateinstitute.ca/climate-impacts-are-getting-worse-canada-must-adapt/

Simmons, D. (2020, July 29). What is "climate justice"? Yale Climate Connections. https://yaleclimateconnections.org/2020/07/what-is-climate-justice/

Smith, L. T. (2012). *Decolonizing methodologies: Research and indigenous peoples*. Bloomsbury Publishing.

Waldron, I. (2021a, July 22). *Centring social justice is sound climate policy*. Canadian Climate Institute. https://climateinstitute.ca/centring-social-justice-is-sound-climate-policy/

Waldron, I. (2021b, July 22). *Environmental racism and climate change: Determinants of health in Mi'kmaw and African Nova Scotian communities*. Canadian Climate Institute. Retrieved from https://climateinstitute.ca/publications/environmental-racism-and-climate-change/

Walker, P. F. (2021). *Young Canadians and climate change: Vulnerability, adaptive capacity, education, and agency* [Master's Thesis]. York University. https://yorkspace.library.yorku.ca/xmlui/bitstream/handle/10315/38568/MESMP02121_Walker_Patricia.pdf?sequence=1&isAllowed=y

Weng, S. S., & Lee, J. S. (2015). Why do immigrants and refugees give back to their communities and what can we learn from their civic engagement? *International Journal of Voluntary and Nonprofit Organizations, 27*(2), 509–524. https://doi.org/10.1007/s11266-015-9636-5

Zaidi, D. (n.d.). Food prices climbed during the second year of the pandemic—and climate disasters contributed. *CTV*. Retrieved February 10, 2022, from https://www.ctvnews.ca/climate-and-environment/food-prices-climbed-during-the-second-year-of-the-pandemic-and-climate-disasters-contributed-1.5755815

Zimonjic, P. (2021, November 25). Canada's climate change efforts going from "failure to failure," says commissioner's report. *CBC*. https://www.cbc.ca/news/politics/environment-commissioner-report-failure-to-failure-1.6262523

CHAPTER 14

Aligning Anti-Racism Efforts with Decolonization: Reflections from Organizing in Vancouver's Chinatown

Yi Chien Jade Ho

In this chapter, I draw reflections from my experience organizing with the working-class senior residents and allies in Chinatown, specifically on how we learn to align our anti-racism and anti-gentrification organizing with decolonization. I will foreground the reflections with an analysis of Asian/Chinese racialization's role in the perpetuation of settler colonialism. This analysis allows us to recognize the invisible connection between racism and colonialism and how we can actively work to undo it. As Bonita Lawrence and Enakshi Dua (2005) caution in their foundational work *Decolonizing Antiracism*, without an understanding of this connection, anti-racism efforts run the danger of perpetuating ongoing settler colonialism. In the context of fighting against anti-Asian racism, without aligning with decolonization, these efforts can many times become dependent on the colonial legal immigration system that perpetuates further erasure of Indigenous people and lands or buying into the false idea of the model minority and upward mobility. Therefore, decolonization cannot be a mere metaphor (Tuck & Yang, 2012) nor representational in building an anti-racist community. This chapter aims to show that this work is not only possible but necessary. The work that we have been doing in Vancouver's Chinatown is by no means perfect and we still have so much to learn. But I hope Chinatown as a site of struggle can inspire us to not only learn how to tease out the intricacy of the oppressive systems, but more importantly about how we can collectively and concretely resist, heal, and flourish despite these systems.

POSITIONING MYSELF

I was born in Taiwan as a third-generation Han settler. I did not realize my family and my position in Taiwan as settlers and Taiwan as a settler colonial nation until I started learning about Indigenous struggles and our responsibilities to decolonization in so-called Canada. I believe the commitment to decolonization in one place also propels one to pay attention to all the places and lands they have lived in or been to. Certainly, that has been the case for me.

When I was 13, my mother and I immigrated to Belize so that I could learn English and one day move to the United States. My mother calls Belize our "jumping board" to America. Later I moved to Mexico as a student and became a teacher there after university. As an East Asian woman living in the Caribbean, I faced daily racist and sexist remarks and exclusionary treatment, but I also realized our own racist socialization against Black and other people of colour. In 2013, I came to Canada as a graduate student. As an international student, I experienced further exclusion and exploitation, but more importantly at the same time I started to learn about collective organizing as a way of making change. I believe it is because of these experiences that I became interested in the work of feminists of colour, anti-racism, and decolonization, and how we can enact these efforts through educating, organizing, and building a community of change and care.

RADICAL REORIENTATION: COMING TO CHINATOWN, COMING TO LUK'LUK'I

In 2016, I was fortunate to be welcomed into an intergenerational group organizing against gentrification and racism in Vancouver's Chinatown. At the time, the group, alongside many working-class Chinatown residents, was pushing back against a corporate landlord's (Beedie Living) development application in the heart of Chinatown: 105 Keefer St. If the development were to go through, it would add a luxury condo tower in the already rapidly gentrifying neighbourhood.

Chinatown, historically and presently, has often been defined against a backdrop of colonialism, capitalist gain, and white supremacy. The area was formed out of anti-Asian racism on dispossessed Indigenous land, a Squamish site called luk'luk'i, a name attributed to the groves of beautiful maple trees that were there before it was clearcut and the community displaced by colonial settlement (Chinatown Action Group, 2017). The notion of "Chinatown" itself stems from a European idea of "an unfavorable neighborhood characterized by vice and populated by an inferior race" (Li, 2003). In the 1800s, Chinese immigrants and migrant workers for the railroads and other infrastructures of capitalist expansion were restricted within the boundaries of this neighbourhood. Canada as a colonial state continues to depend on cheap migrant labour to exploit and extract "resources" from Indigenous lands. But, in resistance and a fight for survival, Chinese immigrants built Chinatown into a place of survival and shelter from white supremacist violence, at least as far as they were able. Therefore, the history of Chinatown is not merely one of exclusion or of an ethnic enclave, but one of resilience, solidarity, and, consequently, "indebtedness" to the support of Indigenous people (Phung, 2015).

Today, in Chinatown, one can easily observe how gentrification brings a new class of wealthier residents with capitalistic values, driven by the redevelopment of land to generate profit. This is a continuation of this city's colonial legacy. Chinatown's history cannot be separated from what is happening now. Learning about Chinatown's history and present, as well as being adjacent to the Downtown Eastside, where many urban Indigenous people reside, has pushed those of us who organize in Chinatown to question how our fight for belonging in this colonial context has been predicated on the displacement and eradication of Indigenous people. Therefore, the fight for Chinatown requires an understanding of the violent history of colonial displacement and the responsibilities immigrant settlers have on Indigenous land. We desperately need a critique of settlers of colour/immigrant settlers, of people who benefit daily, either through coercion or willingness, from the erasure of Indigenous people and land, but at the same time experience oppression. We need to examine the role Asian immigrants play in the reproduction of settler colonial structure. I contend that teasing out this role is essential to our liberation and to our solidarity with Indigenous, Black, and other marginalized people. To do this we need not only to understand our own cultural resources, to connect with our histories, but to also learn about our complacency and formulate a framework on how the colonial structure manipulates our relationship to the state, other marginalized groups and to one another. As Day et al. (2019) posit, this kind of "critical reorientation" calls us to

> grapple with the complex interplay of race and Indigeneity, compelling us to challenge Asian settler mythologies—particularly those that celebrate early Asian labor migrants as "pioneers," while ignoring their complicity with colonial expansion and the genocidal elimination of Native peoples and cultures. (p. 2)

This reorientation has taught me I have not come to "Vancouver, Canada" but I have arrived at Musqueam, Squamish, and Tsleil-Waututh lands on Turtle Island that hold a history of flourishing, survival, and struggle that concerns each person who has come to this land, and all of us are implicated in it. This is a reorientation of our relationship as newcomers and immigrants to this land, and it echoes the question Rita Wong (2008) asks: "What happens if we position Indigenous people's struggles instead of normalized whiteness as the reference point through which we come to articulate our subjectivities?" (p. 158).

For me, this radical reorientation calls us to question the larger rhetoric of inclusion and belonging through nationalistic immigration processes built on settler colonial logics (Toomey et al., 2020). Belonging and inclusion look for a seat at the table but do not question the stability of the table or who set it up in the first place. Instead of belonging and inclusion, I want to focus on a reorientation towards connection and responsibility that centres on building accountability and relationship to land and Indigenous people and a recognition that margin is a place of "radical opening and possibility" (hooks, 1990, p. 22).

ASIAN RACIALIZATION IN SETTLER COLONIAL CAPITALISM

On a December afternoon in 2018, a surprisingly sunny day for the usually damp Vancouver winter, a group of us gathered at the intersection of Gore and Keefer to meet Mrs. Kong, a Chinatown resident. Mrs. Kong has lived in Chinatown for more than 30 years. That afternoon she took us on a short tour around Chinatown and told us stories through her own lived experience to highlight the rapid changes of the past few years. We called this a "gentrification tour." She began the tour by saying, "it feels like this city is trying to push us out, to erase us, but we are still here making sure Chinatown is safe for everyone." On the tour, Mrs. Kong passionately pointed out where she would practice Tai Chi with her friends, as well as her favourite grocery store, now closed and awaiting a future condo development. Many other affordable and culturally appropriate grocers, restaurants, and businesses have also been forced to close in recent years, and in their place: hipster coffee shops, artisanal patisseries, and restaurants of "elevated" East Asian street foods. We finished the tour back on Keefer Street by the Chinese Railway Worker and Veteran Memorial, right beside 105 Keefer St., which had been fenced off by the developer. Mrs. Kong emphasized that this is an important place for her in Chinatown because the monument reminds her of the mistreatment Chinese workers face and the effort early Chinese immigrants put into fighting for belonging in this country. She lamented their belief that building the railroad and going to war for Canada would ensure their belonging, but years after we are still struggling. However, through her own involvement in the housing struggle at 105 Keefer St., she told us how important it is for the community to come together and for marginalized people to raise their voices.

Mrs. Kong's lived experiences and remarks at the Chinese Railway Worker and Veteran Memorial call attention to the specific ways Chinese immigrants and their racialization have been positioned in the settler colonial capitalist system. Many Asian American and Indigenous scholars (Byrd, 2011; Day, 2016; Fujikane & Okamura, 2008; Phung, 2015; Tuck & Yang 2012) have been mapping out the relationship formation underlying settler colonialism. Their formulations take the conversation on settler colonialism beyond the mere binary relationship between Indigenous peoples and white settlers to include an interrogation of the roles racialized others play within the system. Amongst these scholars, Iyko Day (2016) contends that the process of racialization is essential and internal to settler coloniality and its fellow traveller, capitalist progression. As capitalism strives for limitless market expansion, settler coloniality supports that goal and seeks to seize Indigenous lands to be commodified, often through the exploitation of racialized labour. In this conception, settler colonial relations are, as Glen Coultard (2014) posits, "the inherited background field within which market, racist, patriarchal, and state relations converge" (p. 14). By clarifying the process of hierarchical racial formation within settler colonial capitalism, we can understand the interconnection as we fight in different areas of this process and move away from resistance approaches that perpetuate the continuation of settler colonial capitalism.

Based on this formation, Day (2016) proposes a triangulated settler colonial capitalism relation, settler-Indigenous-alien. The term "alien" is to emphasize African slaves, Asian migrant labour, and other racialized labour's "historical relationship to North American land, which was exclusive and excludable to alien labour forces" (p. 26). This formulation is not to equate the experiences of Black people and Asian or other racialized people but to understand settler colonialism's inherent dependence on racialized alien labour, in the forms of forced migration and deportable labour, for its reproduction and continuation of Indigenous dispossession. Day's framework offers a nuanced understanding of the process of racialization in the settler colonial triangulation and how each positionality either assists or hinders the reinforcement of white settler colonial capitalism. Day (2016) further emphasizes that the categories are not meant to be fixed but to point out "the role of territorial entitlement that distinguishes them. In this sense, these positions should not be understood as identitarian categories but rather a political orientation to Indigenous land" (p. 10). With this background in place, I will now dissect the specific ways Asian racialization has manifested and the particular role it holds within the relational system of settler colonial capitalism. I add to this conversation by proposing *manipulability* and *commodifiability* as two of the key features of Asian racial formation.

Asian racial formation manifests in two prominent racial stereotypes: on the one hand, we are the "model minority" succeeding in climbing the ladder of class mobility. On the other hand, we are the "yellow peril" that infests the pure white society with our foreign and uncivilized customs. Although being praised as successful, we are also perpetually foreign and can be expelled anytime. The racial imaginary of the "yellow peril" in English-speaking colonial North America developed in the 19th century when Asian immigrants came in larger numbers as cheap labour (Kawai, 2005). The term conveys fear and undesirability of Asian migration by equating the population with "diseases, vice and destruction" (Day, 2016, p. 7), and thus a threat to white colonial nation building. Early Chinese immigrants faced extreme legal, spatial, and material limitations, such as the Chinese head tax and Chinese exclusionary act, and were relegated to the ghettoized Chinatown. This racial imaginary entered a new stage at the end of WWII by positioning Asian immigrants as a "model minority," able to achieve economic success while standing out as exemplary citizens of their purported hard-working and law-abiding nature. Although this racialization process of yellow perilism and the myth of model minority may seem to represent two distinct historical stages, in actuality they exist on a spectrum forming a racial limbo with fluidity to be both model minority and yellow peril. Day points out the two stereotypes work together as "complementary aspects of the same form of racialization, in which economic efficiency is the basis for exclusion or assimilation" (2016, p. 7). In other words, we should understand these two seemingly oppositional racial imaginaries, one denotes positivity and the other negativity, as existing in an inseparable dialectic relationship, holding each other accountable for the maintenance of white supremacy (Kawai, 2005; Okihiro, 1994).

As a result, people racialized as Asian assume a position of what I call a "racial limbo," a racial space with the illusion of upward class mobility and proximity to whiteness through seemingly voluntary assimilation, but at the same time living under the threat of removal, creating what Harsha Walia (2021) calls a "fantasy of inclusion" that requires high dependency and buy-in into the settler colonial state processes. This "vague purgatory status" (Hong, 2020, p. 20) makes the Asian racial role highly manipulatable to be used to pit against other racialized groups or to take the blame for capitalist failures, evident in the Vancouver housing crisis and the call for the ousting of Chinese foreign buyers, as well as the COVID-19 pandemic and the rise of anti-Asian violence. It is an insidious design that makes it attractive for many of us to opt in. It is a design to erase who we are and self-police when any of us act outside the parameter of a good immigrant. In 2020, after a Filipinx labour organizer did a CBC interview to raise a concern about the inadequacy of short-term assistance like the Canada Emergency Response Benefit and to advocate for long-term solutions to make workers' lives better, she faced strong racist and misogynist blowback with many calling for her deportation. The loudest opposing voices in the campaign were mainly other Filipinx immigrants saying that she has shamed her immigrant community by being "ungrateful" to the Canadian state.

What this smear campaign revealed is not only the buy-in and the obligated gratefulness to the colonial state but an active concealing of the Asian working-class struggle and existence which was made more urgent and apparent by the global health crisis. Asian immigrants are dispersed throughout the class spectrum, but issues of working-class immigrants, migrant workers, seniors, and refugees are rarely discussed in mainstream discourse. This concealment allows the continuation of exploitation of labour power and commodification of Asian culture to be further exploited in the settler colonial capitalist expansion. State policies prioritizing multiculturalism also abet the process of commodification and further colonial exploitation by constructing deterministic cultural and racial differences and identities to fit into "unproblematic neat cultural packages" (Valle-Castro, 2021, p. 96) to be consumed and controlled. Canada was the first country to implement multiculturalism as a state policy in 1971, around the time the model-minority myth emerged. Both the adaptation of multiculturalism and the idea of the model minority conveys an end to the overt exclusionary immigration rules and racist treatment such as the Japanese internment camps that caused havoc in the lives of Japanese immigrants and families. However, as Walia (2021) points out, multiculturalism works in tandem with other racial formations to mask racial hierarchy and elevate national unity by using "grammars of culture and ethnicity," (p. 194) thus boiling down historical and present colonial capitalist violence and expansion into mere discussions of inclusion, diversity, culture, and ethnicity.

Chinatown becomes one of the prime locales for the culmination of these intersecting and interdependent processes. The ongoing gentrification depends on the erasure and invisibilization of working-class Chinese and other marginalized people to ease the process of displacement, while commodifying orientalist ideas of Chinese culture for capitalist gain, such as real estate development. Many new condo buildings or luxury businesses going into Chinatown would make sure they have a splash of red paint, an auspicious colour in the Chinese tradition, or a Chinese translation of the business, but with no working-class Chinese people in sight. In 2017, working-class residents organized to oppose a new city plan, Chinatown Economic Revitalization Action Plan (abbreviated as CRAP)[1]. This plan used language such as "revitalization" and "preserving Chinatown's unique heritage," but in reality, it would heighten displacement and increase land grabs by removing barriers to development permits with no requirement for affordable and social housing. It would also further remove community members from decision-making processes. The open houses held by the city to discuss this plan were marked by inadequate notice for residents, a lack of translation services for the multitude of residents who don't speak English, and the blatantly disrespectful decision to hold them during Lunar New Year. One senior activist, Godfrey Tang, expressed that the city's plan to revitalize Chinatown, in reality, is a replacement—"replacing Chinatown with another culture" (Chinatown Action Group, 2017). This proposed replacement process was occurring alongside the proposed development at 105 Keefer St. Neighbourhood activists had been pushing back against the condo development since 2014 as working-class residents and other community members of the Downtown Eastside rose up to fight for their survival, showing their strength and a rooted presence that cannot be erased despite the insidious systems working against them. In 2017, the campaign had a historic win when the development proposal was rejected by the city for the fifth time. This victory and the process of community organizing signals a collective critical consciousness of the marginalized as well as a refusal to be manipulated, commodified, and replaced by an empty colonial and capitalist redefinition of place and culture.

LEARNING TO DECOLONIZE OUR STRUGGLE

At the debriefing meeting following our win, one of the seniors stood up and shared that she had not previously believed that anyone would listen to what Chinese immigrants have to say. She thought we should just be quiet, keep our heads down, and not make waves, but throughout the campaign, she learned that we have something important to say and when we say it together, we are powerful. Another senior shared that she used to feel isolated and alone in the city. She always thought there was animosity between Chinese and Indigenous community members. But experiencing support from Indigenous people and other allies from the Downtown Eastside in the 105 Keefer St. fight, she felt we had gained important friendships and that we needed to fight for them just as they fought for us.

The process of 105 Keefer organizing also became our collective journey to learn to decolonize and align our struggle with Indigenous struggles. This journey includes both our own empowerment as well as repositioning our relationship with the colonial state and with our Indigenous neighbours. We had to learn to re-establish our intergenerational relationships between elders and youth and had to find ways to facilitate relationship building and knowledge exchange. Together, we needed to re-envision and reclaim Chinatown not as a mere ethnic enclave, but as a place of safety, collective care, and connection. We also needed to refuse the demarcation imposed by multiculturalism and embody the history that Chinatown has not been an exclusive space only for Chinese people, having always been shared by Japanese, Black, Indigenous, and other marginalized people. Its boundary has been porous and flexible although the official border has been restricted.

Throughout our years of organizing together, we began to set up practices and make conscious space in our meetings, actions, and gatherings to facilitate discussions and decision-making processes that allow all of us to imagine and grow together as a community of resistance and care. Khasnabish and Haiven (2014) describe this as the development of radical imagination, as imagination is not an individual possession but a process to be practised collectively and co-inhabited through sharing of experiences, stories, and ideas as well as learning of the past and history and constructing what the future can look like. In 2017, after two years of hosting teatime discussions and house visits, the seniors and youth organizers put together the *People's Vision*[2], outlining a strategy for Chinatown's social and economic development that centres on the needs of marginalized people in and around Chinatown. Throughout this process in conjunction with the 105 Keefer St. campaign, members also got together to carry out power analyses of different levels, so that our vision was not narrow but included an understanding of the systemic issue underlying our struggle, to understand where we should apply the pressure of our collective power.

On the other hand, to loosen the colonial hold means to decentre the dominance of English in our organizing and to make our space accessible to the seniors. The members of our group spoke mainly three different languages—Cantonese, Mandarin, and English. Some can understand all three, some only speak one or two—all at varying levels of proficiency. All our meetings and gatherings were conducted alternating Cantonese and Mandarin with whisper interpretation to people who need a translation. This helped our members feel comfortable speaking up without worrying about challenges in communicating in English. Language accessibility was also one of the biggest struggles when we participated in city processes. Every open house, city council hearing, and development board meeting, we had to fight tooth and nail for the city to provide proper translation and interpretation. When they failed to do so, the youth organizers provided interpretation for our seniors on our own, just to be scolded by white meeting attendees saying we were disrupting their meetings. When our seniors spoke in the city council hearings, they were restricted to the same time limit as English speakers, even though they needed more time for interpretation. The lack of language accessibility at the city level unmasks the racist foundation that Vancouver is built on. However, our members did not waver; our seniors took up every space possible and spoke loud and clear in Cantonese and Mandarin, condemning the city for its lack of accountability and for allowing gentrification and displacement to wreak havoc on people's lives.

Being able to communicate in their own languages and participate in city processes and collective actions, members of our organizing group felt more and more emboldened to share their own lived experiences and place-based knowledge. At the same time, we were also able to have meaningful discussions about how to ensure our fight to remain in Chinatown is not exclusionary but connected to the larger decolonization effort. We needed to first interrogate and unlearn what the colonial state has taught us about each other and undo the prevailing racial stereotypes about Indigenous people, other marginalized people, and ourselves and the land we are on. We began to read territorial acknowledgements out loud in unison together at the beginning of all our meetings and gatherings[3]. We translated the land acknowledgement to Mandarin and Cantonese. Since it was difficult to find the exact translation, "acknowledgement" becomes "we give our thanks out loud" for being on Coast Salish lands belonging to the Musquam, Squamish, and Tsleil-Waututh nations, and "unceded territories" became as literal as "lands that have been taken without agreement." We started doing this practice not just because it is a necessary protocol but also because it grounded our meetings and all our collective decisions while creating room for questions and discussions. When we started this practice, we did not hear any of the seniors comment on it, but everyone agreed to keep doing it. Finally, one day in one of our regular weekly meetings after we read the territorial acknowledgement together, one of the seniors raised her hand and asked, "what do we mean when we say Chinatown is on the land that was taken without agreement from Indigenous people?" She went on to ask, "does this mean that Chinatown is not Chinese people's, but we are on someone's land that was stolen from them?" From there, the group got into a discussion on the history of the traditional land Chinatown is on and how Chinatown was formed. We then proceeded with our meeting. One of the agenda items that day was to give a response to the city about a temporary modular housing being built on the edge of Chinatown. Different members were giving their thoughts, and then the same senior once again spoke up, "As per our discussion earlier, we should ask the Indigenous people about what they think about this since this is their land. Who are we to make this decision? And if this project is going to prioritize housing for Indigenous people, then it is our responsibility to support it."

That was a particularly impactful moment for me as a young organizer to witness a Chinese elder, who holds a strong sense of place in Chinatown, a place which she depends on, reorient her relationship with Chinatown and open up space for solidarity and Indigenous leadership. Although in many contexts territorial acknowledgement has been co-opted to be tokenistic and performative, when it is practised respectfully and intentionally, it has profound pedagogical and transformative potential. This kind of "reflective territorial acknowledgement," as Malissa Phung (2019) points out, is an important "first step towards building Indigenous and Asian relations, particularly in situations of racial conflict and colonial misapprehensions" (p. 20). This practice enabled us to situate that the ongoing displacement is part of a settler colonial capitalist process that continues to displace and erase Indigenous presence and our indebtedness to the original stewards of the land we are now living on.

Nevertheless, as Phung states, while this is a necessary first step, more needs to be done to bridge the two communities. We realized that it is still difficult for many Chinatown elders to fully participate in Indigenous and other social movements and cultivate any personal relationships with the people they might see in their daily lives in Chinatown due to language barriers and racial trauma. We started organizing social gatherings in which people could come together to share traditional foods and stories through interpretation, building personal relationships in a safe space. We also organized the seniors to attend many important Indigenous-led actions such as the Annual Women's Memorial March that brings attention to missing and murdered Indigenous women and all women and gender diverse people in the Downtown Eastside, so they know that they can be a part of a community of change outside of our own organizing.

Lastly, since a lot of learning opportunities like workshops and reading groups are often inaccessible to the seniors, the youth organizers gathered materials and set up various workshops with the elders to discuss topics like capitalism and the housing crisis, dehumanization, and discrimination, as well as understanding colonialism in Canada. We always had fruitful, and at many times heated, discussions. One of the lessons that I gained from being a part of these workshops was that the elders hold embodied knowledge and lived experiences of being in the oppressive systems. They might not have the same political language to describe them, but it does not mean they cannot have this type of political discussion. They all felt them, experienced them, and resisted them. They just needed a place to name, to reflect, to grow, and to see the possibility for change. Grace Lee Boggs (2016), Chinese American philosopher and activist in the Black liberation movement, emphasizes the importance of reflection in the process of resistance and cautions against thinking of racialized people only as an "oppressed mass" but, rather, people capable of making collective 'moral choices'" (p. 149) and accountable to develop "self-consciousness and a sense of political and social responsibilities" (p. 152). Although our work still has a long way to go and it is often messy and slow, we constantly witness our collective growth, and when many would see low-income Chinese seniors as merely a helpless population steeped in conservative mindsets, the senior members would exercise their own agency in becoming change-makers of their own lives as well as better allies to the First People of the land they now depend on.

CONCLUSION: MOVING FORWARD WITH DECOLONIZING ANTI-RACISM EFFORTS

With the recent rise in anti-Asian rhetoric and violence, it is especially important to draw the connection between colonialism and racism. This surge in violence is not just a momentary condition, but it is situated in the history of the racial foundations of settler colonial capitalism. Without situating our struggle in this connection, our anti-racism effort can be easily co-opted and manipulated. The face of gentrification today in Chinatown is no longer only the white corporate developers but also the Chinatown capitalist elites. They have been using the wave of Stop Anti-Asian Hate to advocate for "cleaning up" Chinatown by adding more police presence to criminalize the unhoused people in Chinatown and neighbouring Downtown Eastside. This is a sinister part of the new form of gentrification in Chinatown, using the seemingly progressive messaging of anti-racism and "cultural revitalization," which activist Vince Tao appropriately names "gentrification with Chinese characteristics" (Lowe, 2019). Without understanding the intricate ways that Asian racialization can be manipulated and commodified to advance colonial capitalist gain, it is very easy to buy into rhetoric such as "cultural revitalization."

However, in our effort to connect anti-gentrification and anti-racism struggle with decolonization, we have learned to radically re-orient the positionality of immigrants to expose manufactured belonging and dependency on settler colonial logic that aims to perpetuate colonial control and capitalist exploitation. We began to rely on community building and collective caring as well as deepening our understanding and relationship with Indigenous people and the land we are on. This is a humbling way to relate to the land we have arrived at, to offer gratitude and assume our responsibility for the care of this land through our own lived cultural resources and strength. This repositioning also offers the potential to open space for solidarity down to the most practical details. This vision has helped us feel less alone and that our immigrant history and resistance are connected and have shared solidarity with everyone else—we are no longer just one group of people fighting for what is good for us, but we are deeply implicated in each other's struggle and survival. For me, this is liberating.

NOTES

1. https://www.thevolcano.org/2017/02/12/cut-the-crap/
2. https://chinatownaction.org/
3. The Chinese translation of the territorial acknowledgement used in our meetings and gatherings: 我們鳴謝我們是在 瑪斯昆, (Musqueam) 史戈米殊, (Squamish) 和塔斯里爾-沃特斯, (Tsleil-Waututh)這些西岸原住民族從來沒有同意交出的領土上

REFLECTION QUESTIONS

1. What do we risk when our anti-racism effort does not align with decolonization?
    a. In what ways might your own anti-racist effort perpetuate colonialism?
2. What role does racialization play in the process of settler colonialism?
3. What are the trappings of the "multiculturalism" policy?
4. After reading the stories in this chapter, what are some other ways you and your community can align your anti-racist effort with decolonization?
    a. Do you have a relationship with the Indigenous nation whose land you are on?
    b. What is the history of solidarity between your community and Indigenous people?
    c. How can you go beyond land acknowledgement?

SUGGESTED READINGS

Academic Journal Articles

- Day, I., Pegues, J. H., Phung, M., Saranillio, D. I., & Medak-Saltzman, D. (2019). Settler colonial studies, Asian diasporic questions. *Verge: Studies in Global Asias, 5*(1), 1–45.

- Saranillio, D. I. (2013). Why Asian settler colonialism matters: A thought piece on critiques, debates, and Indigenous difference. *Settler Colonial Studies, 3*(3–4), 280–294.
- Wong, R. (2008). Decolonizasian: Reading Asian and first nations relations in literature. *Canadian Literature, 199*, 158–180.

Literary Work

- Lee, S. (1990). *Disappearing Moon Café*. Douglas & McIntyre.
- Maracle, L. (1990). Yin Chin. *Canadian Literature, 124–125: Native Writers & Canadian Writing* [Special issue]. 156–161. https://canlit.ca/wp-content/uploads/2015/01/CL124_Maracle.pdf

Documentaries

- Cohen, E. (Dir.). (2017). *Painted red*. Vivacious Pictures.
- Cho, K. (2004). *In the shadow of Gold Mountain*. National Film Board of Canada, CBC News, & Vision TV.

Op-Ed Articles

- Hunter, J. (2015, May 9). A forgotten history: Tracing the ties between B.C.'s First Nations and Chinese workers. *The Globe and Mail*. https://www.theglobeandmail.com/news/british-columbia/chinese-heritage/article24335611/
- Lowe, N. (2019, July 16). Class struggle in Chinatown: Ethnic tourism, planned gentrification, and organizing for tenant power. *The Mainlander*. https://themainlander.com/2019/07/16/class-struggle-in-chinatown-ethnic-tourism-planned-gentrification-and-organizing-for-tenant-power/
- Shi, J. (2020, April 27). The revolution will be translated. *Briarpatch Magazine* (May/June). https://briarpatchmagazine.com/articles/view/the-revolution-will-be-translated

REFERENCES

Boggs, G. L. (2016). *Living for change: An autobiography*. University of Minnesota Press.

Byrd, J. A. (2011). *The transit of empire: Indigenous critiques of colonialism*. University of Minnesota Press.

Chinatown Action Group. (2017). *The people's vision for Chinatown: A community strategy for social and economic development*. https://chinatownaction.org/

Coulthard, G. S. (2014). *Red skin, white masks: Rejecting the colonial politics of recognition*. University of Minnesota Press.

Day, I. (2016). *Alien capital: Asian racialization and the logic of settler colonial capitalism*. Duke University Press.

Fujikane, C., & Okamura, J. Y. (Eds.). (2008). *Asian settler colonialism: From local governance to the habits of everyday life in Hawai'i*. University of Hawaii Press.

Hong, C. P. (2020). *Minor feelings: An Asian American reckoning*. One World.

hooks, b. (1990). *Yearning: Race, gender, and cultural politics*. South End Press.

Hudson, V. M., & Day, B. S. (2019). *Foreign policy analysis: classic and contemporary theory*. Rowman & Littlefield.

Kawai, Y. (2005). Stereotyping Asian Americans: The dialectic of the model minority and the yellow peril. *Howard Journal of Communications, 16*(2), 109–130.

Khasnabish, A., & Haiven, M. (2014). *The radical imagination: Social movement research in the age of austerity*. Fernwood Publishing.

Lawrence, B., & Dua, E. (2005). Decolonizing antiracism. *Social Justice, 32*(4), 120–143.

Li, P. S. (2003). Chinese diaspora in occidental societies: Canada and Europe. In D. Hoerder, C. Harzig, & A. Shubert (Eds.), *The historical practice of diversity: Transcultural interactions from the early modern Mediterranean to postcolonial world* (pp. 134–151). Berghahn Books.

Lowe, N. (2019, July 16). Class struggle in Chinatown: Ethnic tourism, planned gentrification, and organizing for tenant power. *The Mainlander*. https://themainlander.com/2019/07/16/class-struggle-in-chinatown-ethnic-tourism-planned-gentrification-and-organizing-for-tenant-power/

Okihiro, G. Y. (1994). *Margins and mainstreams: Asians in American history and culture*. University of Washington Press.

Phung, M. (2015). Asian-Indigenous relationalities: Literary gestures of respect and gratitude. *Canadian Literature, 227*, 55–72. https://doi.org/10.14288/cl.v0i227.187794

Phung, M. (2019). Indigenous and Asian relation making. *Verge: Studies in Global Asias, 5*(1), 18–30.

Toomey, N., Ho, Y. C. J., Del Vecchio, D., & Tuck, E. (2020). Reconciliation through kits and tests? Reconsidering newcomer responsibilities on Indigenous land. In R. Datta (Ed.), *Indigenous reconciliation and decolonization: Narratives of social justice and community engagement* (pp. 61–77). Routledge.

Tuck, E., & Yang, K. W. (2012). Decolonization is not a metaphor. *Decolonization: Indigeneity, Education & Society, 1*(1), 1–40.

Valle-Castro, M. (2020). Reconciliation as rationalization of state violence: Activist performance as resistance to TRC politics in Chile and Canada. In R. Datta (Ed.), *Indigenous reconciliation and decolonization: Narratives of social justice and community engagement* (pp. 94–105). Routledge.

Walia, H. (2021). *Border and rule: Global migration, capitalism, and the rise of racist nationalism*. Haymarket Books.

Wong, R. (2008). Decolonizasian: Reading Asian and First Nations relations in literature. *Canadian Literature, 199*, 158–180.

PART V

ANTI-RACIST ORGANIZATION REFLECTIONS ON DECOLONIZATION IN PRACTICE

While some anti-racist activities have been recommended by government organizations, many significant systemic barriers to implementation in everyday practice remain, particularly within many immigrant and refugee settlement organizations. This part discusses how an anti-racist organization took a different stand to decolonize its policies and practices with critical anti-racist learning and practices.

1. **Rhonda Rosenberg**, as a settler anti-racist activist and educator, shares her decolonial stories by explaining her responsibilities in building anti-racist and decolonial community(ies).

CHAPTER 15

Responsibility to Build Decolonial Community(ies): A Learning Journey through Anti-Racism Education and Action with the Multicultural Community in Saskatchewan

Rhonda Rosenberg

This chapter will look at the opportunities the author has had to engage in anti-racism education with the multicultural community in Saskatchewan. It will focus on the importance of relationships for learning, unlearning, growing, and making change together. It will share some of the key elements for cultivating relationships in which those involved can learn from and with each other. The chapter begins with positioning the author and the Multicultural Council of Saskatchewan (MCoS) in relation to the land and the Peoples who live here. It provides a conceptual framework of race, racism, colonialism, oppression, privilege, and intersectionality. The author shares stories starting with work she was involved in prior to working for MCoS that began her learning journey and continuing with reflections on some of the programs she has initiated or been part of since becoming Executive Director of MCoS in 2009. The stories the author shares include lessons and inspiration for anyone wanting to engage in anti-racism and decolonization, especially those who are rooted in multicultural and ethnocultural communities.

POSITIONING MY ANTI-RACISM DECOLONIZATION JOURNEY

I write from Treaty 4 Territory and Western Region 3 of the Métis Nation of Saskatchewan in Regina. I will reflect on my current work with the Multicultural Council of Saskatchewan (MCoS) and previous anti-racism community building. MCoS is a provincial, community-based, non-profit organization in Saskatchewan that works in and supports work in territories of Treaties 2, 4, 5, 6, 8, and 10, as well as the motherland of the Métis Nation. I am a cisgender woman who has come to live and work here from grandparents who immigrated from Eastern Europe with their own histories and experiences of oppression and anti-semitism. They settled in Toronto, where I grew up. I first moved to Saskatchewan to teach in Southend, a northern Cree community, and then to Regina in 1994.

All of Saskatchewan is a treaty land, and I strive to be on a continuous learning journey about being and becoming a good treaty relative. We are all treaty people who carry benefits and responsibilities. One of those responsibilities is learning and understanding the harms and injustices of the past and present of ongoing colonialism and working in collaboration with Indigenous peoples to create good relationships with this land and all the peoples on it.

This chapter will discuss my 20 years of anti-racism work with a wide variety of partners and individuals. MCoS has articulated five streams of multicultural work: cultural continuity, celebration of diversity, anti-racism, intercultural connections, and integration. This chapter will look at how and why anti-racism is integral to multiculturalism and decolonization as a process of taking responsibilities. My learning shows that if we maintain the traditional focus on cultural continuity and celebration, the power structures and systems do not change. It is essential to educate and mobilize the community to engage in anti-racism. Focusing on my lifelong work, I will discuss how to engage critical partners collaboratively to describe the power, challenges, and possibilities of community building as an essential aspect of anti-racism, anti-oppression, decolonizing work. In doing this, I will elaborate on why we need to take responsibility to create opportunities for newcomers, established immigrants, Indigenous Peoples, and settlers to understand colonialism on this land, as well as in their homelands in many cases, and the racism that is used to justify privilege and oppression.

Established in 1975, MCoS has been talking about the benefits of diversity and the dangers of racism, supporting members, and engaging in a variety of educational programs. The organization coordinates an annual anti-racism campaign in March to recognize March 21st, the International Day for the Elimination of

Racial Discrimination. On this date in 1960, peaceful anti-apartheid demonstrators were massacred in Sharpeville, South Africa. In 1966, the United Nations began to recognize this day, and since 1989, there have been campaigns in Canada with MCoS taking a lead role in Saskatchewan. Our current campaign typically includes public education youth leadership workshops, community forums, and support for local events.

Anti-racism is a lifelong journey and a process of learning, relearning, and unlearning. We begin work with an introduction to anti-racism, so that we share concepts and language with all participants. The concept of race has only a superficial basis in biological reality, and, as such, has no meaning independent of its social definitions. Therefore, skin colour, hair colour and texture, eye colour and shape, and those visual cues that we identify as being racial features are only .006 percent of our DNA. This insignificant difference has led geneticists to say these characteristics do not legitimate a biological justification to racial divisions (AAPA Statement on Biological Aspects of Race, 1996). "Racial prejudice, historically linked with inequalities in power, reinforced by economic and social differences between individuals and groups, and still seeking today to justify such inequalities, is totally without justification" (UNESCO, 1978).

So, if the race is not genetic, then what is it? Race is a social, economic, and political construct. It has a real purpose. Its purpose is to put people into categories that define and differentiate between groups of people. These categories change over time and location. The purpose of categories is to privilege some through the oppression, exploitation, or exclusion of others (Tator & Henry, 2006). This concept of race, and the hierarchies of racism, were developed as justification for European colonial expansion to legitimize taking land, resources, and people. White supremacy that defines superiority and inferiority continues to be a foundational ideology of Canadian society with facades of concepts such as multiculturalism and diversity built on top. Colonialism continues in our structures and systems, as well as the way we see each other and ourselves (Bonds & Inwood, 2015).

It is important to note that we can all carry racial prejudices in our heads and hearts. We all can carry stereotypes and prejudices against other people. But in the case of what we call racism, power or privilege are required to enact it. Racism is the combination of prejudice plus power. Racism is about power. It seeks to give privilege to some and to oppress others. This results in the economic, political, and social benefit of those with power, often directly from the oppression of others (United Nations, 1969).

MCoS created this model for explaining the ways that racism works and the impacts it has on our lives. It has proven helpful, both for my own learning and to help others learn. I have found in my journey with anti-racism education that many people think only about interpersonal racism when they think about racism, so they think it is conscious, it is intentional, and it is often violent. But we actually know that racism is a whole lot more than that. Even interpersonal racism can be very subtle. It can be microaggressions, and it can be unconscious. It can be unintentional. But that's only one kind of racism. It is essential that we understand the hierarchies of white supremacy–embedded structural racism and the economic, social, and political disparities they have engendered. Each of us has lifelong work with internalized racism to question our thoughts, feelings, and assumptions about people in groups to which we belong and "others." This helps us before we take action and when we recognize harms we may create. This transformational journey can shed light on all levels of racism, including systemic racism in the places we work, educational institutes, businesses we go to, and community organizations. We need to be able to see the policies, programs, processes, and practices that perpetuate racism in systems throughout our communities in order to instigate alternatives.

It is important to understand the relationship between colonialism and racism on the land where we live. The Doctrine of Discovery is a papal bull from 1455 that was only just repudiated by the Vatican in 2023. "The Doctrine of Discovery was the framework Spain, Portugal, and England used for the colonization of many lands, including North America. ... The Doctrine of Discovery was the international law that gave license to explorers to claim vacant land (*terra nullius*) in the name of their sovereign. Vacant land was that which was not populated by Christians. If the lands were not occupied by Christians they were vacant and therefore could be defined as 'discovered' and sovereignty, dominion, title and jurisdiction claimed" (Indigenous Corporate Training, 2020). It reinforces the hierarchies of both Europeans and Christianity as superior, and therefore, entitled to the land and labour of all they encountered.

When we look at land on the prairies in the provinces known as Manitoba, Saskatchewan, and Alberta, we see that Indigenous Peoples were seen as an impediment to Canadian nation building. Traditional ways of life and economies were disrupted and undermined, treaties were interpreted to dispossess First Nations and Métis communities of lands they had cared for, and laws were enacted, particularly the *Indian Act* of 1876, to control and impoverish Indigenous people, while enabling immigrants from Europe to access free or inexpensive land and accumulate wealth over generations.

It is important to understand intersectionality when we think about racism. I understand intersectionality as the interplay between ways that individuals are privileged and oppressed for each of our identities. I like to use the idea of a wheel. Those who carry privilege in the identities on each spoke are close to the centre where the well-oiled axle makes life run smoothly, or at least not be made more difficult as a result of that aspect of identity. The more privileged identities a person carries, they will encounter fewer barriers, resulting in reduced awareness of the challenges faced by those oppressed and marginalized by the obstacles created by hierarchies. The more identities that a person carries that are oppressed, the more ways in which discrimination plays a role in making life more difficult, symbolized by the crush of the wheel as it rolls around each spoke identity. People who are marginalized, in contrast to those with privilege, are often aware of those with privilege and their own experiences.

We may then ask where the privilege-oppression spectrums come from in our identities. Colonial ideology creates categories and hierarchies (Pihama, 2019). My experience has shown me that these include human over nature, men over women (and other genders are ignored or considered "perverse"), Christianity over other faiths, heterosexuality over all other sexualities, able-bodied over disabled, neurotypical over neurodivergent, and more. There are innumerable aspects of human identity that can be seen in terms of who is privileged and who is oppressed and marginalized. A decolonizing approach to anti-racism must maintain awareness of intersectionality and build relationships with those working to identify and eliminate oppression.

ACT! (ANTI-RACIST CROSS-CULTURAL TEAM DEVELOPMENT)

My experiences with community building and anti-racism work began with my involvement with ACT!, Regina Public Schools' Anti-racist Cross-cultural Team development program. A friend with extensive experience in popular theatre and community development who I was connected to through global education work initially invited me to explore transformational drama work, including training teachers. This started a long journey for me in using drama as a way to engage with racism and other topics for social change and social justice. It is a way to explore our own experiences that is very validating, creates opportunities for empathy, and playfully explores opportunities for transformation. It lets us get beyond words and be in our bodies and hearts, connecting with each other deeply, sharing what is hard to express in words, and enabling us to come together across multiple languages.

In the context of the ACT! program, a small group of interested Regina public school staff and community educators put together a team of adults and youth that functioned as a steering group. We did not even have a name, but the sense of community that was born in that process was powerful. I remain connected to some of the young people and adults that were involved at that time. Many high school students came to ACT! retreats expressing the freedom to remove masks (figuratively) and be fully authentic in all their identities at retreats. Two student leaders shared powerful experiences of finding their voices. It was the first time one young man with a speech disability was recognized for his strengths. A young woman shared with teachers that when she was first at an ACT! retreat, she was so painfully shy that she would not talk to peers, even though she knew her silence was hurting them.

ACT! creates powerful experiences of coming together across many kinds of differences and sharing ideas, deeply listening to each other, and developing trust and deep respect. Intentional creation of community requires trust. Many youth programs include trust games; we began to recognize that some of these are, in fact, trust-testing games. While fun and effective for some, these can create deep discomfort and lack of safety for others. I have learned that challenge by choice is a key concept in engaging all participants where they are (Schoel et al., 1988). We carefully selected activities that gently built trust in ways that all people could feel comfortable participating and contributing to the community. I continue on my journey of transforming some of those trust-building activities so that they are ever-increasingly safe.

One of the young women began her journey with ACT! in elementary school and became a significant leader in high school. Her school attendance was inconsistent due to family responsibilities. The way she excelled in ACT! contrasted with the ways some school administrators saw her attendance and academic performance. The principal actually prevented her from coming to one retreat despite a distressing meeting between him, the school division's equity consultant, and me. As a young mother in Saskatoon, she was co-facilitating with me at the session where I first met Dr. Ranjan Datta, the editor of this book, and his family. I am proud to say that she is now a dynamic and inspiring middle-years teacher in a reserve community outside of Regina, as well as a fierce, funny, and caring parent.

ACT! was a formative experience for me. I learned how important it is to have community in this work. Anti-racism work is hard. We deal with heartbreaking topics, topics that people challenge. Sometimes we deal with audiences and people with power in systems that don't want to accept that racism exists or that they might be benefiting from it, and so having community, having people to go to for a hug or to debrief with, and having very vulnerable conversations is essential in anti-racism work.

YOUTH LEADERSHIP WORKSHOPS

When I started working for MCoS, I was able to bring the work that I began with ACT! forward. I had the opportunity to work with the Ministry of Education, which was interested in supporting anti-racism work with youth.

It started in 2010 with a one-day workshop in Regina, engaging ACT! facilitators, especially some of the youth leaders who had graduated. We continued to develop the relationship with the Ministry of Education, which supported growth to multiple communities. We fostered relationships with school divisions, with teachers, with students, with Elders and Knowledge Keepers, with municipalities who offered spaces and more, with settlement organizations whose Settlement Workers in Schools (SWIS) facilitate and often bring students, with multicultural councils, and with friendship centres. These connections and this sense of community were essential to the success and impact of the program.

One student (who uses they/them pronouns) began as a participant early in high school. When the student was in Grade 11, they trained as a facilitator and became one of the most effective and reliable members of the community. They have continued facilitating and shaping the program through their education degree at SUNTEP and beyond. I have also enjoyed long conversations with them, exploring ideas around racism, anti-oppression work, and culture as they embraced their Métis identity.

Part of what broadens the outcomes of these youth leadership workshops is that we train facilitators from the host community one day, and then they work with high school students in small group work the next day. This programming has continued to grow, and until 2020, we were often doing four or five workshops around the province. In 2021, we were able to offer virtual workshops, but the capacity to build relationships online was greatly reduced.

We expect students and teachers to take what they have learned back to their schools, either replicating some of the activities or developing their own. Students have the opportunity to complete a form with how they have applied the learning, after which they receive a leadership certificate. This also helps us to measure impact and maintain connections with students.

Conversations about racism have evolved over time. One of the other benefits of this community is having a safe space to be vulnerable. Gender and sexuality are very often identities that come to the forefront in settings where youth can explore and find acceptance for all their identities. We are sharing a lifelong learning journey and the work that we do can always be improved. We have a greater focus on colonization that has been influenced by facilitators, students, and other partners. Facilitators offer suggestions and we engage in ongoing learning together. This is another key element of the benefits of building and engaging community for anti-racism work.

The facilitators not only worked with young people and had the young people take their learning back to their schools and apply it, which was really what our core hope was, but we also found that the facilitators took this to other parts of their lives as well.

COMMUNITY SPREAD: THE RIPPLE EFFECT OF TRAINING FACILITATORS

One example of the sense of community built through these workshops is my relationship with Dr. Jebunnessa Chapola and Dr. Ranjan Datta, anti-racist and decolonial feminist colour settler scholars and community activists; both were working at Mount Royal University. I first met them and their children at an anti-racism workshop in Saskatoon in 2011. The next year, they volunteered as facilitators at an anti-racism youth leadership workshop and continued to return annually to Saskatoon, and later travelling to facilitate in Prince Albert and La Ronge, Saskatchewan. We have continued to learn from and with each other. They have taken the knowledge and methods we shared to other community settings, including Ness Creek Music Festival, community gardens, and community radio. This demonstrates the importance of ensuring that facilitator training is a robust part of the youth leadership workshops.

In my personal communication with Chapola in March 2022, I learned that this work is an integral part of her life and has led to her doctoral work. I recently had the honour of sharing an anti-racism presentation in her Community and Society class at Mount Royal University. We continue to connect with conversations and opportunities to think, feel, and learn together.

Hearing that facilitators took their learning back to their organization or community involvement or faith group became more common. It was a significant indicator for me that I was building that sense of community with these leaders, these facilitators, these people who are interested in not just learning about anti-racism but actually leading work in it. That sense of community is inspiring to me. The intention for the workshops has always been for high school students to take it forward, but we saw the facilitators grow their capacity to share in new contexts with confidence because of that sense of community.

COMMUNITY FORUMS: LOCAL GATHERINGS FOR LEARNING, PLANNING, AND ACTION

MCoS coordinates regional community forums in five to seven areas of Saskatchewan each year. Initially, we developed a formula for the forums that we used in each location. We contacted our awesome local partners in that place, and we just worked with them to identify local Elders or Knowledge Keepers, and local speakers that might be appropriate to fit the program.

Many organizations that are members of the multicultural community have traditionally focused on cultural continuity and celebrations of diversity streams. Others have been working in anti-racism and intercultural connections for many years. It has taken time and intention to invite multicultural partners to see their role in anti-racism and decolonization. Some factors that have made a difference are a shared vision and common goals; trust in the organization and in me as a person; provision of tools, resources, advice, and funds; reciprocity; and increasing ownership.

As I wrote this chapter, I had the honour of participating in forums hosted by the Truth and Reconciliation Committee that serves the southwest part of Saskatchewan. The leadership and instigation for this comes from the Southwest Multicultural Association. This is an example of the drive to recognize the harmful impacts of racism and engage widely to promote change.

As we became more interested in decolonization and deepened community relationships, we moved into a more collaborative approach. The anti-racism coordinator has been able to work with partners in every community ahead of time to talk about what issues around racism are currently most important. These valuable relationships and conversations result in every community forum having a different focus.

The pandemic pushed many of these online, but we have found that this can increase access for some people, including those from rural areas, and those interested in the topics hosted by other regions.

One of the challenges is timing of funding notification. When they come late, it makes the conversations rushed, which has an impact on the sense of community and on the outcomes. The reliance on project and event funding for anti-racism work can be an obstacle to building and maintaining community. We do not want to cause harm. Funders who offer sustainable funding are partners in building anti-racism community by recognizing the long timelines needed for trust and action.

We also find it important to consider who is participating in this community as staff, and therefore being paid, and who is a volunteer. The voices of community members, artists, and others who join this work are extremely valuable, and we are building budgets that allow us to recognize their time and contributions with honoraria, contracts, and other acknowledgements.

We try to maintain frequent or regular communication with organizational partners. When we do, it is easier to plan community forums quickly, because the relationships are there. Prince Albert Multicultural Council is one example of ongoing interaction. I put effort into cultivating relationships and making sure partners know they are valued. Taking the time for conversations that allow us to know each other as people, to deeply engage with complex issues, and to support each other's growth requires intentionality and time.

SUPPORT FOR LOCAL EVENTS

We are able to support local events organized by partners with modest funding and promotion. The working relationships do not need to be as close, but we need trust in the value of the activity. The work that Rock Against Racism has done, for example, has attracted large audiences to music and speakers with important messages. I first met the primary organizer when he was the executive director of a regional multicultural council.

One of the aspects of building anti-racist community is listening. And learning. And shifting perspective when you need to. Normally anti-racism work is focused on power and privilege. When our partners in the southwest of Saskatchewan brought us their idea for an anti-racism project, my first reaction was, "that's not anti-racism, that's cultural awareness, maybe building intercultural connections. Those are important things, but that's not anti-racism work."

When we met on Zoom, they shared that they'd "been doing community forums in person and online." "They've been great." "We've had excellent people." "We've had good attendance." "They've all been people who are either already engaged with anti-racism or, at least, already open to learning and acting for anti-racism." That is important in building our local and regional community.

They continued that what is important now is to reach folks in this mostly rural, relatively conservative part of the province. Most of this target audience are never going to come to an anti-racism community forum, so we want to do something really different and it's going to be soft and it's going to be gentle and it's going to start out very simple, but it's going to be real outreach.

I was able to hear and understand this approach, and so MCoS is supporting an experimental multiyear initiative. The Southwest Newcomer Welcome Centre created pop-up display units that they can put anywhere, including malls, schools, hockey rinks, and rodeos, not only in Swift Current but also in different communities around their region. The displays will share information, questions to spark thinking and conversations, and a QR code that takes people to a survey. The survey serves to both encourage thinking about the role of culture and intercultural relationships in their lives and communities, as well as to collect data. It looks at knowledge, openness to other ways of doing things, and connections. Future surveys will begin to pose questions about privilege, and eventually racism, oppression, and action.

It is so important within an anti-racist community to be aware of power relationships and intentionally reduce hierarchies. In this case, MCoS has power in the form of both funding to distribute and expertise. It was crucial that I took the time to listen to an idea that serves a goal widely shared in the anti-racism community to reach people who do not currently see the importance of this work. If successful, this longer-term project may be a model for other regions.

EDUCATION OFFERED BY MCoS INCLUDES RECOGNITION AND REJECTION OF RACISM

MCoS offers education, primarily through five modules. We have trained a network of facilitators across Saskatchewan that are part of this anti-racist community. One module is Recognition and Rejection of Racism, and it was rarely requested. The interest was more in cultural awareness, diversity, inclusion, and equity. I have often called equity my "Trojan horse," because it was the way that I would be able to talk about anti-racism and anti-oppression work. Since racism became a bigger part of the public conversation in the wake of the murder of George Floyd, we have started to see change. Corporations, government ministries, and community organizations have started expressing interest in anti-racism education. This is rewarding, if difficult, work for all facilitators, so connections with others engaged in the work are important for our mental health and professional growth.

ANTI-RACISM NETWORK: OPPORTUNITY FOR ADVOCACY, LEARNING, SUPPORT, AND COLLABORATION

The Anti-Racism Network started in Saskatoon as a way for anti-racism practitioners to support each other and learn together. It has evolved to develop in-depth education, its own facilitators, and to be more provincial. Monthly meetings include opportunities to share activities, learning, frustrations, and questions. I greatly value relationships with leaders engaged with municipalities, health, education, criminal and legal systems, evaluation, and more. My involvement with this group leaves me feeling both inspired to continue this work and stronger in the connections to a larger movement.

RECONCILI-ACTION: THE POWER TO CHANGE: TRAINING VIDEO ON SYSTEMIC ANTI-INDIGENOUS RACISM FOR BUSINESSES

We became involved in a project that started from an incident at a Canadian Tire in Regina. Kamao Cappo had gone to Canadian Tire as a customer to buy a chainsaw. He was physically kicked out by an assistant manager who accused him of stealing. He filmed the incident and took it to both the media and the Saskatchewan Human Rights Commission (SHRC). Francois Brien is the dealer, which is the franchise owner, for the Canadian Tire store where this took place. With support from SM Solutions, Brien took the opportunity to take leadership in understanding systemic racism and making his store a safer and more welcoming business (CBC News, 2019).

They went through mediation with the SHRC that led to engaging community partners, including MCoS, the Office of the Treaty Commissioner, and Buffalo People Arts Institute, to develop a training video. These partners continue to work together. We have attracted funding to develop a workshop for business audiences to learn about systemic racism, especially as it impacts Indigenous Peoples, and to support them in creating and implementing action plans for change. The SHRC honoured Kamao Cappo, Francois Brien, and me as the inaugural recipients of Human Rights Champion in 2020.

ANTI-RACISM AND DECOLONIZATION AS A LIFELONG JOURNEY

In my journey, I have seen many people begin learning about racism and the harms of colonialism in fear. Fear of change, fear of complicity or guilt, fear of doing something wrong, and so on. Once my eyes were opened, however, I could no longer pretend not to see. I see the financial costs we all pay as a society in the criminal legal system, in healthcare, in remedial education. Even more important, it costs us by losing people's gifts by discounting their contributions. We all gain by seeing each other as people who have perspectives, gifts, experiences, and knowledge to contribute.

As I and those I work with in various ways move through the fears and build empathy, our desire to learn strengthens, and we can begin to fully engage with learning that expands our perspectives. Regardless of our positionalities with privilege and oppression, we may experience cognitive dissonance and the need to unlearn what we have been taught. We start to become more comfortable with discomfort.

I listen to the experiences of others and take responsibility for my own learning without retraumatizing those most impacted by racism and other oppressions to repeat their stories. I am able to be vulnerable about what I do not know, my mistakes, and my own trauma. I choose to spend time with others on similar journeys—planning, working, eating, laughing—and we gain deeper appreciation of each other, which becomes affection and caring. We learn to be trustworthy. These are the processes that build the trust necessary for authentic relationships that are the foundation for solidarity.

In these relationships we learn and I witness readiness to take action in myself and others. This may begin with working with MCoS to host a session and grow to having the knowledge, tools, and confidence to speak up against injustice. I recognize power and privilege and question the systems that bestow it. I work to liberate myself from supporting and benefiting from hierarchies and oppression. I am an advocate and create spaces for others to speak, to advocate for themselves, and to act for change. When I make mistakes, I work to have the emotional capacity to be in discomfort and learn from them. I strive to be able to apologize, change, and forgive myself and others as I grow.

This is how I nurture individual relationships and a community that is always open to those who wish to join from wherever they might be in their journey, for all the experiences they bring. At MCoS, we honour and respect difference and foster solidarity. We build relationships based in reciprocity—we all give and receive as we are able. The sense of community that arises from these connections and networks inspires, supports, challenges, and nurtures us to act on our own power.

Decolonization, anti-racism, and anti-oppression are lifelong processes for me personally and professionally. I join with others on this journey towards change. It helps to understand our own identities, roots, history, connections, and how they relate to our privileges and oppressions. This allows us to take responsibility for understanding our colonial legacy and making change to build communities that recognize and reject racism and oppression.

REFLECTION QUESTIONS

1. Can you comment on past social movement struggles and whether or not you saw them as engaging in the process of decolonization as you understand it today?
2. How does decolonization take place within anti-racist and anti-oppressive struggles?
3. What political ideas and frameworks influence your own engagement in the process of decolonization?
4. What effect does the current historical, political, and economic (especially neoliberal) context have on your practices of decolonization?
5. What is the role of the state in the process of decolonization?
6. What do you believe are the relationships between struggles against heteropatriarchy, racism, misogyny, ableism, capitalism, and the struggle for decolonization?

SUGGESTED READINGS

- Corntassel, J. (2012). Re-envisioning resurgence: Indigenous pathways to decolonization and sustainable self-determination. *Decolonization: Indigeneity, Education & Society 1*(1), 86–101.
- Creese, G. (2019). "Where are you from?" Racialization, belonging and identity among second-generation African-Canadians. *Ethnic and Racial Studies, 42*(9), 1476–1494. https://doi.org/10.1080/01419870.2018.1484503
- Datta, R. (2018). Decolonizing both researcher and research and its effectiveness in Indigenous research. *Research Ethics, 14*(2), 1–24.
- St. Denis, V. (2007). Aboriginal education and anti-racist education: Building alliances across cultural and racial identity. *Canadian Journal of Education / Revue canadienne de l'éducation, 30*(4), 1068–1092. https://doi.org/10.2307/20466679

REFERENCES

AAPA statement on biological aspects of race. (1996). *American Journal of Physical Anthropology, 101*(4), 569–570. https://doi.org/10.1002/ajpa.1331010408

Bonds, A., & Inwood, J. (2015). Beyond white privilege: Geographies of white supremacy and settler colonialism. *Progress in Human Geography, 40*(6), 715–733. https://doi.org/10.1177/0309132515613166

CBC News. (2019, July 24). First Nations man and Regina Canadian Tire settle over racial-profiling allegation. https://www.cbc.ca/news/canada/saskatchewan/kamao-cappo-canadian-tire-human-rights-commission-1.5222999

Indigenous Corporate Training. (2020, January 26). *Indigenous title and the Doctrine of Discovery.* https://www.ictinc.ca/blog/indigenous-title-and-the-doctrine-of-discovery

Pihama, L. (2019). Colonization and the importation of ideologies of race, gender, and class in Aotearoa. In E. A. McKinley & L. T. Smith (Eds.), *Handbook of Indigenous education* (pp. 29–48). Springer. https://doi.org/10.1007/978-981-10-3899-0_56

Schoel, J., Prouty, D., & Radcliffe, P. (1988). *Islands of healing: A guide to adventure based counseling.* Project Adventure.

Tator, C., & Henry, F. (2006). *Racial profiling in Canada: Challenging the myth of a few bad apples.* University of Toronto Press.

UNESCO. (1978). *Declaration on race and racial prejudice.* http://portal.unesco.org/en/ev.php-URL_ID=13161&URL_DO=DO_TOPIC&URL_SECTION=201.html

United Nations. (1969). *The International Convention on the Elimination of All Forms of Racial Discrimination.* https://www.ohchr.org/en/instruments-mechanisms/instruments/international-convention-elimination-all-forms-racial

What Is Next? (Moving Forward)

Now that you are done reading our collective decolonial stories, you are responsible for becoming part of our collective decolonial movement. I hope our decolonial stories inspire you to reflect and reshape who you are and who you need to be, learn how to do things differently, and change your everyday actions to achieve social and environmental justice on the Indigenous land on which you are currently living.

I hope our collective decolonial stories about building decolonial communities may show you how to take responsibility in your everyday practice, help you learn why and how to honour and respect Indigenous treaty rights and land-water rights, and show you how to celebrate diversity and differences, speak up for justice, and acknowledge and challenge ongoing racism. By fulfilling our responsibilities, we become more potent and closer to each other.

Despite our different cultural communities, such as Indigenous, settlers, Black, transnational immigrants, new immigrants, and refugee communities, we hope our collective decolonial stories may inspire you to collaborate and work together to create the society that we all dream of.

Your everyday responsibilities are a perfect starting point to be responsible, to be different, to be anti-racist, to be Indigenist. My hope is that, along with your family, community, colleagues, students, and communities, you keep inquiring about the consequences of everyday actions within your community and profession, as I will.

Index

4Rs, 160, 162–163

acceptance and respect, 146–147
ACT! (anti-racist cross-cultural team development), 263–264
Anishinaabek, 12, 14
Anti-Racism Network, 270
anti-racist, being, 3–4
anti-racist and decolonial disability, 219
Asian racial formation, 246
Asian racialization, 244

Beardy's & Okemasis' Cree Nation, 50, 58–59
BIPOC (Black, Indigenous, and people of colour), 116, 225–227
Black, 1, 223
Black and Asian immigrants, 223
Bridge, 163
Bridge Framework, 159–163

child with disabilities, 209
children's artwork, 181–182
citizen science, 150–155
classroom-based education, 179
climate change, 154–155, 163, 166–167, 182, 201, 225–238
co-creating solutions, 162
colonial Canada, 66
colonization, 15, 32–33, 68, 78, 82, 88, 131, 132
colonized mindset, 77
colour settler woman, 115, 197
community building, 178

community engagement, 161
community-based participatory research (CBPR), 150–155
COVID-19, 150–157
Cree culture and heritage, 48, 49, 51, 56
crisis of disbelief, 14–15
cross-cultural communities, 1
cross-cultural dancers, 178
cross-cultural youth, 178
cultural intersections, 18
cycle of ceremonies, 98–101

dance, 11–24, 181–182, 184
data ownership, 164
decolonial data analysis, 228
decolonial reflective stories, 206
decolonization in practice, 1, 8
decolonization is relearning, 68
decolonized dreams, 77
Decolonizing Antiracism, 241
decolonizing pedagogy, 31
decolonizing phenomenology, 225–229
decolonizing university, 29
digital citizen science, 155, 158
disability and education, 210
Disability Critical Race Theory (DisCrit), 215–218

Elder involvement, 55

first nations schools, 55
food security, 55
food sovereignty, 55

gender equality, 57
grand entry into academy, 17
growing food, 181–182

healing, 18
health and food systems, 163

identity, 12
Indigenist, 4
Indigenist theoretical framework, 180
Indigenous
    awareness training, 56
    education, 51, 54, 108
    Elders and Knowledge Keepers, 183
    identity, 79
    journey, 77
    land-based education, 94–101
    meaning of Land, 115
    methodology, 35
    storying, 29
    treaty rights, 144
    settlers, 1
innovative educational learning, 6
insects, 182
integrated knowledge translation, 162

kastowas, 101
kawenna'ón:we, 94, 101

land acknowledgements, 126
land-based education, 48–55, 94
land-based learning, 3, 181
land-based stories, 183
learning, 134
    awareness, 143
    challenges, 139
    from art, music, and dance, 184
    parents' stories, 184

Miyo-Pimatisiwin, 35
Mohawk immersion school, 101
music, 179

Nehiyaw, 35
new immigrant, 1

Ohén:ton Karihwatéhkwen, 93, 98–99, 102–103

pedagogical approach, 40, 63
people of colour with disabilities, 213
plants, 183
Pow Wows, 53

racialized woman with disabilities, 212
racism and ableism, 205
reflective learning, 4, 116
relational decolonial autoethnographic research, 116
relational stories, 182
relationship building, 126
relearning, 136
residential schools, 83
resilience, 37, 41
responsibilities for decolonization, 64, 196
responsibilities for reconciliation, 72, 143–156, 200
responsibility, 1–4
    for awareness, 70
    to be a lifelong learner, 3
    to build a decolonial community, 131
Rotinonhsonníh Land-based education, 96–98
rural and remote communities, 157

self-decolonization, 159–165
self-determination, 83
Shia Hazara family, 194

Shiibaashka'igan, 12, 18–23
Situating self, 12
soul and spirit, 17
spiralling, 91–96
stereotyping race and disability, 216
Sub-Saharan African Immigrant, 225
systemic challenges, 208
systemic racism, 30

teacher passion, 57
traditional ecological knowledge (TEK), 50
traditional storytelling, 181
transformation, 40

transnational immigrant, 1
TRC's calls to action, 4, 140

university learning, 38
unrelated learning, 179, 180

Wampum theories, 101
ways of knowing, 48
Western education, 179
Western-centric research practices, 158
Wilson, Alex, 128

youth leadership, 265